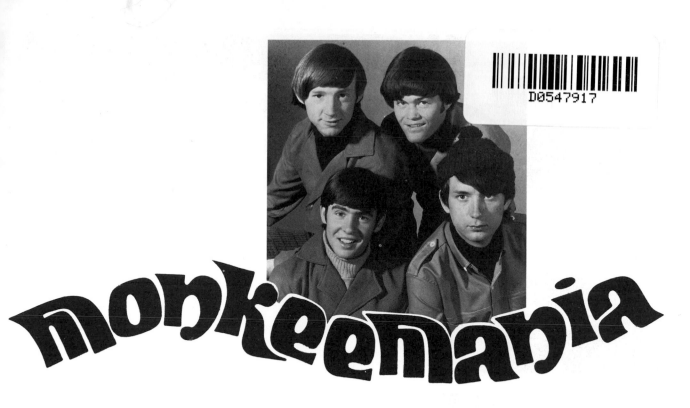

monkeemania

The True Story Of The Monkees

Glenn A. Baker

assisted by
Tom Czarnota and Peter Hogan

Plexus, London

This edition copyright © 1986 by Plexus Publishing Limited
Text copyright © 1986 by Glenn A. Baker
Published by Plexus Publishing Limited
30 Craven Street
London WC2N 5NT
First printing 1986
Cover design : Phil Smee
Book design : Phil Smee

Baker, Glenn A.
    Monkeemania! : the story of the Monkees.
    1. Monkees
    I. Title   II. Hogan, Peter   III. Czarnota, Tom
    784.5′0092′2   ML421.M6/

    ISBN 0-85965-090-1

Manufactured in Great Britain by Hollen Street Press

contents

preface

Like an illegitimate child in a respectable family, the Monkees are destined to be regarded forever as rock's first great embarrassment; misunderstood and maligned like a mongrel at a ritzy dog show, or a test tube baby at the Vatican. The rise of the pre-fab four coincided with rock's desperate desire to cloak itself with the trappings of respectability, credibility and irreproachable heritage. The fact was ignored that session players were being heavily employed by the Beach Boys, the Beatles, the Mamas and the Papas, the Byrds and other titans of the age. However, what could *not* be ignored, as rock disdained its pubescent past, was that a group of middle-aged Hollywood businessmen had actually assembled their concept of a profitable rock group and foisted it upon the world.

What mattered was that the Monkees had success handed to them on a silver plate. Indeed, it was not so much righteous indignation but thinly disguised jealousy which motivated the scornful dismissal of what must, in retrospect, be seen as an entertaining, imaginative and highly memorable exercise in pop culture. *The Monkees* television series was the creative expression of Hollywood's young mavericks – visionary producers, directors, script writers, film editors and set designers. That an innovative television concept was able to spill over into the rock/pop sphere is a testament to the high calibre of talent employed in all areas of the project. The metamorphosis from a pretend playgroup to a quartet of real live rock'n'roll superstars had much to do with the fresh and vital contributions of such formidable talents as Carole King, John Stewart, Harry Nilsson, David Gates, Tommy Boyce and Bobby Hart, Neil Diamond, Paul Williams, Carole Bayer-Sager, Michael Murphy, Jeff Barry and Chip Douglas.

In a whirlwind Blitzkrieg which spanned little more than three years, the Monkees notched up six American and three British mega-hits, shattered album sales records held by the Beatles and Elvis Presley, won an Emmy Award, established a new standard for rock performance, created an innovative television series compared favourably to the Marx Brothers' classic films, were hailed by the likes of John Lennon and Frank Zappa, leaving behind a feature film held in enormously high regard in serious cinema circles.

The saga of the Monkees reaches far beyond hit charts and a thousand trashy trinkets. It is also the story of a burgeoning film community which gave the American cinema of the seventies some of its finest achievements; of the inner workings of the once powerful record industry; and of the social and cultural explosion that was the sixties. This book deals with not only Davy, Micky, Peter and Mike, but with Jack Nicholson, Charles Manson, Jimi Hendrix, Stephen Stills, Don Kirshner, Bob Rafelson, Paul Mazursky, Lowell George, Bones Howe and many other notable figures who went on to leave an indelible mark on society and art.

Here we come walking down the street

When Richard Lester delivered *A Hard Day's Night* in July 1964, he and his protagonists effectively transformed a musical phenomenon into a cultural blueprint for the sixties. The language, the dress, the behaviour – all were irresistibly laid out, to be adapted and mimicked by the first huge wave of post-war 'baby-boom' teenagers, ravenous in their appetite for elitism and new thrills, be they cheap or otherwise.

If young males in western society thought about forming or joining beat groups when they first heard Beatles records, they were soundly convinced by a visual representation more accessible than Elvis Presley diving off the cliffs of Acapulco. Just watching frenzied girls in lustful pursuit of four young musicians was an enormous adrenalin rush to a generation unashamedly seeking hedonistic values. Girls flocked to movie houses to scream and cry, males to learn and emulate. The fact that such a film made $12 million at the box office did not go unnoticed either.

At the same time as the perceptive and innovative Lester was adding another notch to the fine tradition of aware, honest British cinema, the seeds of a very real revolution were being sown within the film and television colony of Hollywood, California. American cinema throughout the fifties and early sixties was a never-ending scenario of champagne romances among heavily-jewelled beautiful people to a background of Henry Mancini melodies. Kissing was old hat and screwing was not yet allowed, so many miles of celluloid were wasted on indefinable practices located somewhere in the middle.

At the core of a seditious movement which sought to unseat the likes of Capucine, Audrey Hepburn and Rock Hudson was a thirty-year-old writer/producer/director named Bob Rafelson, who had recently been sacked as an associate producer at Universal Pictures for overturning Lew Wasserman's desk during a spirited defence of a script he felt was being violated. A compulsive drifter, he was a rodeo rider in Arizona at fifteen, worked on a European-bound ocean liner at seventeen, played drums in an Acapulco jazz band at eighteen, and wrote prize-winning plays at Dartmouth

Film director Richard Lester with John Lennon.

College by the age of twenty. As a serviceman he worked as a disc-jockey on a Japanese military radio station, picking up bucks on the side translating Japanese films and advising Shochiku Films on which Nipponese flicks were suitable for export to America. Back in the States, he was hired as a reader and story editor for the two and a half hour *Play Of The Week* telecast. He recalls reading more than a thousand scripts in a year and writing additional dialogue for Shakespeare, Anouilh, Giraudoux and others, his efforts triumphantly undetected by critics.

For five years Rafelson gravitated towards the fringes of the film industry, tackling myriad tasks and developing a healthy fascination for plastic trash culture. In 1962 he created the excellent *Hootenanny* series for ABC Television and was associate producer on *The Wackiest Ship In The Army*, *Channing* and *The Greatest Show On Earth*. During this period he also began conceptualising a music related drama series based around a folk singing group.

Bob Schneider (left) and Bert Rafelson.

By 1964, Rafelson had become associated with Bert Schneider, the financial vice-president of Screen Gems Television, and son of Abraham Schneider, president of Columbia Pictures. Together they formed Raybert Productions, an independent enterprise for experimental film projects. The two mavericks took their concept to former child actor Jackie Cooper, the senior executive of Screen Gems, the television arm of Columbia Pictures. 'Hollywood has a thing for making pictures that talk down to young people,' the pair reasoned. 'We want to do a series in the new-wave style, a very far out show.' Cooper was sympathetic to the boss's son, allocating $225,000 for the production of a pilot episode of a situation comedy series based around a Beatles-type rock quartet, without even a written outline being submitted.

Jackie Cooper, head of Screen Gems Television, as a child actor/musician.

There was really no precedent for Cooper or his fellow executives against which to judge the proposal. Up until 1965 television had not acknowledged any audience pockets outside of 'children' or 'adults'. Those who screamed at the Beatles were, in adult eyes, children who sucked lollipops and wore party frocks. Teenagers were merely troublesome children and did not merit any particular attention. There was no minority programming because, in Hollywood's ivory towers, there were no minorities. Gays, feminists, blacks, hippies, bikers, protestors and academics were seen on the same level as albino dwarfs – sad mutations of nature to be pitied. If any individuality in youth was acknowledged at all, it was deemed to be 'juvenile delinquency'. The only show on TV which made an intelligent attempt to cater to teenage taste was *Shindig*, the brainchild of visionary British producer Jack Good.

Schneider and Rafelson did not waste energy in trying to topple the prevalent school of thought; they merely sidestepped it. Within their select community were other talented mavericks also looking for an avenue to liberate their crafts. Scriptwriters Paul Mazursky and Larry Tucker, underground film director Jim Frawley, and film-maker/cameraman Mike Elliot all offered their support to the new project from Raybert Productions.

Schneider opted against hiring professional actors, feeling that wholesome American boys-next-door like Frankie Avalon or Troy Donahue would only provide the standard Hollywood image of adolescents. Television had traditionally cast teenagers as basically conservative and subservient, even if they were meant to be 'kooky'. Certainly there was nothing seditious about Dobie Gillis.

But Schneider wasn't interested in giving the public another version of *My Three Sons*; he wanted to achieve the same natural charm that Richard Lester had showcased so expertly in *A Hard Day's Night*. 'We didn't want the usual type of smart know-alls who were into camera angles and scripts and were professional at *playing* teenagers,' he explained later. 'We wanted guys who could act themselves. If we'd hired professionals we wouldn't have got the primitiveness we were looking for.' What they really wanted was four unknowns who would not command a large salary and would not rock the boat with their own self-interest.

So, highlighted by a flurry of asterisks and exclamation marks, the following advertisement was placed in *Daily Variety* in August 1965:

And so they came to pit their various skills against each other: Paul Peterson from *The Donna Reed Show*, Micky Braddock from the old *Circus Boy* series, guitarist Stephen Stills, recording artist Michael Blessing, elfin singer-songwriter Paul Williams, recording artist and producer Danny Hutton, stage musical star David Jones, road musician Peter Thorkelson, television actor Don Scardino, guitarist Jerry Yester, writer Rodney

MADNESS!!
AUDITIONS
Folk & Roll Musicians-Singers
for **acting roles in new TV series.**
Running parts for 4 insane boys, age 17-21.
Want spirited Ben Frank's-types.
Have courage to work.
Must come down for intervie
CALL: HO. 6-518

According to songwriter Tommy Boyce, 'Ben Frank's was a late night restaurant on Hollywood Boulevard where you'd go in the morning after the Whisky Au Go Go closed, and drop drugs.'

The advertisement seemed to capture the attention of every young male in Los Angeles (and a good many in New York) who were involved in music or acting. Some 437 hopefuls submitted applications and were summarily auditioned by Schneider and Rafelson. The general street feeling was that the project was going to be big, though nobody really imagined that the group or their music would expand beyond the television format.

Not all of those who auditioned came forward as a result of the press advertisement. A casting call was sent out to agents, managers and Columbia film and television production offices. As it turned out, only one of the four Monkees chosen applied as a result of its appearance. According to *Newsweek*, 'So frantic was the talent hunt that Screen Gems studio guards were instructed to send in likely looking lads off the Hollywood streets, and they did – including one bewildered kid carrying a sack of laundry to the laundromat.'

Two of the four hundred and thirty-seven contendors – Micky Braddock and Bill Chadwick (right)

Bingenheimer and (if certain auditionees are to be believed) general weirdo Charles Manson among them.

Two of the strongest contenders from the outset were songwriters Tommy Boyce and Bobby Hart. Boyce had recorded solo for RCA and MGM, charting moderately in 1962 with *I'll Remember Carol*, and Hart was writing hits for Little Anthony and the Imperials and Tommy Sands, with Wes Farrell. It was originally intended to cast them as the Lennon/McCartney of the Monkees, but their publisher, Don Kirshner, opposed the idea. They had only been signed to Screen Gems Music for a year and, although they had several hits prior to signing, they had spun very little coinage for Kirshner. As a consolation, Lester Sill, Screen Gem's vice-president on the west coast (and former partner in Philles Records with Phil Spector) arranged for the pair to be given initial musical production rights for the series; an offer they readily accepted.

The first auditions were held during September 1965 both at Lester Sill's Colpix Records office in Los Angeles and in Raybert's office on Sound Stage 7 at Screen Gems Columbia Studios (from where *The Farmer's Daughter* originated). Once the hack folkies, mediocre actors and mentally unstable extroverts were weeded out, the thirty remaining hopefuls were subjected to a series of bizarre mind games, in order to sort

Above right: David Jones had an inside run in the auditions. He was under contract to Screen Gems/Columbia and they were looking for a suitable vehicle for his talents.
Below: Songwriter auditionees Tommy Boyce (left) and Bobby Hart.

david jones

WHAT ARE
WE GOING
TO DO?
b/w
THIS BOUQUET

CP 784

out the true eccentrics and strong characters. A series of impossible questions were posed, such as, 'Suppose you were on Mars, where would you go for a hamburger?' or 'Do you like the colour of the carpet?' or 'How would you like to be sitting in my chair?' Often they would be unsettled by taunts like, 'What a ridiculous pair of boots! Hey man, where'd you get those dumb boots?' and occasionally the interviewers would simply ignore them as they staged mock arguments or played catch with a golfball. Tommy Boyce recalls that some of the applicants were even stranger than the questions they were supposed to answer. 'One guy came in carrying two bags of groceries. He was about forty years old, six foot seven and weighed about 400 pounds. A real live white hulk.'

At one audition, Micky Braddock found Schneider and Rafelson absorbed in balancing a pile of bottles, paper cups and glasses on a desk. Figuring they were props, he grabbed a spare object, stuck it on top of the stack and triumphantly claimed 'checkmate.' On another occasion, Peter Thorkelson found them juggling balls and observed the proceedings in intense silence, his face displaying Harpo Marx-like expressions. Michael Blessing was a little more forthright. As interviewee 274, married with a child, he was very much a dark horse. He strode purposefully into the room wearing a green wool hat (to keep his hair out of his eyes when riding a motor bike) and cowboy boots, thumped the desk and demanded in a slow Texan drawl 'What's all this about?' Impish David Jones turned the tables on the erratic interviewers by tossing a relentless series of questions at them in a broad north country English accent.

The survivors of this third degree process were then herded into proper sound stages for personality tests – filmed conversations with an intimidating off-camera inquisitor. 'All of this was enormously revealing about what I was looking for, when and if they made it into the group,' explains Rafelson. 'Did they listen? Did they compete? Did they challenge? Who was the natural leader? Who could be stupid? Who could be smart? Who could be funny? Who needed lines and props? I felt like a marriage broker. I couldn't figure out who would dig each other, but I knew who wouldn't make it.'

Such brutal culling reduced the field to eight finalists. Schneider and Rafelson personally selected their four but held off until Audience Studies Inc., a Screen Gems market research subsidiary, screened all eight screen tests to a random gathering of mixed kids aged six to eighteen. Four shattered lads were dismissed with a handshake, among them Danny Hutton, who would survive a stint as Kim Fowley's chauffeur to go on to superstar fame as leader of Three Dog Night; Bill Chadwick, who would stick around the project as a stand-in, roadie, sound mixer and songwriter; Don Scardino who, having been offered a final berth, was deemed ineligible because of his current contract with the afternoon soapie *The Guiding Light*; and later RCA

The first publicity photograph of the group. Clockwise from top: Michael Blessing, Micky Braddock, David Jones and Peter Tork.

chart failure 'Miki', who proved to be one Britisher too many.

The victors were signed to far-reaching iron clad contracts late in October 1965. They were Micky Braddock, David Jones, Michael Blessing and Peter Tork. They were first called the Inevitables and then the Turtles. 'Then we kind of fooled around with the Creeps but decided that was all too negative,' reveals Schneider. Raybert finally came up with the Monkees, mis-spelt in the obvious tradition of the Byrds, the Beatles and Cyrkle. 'I don't know why,' Schneider said, 'I'll have to ask my analyst.'

The four actors had no natural affinity, save that two were musicians of little achievement and two were actors of moderate achievement. In Micky's opinion; 'They cast us to be contradictory rather than similar. They wanted four diverse personalities, which they certainly got.' Peter was the docile and loveable Ringo, Davy was the cuddly and wholesome Paul, Micky and Mike were interchangeable with John and George, each suggesting characteristics of both. Even the Monkees communal house bore a resemblance to the Beatles' pad in *Help*.

Davy, Micky, Peter and Mike had seen each other at the various auditions and screen tests, and Peter and Mike knew each other vaguely from the Troubadour, but there was no real familiarity or friendship in evidence. Manchester, Los Angeles, Connecticut and Texas – and not a common taste or interest between

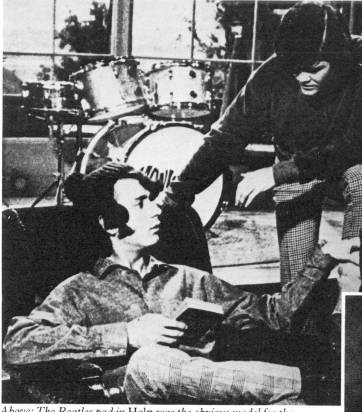

Above: The Beatles pad in Help *was the obvious model for the Monkees' house at 3434 Beechwood Drive.*
Right: David Jones (left) and Peter Tork in the pilot episode.

them, apart from a wide-eyed expectation of riches and fame. 'They sent us down to this town called Delmar to film the pilot episode,' relates Davy. 'We all travelled in the same car so that we could get to know each other, but there was no rapport at all, we just sat in the car looking out the window. It was Bert and Bob's idea and it made sense, all of us travelling like a theatre troupe. It was on the way down that I became aware of Micky's table manners, which were the worst in the world. He eats like it's his last meal and when he finishes with his plate it has to be thrown away because there are chips out of the bottom of it. Now I couldn't believe this so I said to him "I've never seen anybody eat like that in my life man. You're a pig." Suddenly a dead silence came over the table. Mike looked at me, then Peter looked at me and they were obviously thinking "what's going on with this little Manchester jockey, where's he coming from?" They all slowed right down because they were a little worried about their own table manners. What was I going to get upset about next? So I started cutting up the salad on my plate. Three minutes went by, it felt like ten. I put the dressing on, and they were all just staring at me. Then I put my knife and fork down, grabbed two handfuls of this chopped salad and rubbed it all over my face. Well, that cracked them all up and it kind of broke the ice, we all felt a bit looser after that.'

With four untrained and mostly inexperienced actors, the producers confined the pilot to rudimentary slapstick sequences, hoping to capture some natural chemistry that would give the network an indication of what could later be achieved under optimum circumstances. To give the pilot an edge, Raybert incorporated some arty tricks. Film was under or over exposed, turned upside down and sequences reversed. Action switched abruptly from a slow motion scene of the four Monkees riding camels in the Sahara desert to four Keystone Kops racing disastrously up a hill, to mimed performance sequences. For television in 1965, this was a little beyond state-of-the-art. The script, which centred around a 'sweet sixteen' birthday party, was written by Mazursky and Tucker, who had it checked for correct jargon by typists and Schneider's eight-year-old son, Jeffrey. Rafelson aside, Mazursky was the most proven talent involved with the project. An actor since 1951, he had appeared in many films, including *Blackboard Jungle*, *Fear and Desire* and *Death Wish*. Between 1954 and 1960 he worked as a nightclub comic and then moved on to directing live theatre and playwriting.

Feature songs for the pilot episode were prepared by failed auditionees Tommy Boyce and Bobby Hart who wrote the exceptionally commercial *Last Train To Clarksville* during a twenty minute coffee break, using a 'No No No' refrain as a counterpoint to the Beatles' Yeah Yeah Yeah'. With their own musician friends they recorded *Last Train to Clarksville*, *Let's Dance On* and *Theme From The Monkees* for insertion into the show and afterwards, the Monkees lip-synched to all the tracks. At the time, Mike confided that the theme song struck him as 'hey hey we're the Beatles' in intent. Like most professional film people, Raybert had no deep interest in the musical aspects of the show, because there were people paid to do that.

Once chosen, the four young actors were expected to stand quietly off to one side and lurk unobtrusively until they were issued with instructions to obey. Still thunderstruck and reeling, there were no objections on their part. 'When we first came face to face with the big men behind the scenes we felt pretty damn nervous,' recalls Micky. 'They talked so fast and so dynamically that we felt what we probably were – greenhorn kids suddenly in the middle of a million dollar deal. We had little to say for ourselves. We knew our own limitations but it was pretty tough hearing them expressed publicly at meetings. Big time showbiz was going on all around with us in the middle trying to learn about all the things we didn't know. And everything we did was on the secret list, we couldn't tell anybody.'

The unconventional pilot was sent off to Audience Studios Inc. for appraisal before a sample audience. Raybert were expecting a rating of at least 700, which was actually considered dangerously low by most television executives. *The Monkees* scored barely 600. Screen Gems were prepared to scrap the project but Schneider and Rafelson asked for a twenty-four hour stay of execution. They realized that they had taken the wrong approach in making the pilot. Their clever scenes were too long and too complex for young America and the show had sailed right over their audience's heads, exceeding their lamentably brief attention span. In one easy lesson they graduated from film-makers to television producers.

As they pored over the survey report, they isolated the factors which had produced a negative response from the audience. Then they moved a Movieola film editing deck into one of their living rooms and began an all night rescue project. Scenes that were thought to be confusing were either deleted or relocated in the print.

To fill the gaps the unscripted personality sequences of the final audition screen tests were examined and those of Mike and Davy were spliced in. 'In the end they threw it all on the kitchen floor,' relates Davy, 'jumped up and down in rage and almost set it alight. Then they felt sorry for what they'd done and cut it all up again. We became the Marx Brothers, then the Three Stooges; nothing that the kids would have to concentrate on for very long.' Peter adds, 'They worked at it feverishly all night. I have to hand it to those guys, they were dedicated. They weren't just a couple of cigar chompers who said "the kids'll love it whatever we do," they really cared about the quality of what they were doing. They wanted to be a part of the new wave themselves. You see, they didn't even mind guys who were gonna give them trouble. That was all right, they'd rather have some personality clashes and get a sparkling show. For a while that was the tradeoff they did get.'

In the morning the edited film was sent back to ASI for a second appraisal. This time the audience rating neared 1000. 'We went from failure to success in twenty-four hours,' boasted an ebullient Schneider. Screen Gems placed the show with NBC that day and national sponsors were secured within seventy-two hours. The corporate wheels turned and the show was locked into the network's 1966 schedule, due to begin in September.

That accomplished, Mike, Peter and Micky were given small salary advances and told to come back in three months. Davy had to be handled differently, as he was already under a retainer contract to Columbia Pictures and had not been signed to a specific Monkees contract. 'I needed some money,' he recalls, 'so Bert gave me $15,000, put a bunch of papers in front of me and said "just sign here Davy." Unknown to me at the time, that meant a flat $450 a week, including merchandising and everything, and all sorts of "you can't talk to these people, you can't do this or appear there without our consent" clauses. All this stuff that I didn't read inside a twenty-five page contract. All I had in mind was home, sisters, dad. I used the money to get back to Manchester for Christmas, buy a car for my sisters and a house for my dad.'

A fantasy sequence from the pilot episode with David Jones.

origins of the species

David Thomas Jones was born on 30 December 1946 in Manchester, England, the fourth and final child of Harry and Doris Jones. Harry worked for British Rail and struggled to raise Davy and his sisters Hazel, Beryl and Linda on a weekly wage of a little over ten pounds. The Jones family lived in a 'two up-two down' terraced house in Leamington Street, Higher Openshaw, the poor section of Manchester. The house had an outdoor toilet and no bathroom at all. 'I remember I had to wash myself in the kitchen sink,' he recalls. 'We all had to do that. Some of my relatives still do. But it wasn't like we were poor in a rich neighbourhood. Everyone was poor in Higher Openshaw. Dad had to struggle to buy us clothes and food, but so did every other dad in the area.'

The Jones family was very close; Davy was surrounded by an aura of affection, unity and loyalty that shaped the course of his life. 'Every year we used to go away on a two week holiday,' he recalls proudly. 'We were the only kids in the neighbourhood who got to do that. We used to go to a place called St. Annes, near Blackpool, but cheaper. Everybody else was busy

The Jones Family on their annual seaside holiday at St. Annes near Blackpool.

13

buying furniture and new televisions and all that, but my father was busy making sure we had a good time.'

Growing up in Higher Openshaw was hard, but growing up small was even harder. Davy had to prove himself time after time, scrapping and warring with bullies to win the respect of the bigger kids. Keepers in Debdale Park, which was behind the Jones house, knew Davy as the smallest (but loudest) of a gang of local school kids. These kids took part in the annual Sunday School pantomime, which one year featured Davy as the Genie in a production of *Aladdin*. At the age of eleven Davy enrolled at Varna Secondary Modern School, where his earlier amateur theatrical activities were expanded. He took a major role in a production of *Tom Sawyer* and plucked some basic banjo in a skiffle band called the Conga Boys. 'I got my first chance to act through answering a BBC advertisement for boys to play urchins. They asked me to audition but I didn't get a job. So I answered the same advertisement a second time. They obviously didn't remember me. I did the same audition and was accepted. So I started acting then, a couple of spots on radio, little plays like *Morning Story*. Everybody at school said I should be a professional actor, but I always said no, I was going to be a jockey.'

Davy was fourteen when his mother died in 1960. The effect on the family unit was shattering. Davy found that he had no further interest in school, 'I really decided that I wanted to be a jockey because I realised it was the one profession in which it was an advantage to be little. . . . Luckily enough, one of my sisters knew a bloke who was friendly with a reporter called Richard Onslow on the *Sporting Chronicle*. Onslow knew Basil Foster, the well-known Newmarket trainer, and wrote to him on my behalf.'

Foster was willing to accept young Jones as an apprentice and even board him in his own house. Davy sampled the life for a couple of weeks during summer holidays, painfully finished the school year, and returned to Newmarket at Christmas to become an apprentice jockey at a wage of twenty-five shillings a week! He was a competent apprentice, although his head trainer Bill Evans once claimed that he rode like a sack of potatoes. He enjoyed the work and also enjoyed the full support of his father, 'Dad didn't want me to spend my whole life like he did and have nothing to show for it. He wanted me to go out and make some money so I wouldn't have to worry when I got to his age. He would even send me spending money while I was training. Most fathers just want their sons to bring their wages home. That's how it happens in England – you give your wages to your parents and they give you an allowance. It's the proper thing to do.'

Although he was very involved in the racing world, Davy had not left behind his interest in theatre or music. Early in 1961, Bobby Vee, who had just scored his first hit with *Devil Or Angel*, became an overnight hero, and when Davy heard Johnny Tillotson's *Poetry In Motion* he rushed out to buy a copy, even though he

Riding 'Largee Duff' at Basil Foster's Newmarket stables, 1960.

didn't own a record player. Davy was also doing live performances during weekend breaks and at one pier concert on the Isle of Wight, was spotted by BBC radio writer Bill Naughton, who took a note of his name.

BBC producer Alfred Bradley contacted Harry Jones and asked if Davy could appear in a radio play being recorded in Leeds, called *There Is A Happy Land*. Harry passed the request on to Basil Foster, who was quite happy to give Davy some time off. Davy, however, was not terribly interested. 'I was quite happy at the stables and acting wasn't as important as becoming a jockey,' he recalls. He finally did accept the offer and managed to get his name in the *Radio Times*. A reviewer noted that it was the longest radio part ever written for a juvenile – almost four hours. Davy made an instant impact with his performance and the offers of acting work began to accumulate. Soon Foster received another letter from the BBC requesting Davy's services in a television programme called *June Evening*, and then Granada Television asked that he go to Manchester for an appearance in the hallowed *Coronation Street*. Then Davy performed in *A Series Of Modern Stories* on radio, and the first episode of the television cop show *Z Cars*. By this time Basil Foster had come to the very astute conclusion that horse riding was not to be David Jones' destiny. Rather than hinder what might divert Davy from his chosen profession, Foster decided to do everything he possibly could to encourage him. 'I realised, after watching him on *Coronation Street*, that he really did have a great deal of talent. In a way I felt sorry for him because he was so much in love with racing and he hated to ask for time off to pursue his theatrical interests. All the same, I felt more confident about his chances in the theatre than in the equally tough world of racing.' Davy, at that stage, was just about to commit himself to a career as a professional jockey. 'I didn't want to leave the stables at all, even for a few weeks. Being a jockey was my big ambition, not acting. But Basil persuaded me to try it for a time so I travelled up to London to audition for the part of Michael in a touring company production of *Peter Pan*. They had me walk about, say a few lines, sing a song, and eventually they said I was fine for the part. They also sent me for an audition for the part of the Artful Dodger in Lionel Bart's West End production of *Oliver*, but the person who auditioned me said I could only have the part if I lost my Northern accent. I had just six weeks to do it, while I was touring with *Peter Pan*.'

Fortunately a young actress called Jane Asher, who had herself crash-learned a smattering of cockney,

Above right: Davy during a performance on the pier at the Isle of Wight.
Below: Ena Sharples and 'grandson Colin' (Davy Jones) in a 1961 episode of the marathon ITV series Coronation Street.

offered to teach Davy enough East End jargon to get him on stage in the West End. 'It was all a bit of a laugh really, but Jane did manage to teach me enough phrases to pass the second audition when I got back to London.'

David Jones performed the part of the Artful Dodger at the New Theatre (now the Albany) for eleven months, from 7 May 1962. He enjoyed the experience but was still unwilling to sever his connections with the turf. 'Once or twice I managed to get time off to go to a race meeting near London and meet up with some of the apprentices. I'd try to collect all the gossip from the stables. I was always interested in the fortunes of a horse called Stonecrackers, which was the first proper mount I'd ever had.' Basil Foster came down to London regularly to see the show and recalls that 'Davy always made me promise that he could come back to Newmarket when the show was over.'

Naturally, Davy was reluctant to accept an offer early in 1963 to repeat his role for David Merrick's production of *Oliver* on Broadway. But Foster's advice was 'Don't be a mug, why work with other people's horses when you can own your own? Go to America and make a lot of money, then come back and buy the best.' So, fifteen-year-old David Jones, a wide-eyed working class lad who had never travelled further than from Manchester to London, flew to New York.

The Big Apple was almost too much to handle. 'People stared at me when I walked down the street,' he recalls. 'I couldn't understand it, then I realised that I had long hair, which suited my role as the Artful Dodger, but all the American males had crew cuts. Everything was so big, so different from England. I'd never eaten a steak in England but in America I had it every meal for a month, including breakfast.'

Davy played the Artful Dodger for one year and seven months, during which time he was nominated for a coveted Tony Award and judged by the *New York Times* to be a 'young Danny Kaye.' His personal following was so strong that by the end of the run, his fan club boasted almost twelve thousand members. When club president Helen Kesnick organised a meeting with fans on Long Island, more than five hundred turned up for an autograph and a kiss.

By the time he was seventeen, Davy was a confident, capable young man with the world at his feet and beautiful girls by his side. The society pages of New York newspapers often sported photographs of the young actor escorting stunning females to ritzy nightspots. Davy's first significant teen-media coverage came in the December 1963 issue of *16* magazine, which gave him a front cover listing. The major stories in *16* magazine were devoted to screen personalities like Elvis Presley, Ann-Margret and Jesse Pearson (*Bye Bye Birdie*), Paul Petersen and Shelley Fabares (*Donna Reed Show*), Patty Duke, Rick Nelson (*Ozzie and Harriet*), Richard Chamberlain (*Dr. Kildare*), George Maharis (*Route 66*), Edd Byrnes (*77 Sunset Strip*), Hayley Mills, Annette Funicello, Connie Francis, Troy Donahue (*Hawaiian Eye*), Russ Tamblyn, George Chakiris (*West Side Story*) and Vince Edwards (*Ben Casey*). So, although stage performers rarely enjoyed coverage in *16*, editor Georgia Winters could not ignore Davy's press notices and the increasing number of enquiring letters from her readers. 'A real show stopper, David Jones has completely won the hearts of all who have seen him. Let's hope he decides to stay in America after he outgrows his part.'

On 9 February 1964, Davy appeared on the *Ed Sullivan Show*, performing a song from *Oliver*. Also on the bill was a brand new act from Liverpool, called the Beatles, who effectively stole much of Mr Jones' thunder. He was far sighted enough to ask for a video of the show, which he counts as one of his most treasured possessions to this day.

Towards the end of 1964, David Merrick asked Davy to join a three month roadshow production of *Pickwick*, starring British comedian Harry Secombe. Ward Sylvester urged him to accept the offer, promising that when the show hit Los Angeles he would have the house stacked with influential people. True to his word, Sylvester gathered half the staff of Screen Gems-

The first Manchester boy ever to play the Artful Dodger on the London stage.

16

Columbia at the Los Angeles Music Centre for the opening night. Davy's breezy performance of snappy show tunes and gentle love ballads charmed the select gathering and, during the Californian run of the show, Davy signed with Screen Gems-Columbia's house label Colpix, and began recording tracks for what would become his debut album. Davy had already signed an acting contract with Screen Gems-Columbia in 1963 but little was done until scriptwriter Larry Tucker saw him at the *Pickwick* opening performance, and told him, 'I want you in my next show.'

The company was obliged to find some work for their contracted star, so they cast him as a glue-sniffing wife beater in an episode of *Ben Casey* called *If You Play Your Cards Right You Too Can Be A Loser*. Davy also auditioned unsuccessfully for roles in some new television shows, *Hogan's Heroes* and *The Wackiest Ship In The Army*. 'I was either too young, too English, or both.'

Christmas 1964 saw Davy back in Manchester unsure of his future. He had nothing more to occupy him in America, no more stage shows, no more recording plans and no television or film openings. 'To tell the truth, I wasn't sure what I was going to do. Things looked so bleak that I was ready to forget showbusiness and just stay at home. Months passed and I heard nothing from my manager or agents in America, so I began thinking seriously about racing again. Then in March 1965 I received word from Ward Sylvester to return immediately to America. Once more I was faced with the decision of leaving England for something unknown. But I felt I had to go back, if only to make my father proud of me.'

Back in Los Angeles, Davy auditioned for some television shows and landed a meaty part in *The Farmer's Daughter*, playing a Congressman's son who forms a rock'n'roll band. He also continued his recording career, laying down tracks for new single releases. Colpix released three singles within the first half of 1965 but none made the charts. However, they did rekindle the interest of *16* Magazine's new editor Gloria Stavers. Stavers began to feature him in the magazine and soon found that the stories and cutesie-pie photographs were stirring up quite a groundswell. This reaction was intensified by the release of his first album.

'David Jones' was a simple teen pop album after the manner of the singer's idols – Bobby Vee, Bobby Rydell and Cliff Richard – barely acknowledging the advent of the Beatles and the British Invasion. A good third of the songs were British music-hall standards – *Maybe It's Because I'm A Londoner*, *Any Old Iron*, *Put Me Among The Girls* – treated in much the same way as Herman's Hermits' version of *Leaning On The Lamp Post* and *Bidin' My Time*. The rest of the album yielded some occasionally tolerable moments. Standing out was a folk-rock treatment of Bob Dylan's *It Ain't Me Babe* which was almost as good as the Turtles' version later that year. Van McCoy's *Dream Girl* was pleasant melodic pop and even a cover of Mann and Weil's Paul

Petersen top ten of 1963, *My Dad*, recorded as an obvious tribute to Harry Jones, was quite listenable. A number of Colpix tracks were issued only on singles, including *Take Me To Paradise* and, the best track of all, Goffin and King's *Girl From Chelsea*.

At this point the Davy Jones chronicle becomes confused, as Davy has never agreed with the accepted story of the origination of *The Monkees* series. However, his own account has offered some contradictions: 'There was a song in *Pickwick* in which I sang "I'm as clever as a monkey in a banyan tree." I thought it would be a good idea to form a group called the Monkeys. I'd sing songs with a monkey on my shoulder, just like one of those guys at a barrel-organ. Then Screen Gems came up with an idea for a show in which I'd have two parts, playing cousins. It was going to be called *The Monkeys* but the idea became *The Patty Duke Show*.'

The following version gets a little closer to the truth; 'The Monkees idea came out of me seeing the Byrds and Sonny and Cher at a place called Ciro's on Sunset Strip during 1965. I was in a penthouse across the street and I saw the Byrds and thought "I want that group to back me, I wanna be in a group." At the same time Ward Sylvester, a friend of Bert Schneider and Bob Rafelson, took to them an idea for a show to be called *The Monkees*. Columbia Pictures was starting to falter a little because of union problems so they started merging and bringing independent companies in. Bert wanted to do his own thing so he brought Bob in and got Larry Tucker and Paul Mazursky to write a script. Then Ward, Bob, Bert and I went out and experienced the new groups – we really liked Arthur Lee and Love, and the Lovin' Spoonful. We needed three other guys for the show so we went to all the clubs in L.A. We found Micky playing with the Missing Links. Yes, there was a press ad, that's how we found Mike.'

The truth of the matter is that Ward Sylvester became aware of the television project which Rafelson and Schneider had conceived and were about to execute. At the same time, Screen Gems-Columbia were trying very hard to find a suitable vehicle for their contracted actor, so they let it be known that it would be desirable to have young David Jones included in the new series. Raybert Productions agreed to audition him, they liked what they saw and gave him the part but not without some reservations. 'Davy had the least contact with rock-'n'roll,' explains Rafelson, 'so I wondered if he wasn't the real gamble of the four of them. I even wondered if he'd be able to get into the spirit of the show.' Davy was not overly excited by his role in *The Monkees* either. It was no different to landing his roles in *Oliver* or in *Pickwick*. 'I don't regard this as a success,' he declared, 'it's just a step up.'

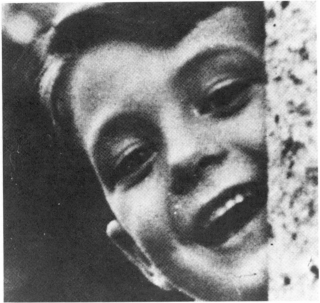

One of the few photographs of Mike as a child. Taken in 1947 when he was five years old.

Robert Michael Nesmith was born on 30 December, 1942 in Houston, Texas, the only child of Bette and Sergeant Major W. A. Nesmith. Six years later his mother broke away from the rigid discipline of army life and relocated herself and Michael in Farmer's Branch outside of Dallas, having inherited some land and property in what was essentially a black ghetto. Stark poverty beset the Nesmiths as mother and son struggled to establish a new life outside the stifling military base community. 'I had a tough childhood,' Mike recalls. 'I remember being hungry a lot. I couldn't keep up with the other kids because I went to a pretty rich school due to the weird zoning of school districts. I was unpopular because I was poor, thin and ugly. Until I was about sixteen I kept trying to make friends but other kids were crummy to me because they were wrapped up in themselves and their huge social system. They just used to laugh at me.'

Without the demands of social activity, Mike developed a voracious appetite for information, experience and introspection. 'I was interested in things like where chalk came from, how much money the janitor made, or how the boilers worked. There was a third grade teacher who let me sit and read all these weird books and never listen to the lesson. She passed me. She was nice. I didn't start failing really badly until high school, which was a real drag.' In high school Mike attempted to compensate for his unpopularity with eccentric behaviour. He found that by organizing dangerous pranks against teachers he could command attention, albeit fleetingly. 'I used to walk out of class a lot, just go whistling down the hall. I'd really make the teachers mad because I'd never get visibly upset, even when they put me on detention for days. I don't really understand why I was never expelled.'

During this struggle for peer acceptance, music began to creep into Mike's life. 'There was this guy who played organ in the window of a Dallas music store and I would stand outside that man's display for hours. As I watched him work, moving his fingers along the keyboard and making these incredible sounds, I thought it was a remarkable way to use thought. As I got into music I found that the only stuff that was really appealing to me on a gut level was black rhythm and blues, which I recognised as a highly evolved music. The white rock'n'rollers just zipped by me. Nothing happened to me with Elvis or Bill Haley or Buddy Holly or the Big Bopper. I liked it, it was hit music and it was part of the social boogie of the time but in terms of something socking me in the stomach, nothing much happened until Bo Diddley, early Ike and Tina Turner, and blues guys like Freddie King and Bobby 'Blue' Bland who were hanging out in the South. I remember when B. B. King had something like six hits in a row. At least they were hits to me because they were what got played a lot on the juke boxes when I was in the back of some bar shooting illegal pool. People like Jimmy Reed, Ray Sharpe . . . hell they lived right there!' But it was not only black blues which affected the young Nesmith. He also latched onto the white country music which dominated the airwaves of the South. The notes on his first solo album state, 'Hank Williams, Jerry Lee Lewis and Jimmie Rodgers are to me something of a musical triumvirate. Somehow I always get back to them. They had a clearly defined musical position, a pure approach to what they sang and wrote . . . alive with their own emotion.' Such was the intensity of his spiritual conversion to music that he was able to land a singer's job with a credible band run by Spinner Martin, on the strength of knowing a handful of Chuck Berry songs.

During his later high school years Mike began running away from home, once by 'borrowing' the family car for a flit to California. Bette Nesmith had remarried Robert Graham, a union which apparently did not receive Mike's full blessing. When he turned eighteen his mother packed him off to a military career in the U.S. Air Force, hoping that it would curb his developing delinquency. His fourteen-month stint is best described by himself. 'As an airman I was a disaster. I tipped over a general's plane one morning while cleaning it, which is not the kind of thing you do if you want to get ahead in the air force. I wasn't the school type and I wasn't the military type either.' The only highlight he can recall from his service days is a concert by Hoyt Axton at an Oklahoma folk club. 'After I got out of the air force I asked my parents to stake me to a guitar. I figured that the easiest way to learn was by trial and error. I played records and tried to pick out the right chords as I listened. People told me I must be mad, that the way to do it was to go to a teacher or at least buy a tutor book. The result was that I could do a lot of things with a guitar that just weren't meant to be done. I'm not what you call an expert technician but I get by.' With increased musical proficiency came an interest in songwriting. 'I tried to learn some folk songs but I couldn't master them so I began to write songs that sounded tonally correct to me. I never understood the science or mathematics of music but I knew how to express myself musically.'

At San Antonio College, where he enrolled after the air force, Mike continued to pursue musical interests as well as involving himself in drama by managing the campus theatre. Like a number of other budding young Texan musicians such as Augie Meyers (Sir Douglas Quintet) and Keith Allison (Paul Revere and the Raiders), he began keeping company with Southern Texas celebrities Denny Ezba and the Goldens. Ezba was a John Mayall-type figure who encouraged young players to climb up on the stage and often participate in recordings. During an engagement at the college theatre Ezba heard and liked Mike's *Go Somewhere and Cry* and offered to record it. He was invited down to the session at Jeff Smith's Texas Sound Studio and contributed some guitar and sagebrush whistling.

Confident enough to work alone, Mike began flogging himself around the local folk club circuit with a slightly more expensive guitar and a kazoo. At this time he met double-bass player John Carl Kuehne who called himself John London, and the two soon began working as a duo. They proved to be well matched and bookings were moderately strong. Mike was the dominant partner from the outset. A classic 'only child' personality had moulded him into an individual who would be later described as 'having no community spirit whatsoever.' Socially, conditions were only slightly altered from grade school days. Women were still not beating a path to his door. 'I couldn't get a date. I'd ring up girls and they'd say "No, I don't like you." It used to shoot me down real bad.' But male companionship was another matter again. Mike began surrounding himself with a tight circle of high school and air force buddies, which included London, Michael Murphy, David Price and Bill Sleeper. Mike finally set his eyes upon Phyllis Barbour, another military child, three years his junior,

John London and Mike Nesmith

who had spent her childhood in army camps around the world and the United States. Mike asked Phyllis to marry him before he had even taken her out. She declined, but his persistence paid off. 'You feel certain things about certain people and that was the way I felt about Phyllis immediately I met her. I waited a while, asked again and she said yes.' They were married in San Antonio on 16 March, 1963 and on 31 January, 1964 became parents of a son who they named Christian Du Val.

Bored with his academic pursuits and the stagnation of his musical activities, Mike purchased an MG Sprite sports car, loaded it with Phyllis (whom he called April), John London and various oddments of luggage, and headed off for California. Outside Bob's Restaurant in Van Nuys the intrepid trio picked up a copy of the *Valley News*, a North Hollywood newspaper filled with advertisements for apartments and employment. They moved into the first apartment they looked at, the landlord of which happened to have a daughter who was Frankie Laine's business partner. This helpful soul wasted no time in directing Mike and John, as the duo called themselves, to the Laine office for an audition. 'This lady asked me what I did and I told her that I was a singer, a songwriter, a guitarist and an actor. She said, "You're terrific, we'd really like to put some money into you and develop you as an entertainer," which sounded OK to me.' The first assignment arranged by the Laine office sent them right back to Texas, on a three month tour of Southern School Assemblies.

'When we got back,' explains Mike, 'We were just about dead and we didn't have much money to show for it either. We weren't sure what we wanted to do but we knew we weren't going to do any more road tours. As a folk singer, it became swiftly apparent to me that the folk era was waning. The Beatles were hot news and electric rock'n'roll was starting to happen. The Laine office suggested that I get a band together so I called up this drummer in Dallas called Bill Sleeper and said, "C'mon let's make some rock'n'roll." We went off and thought real hard for two or three days about what to call the new act and finally we came up with Mike, John and Bill.'

Mike, John and Bill were but a brief twinkle in rock's firmament. They played very few gigs but did manage to persuade Laine to let them record a single, *How Can You Kiss Me?/Just a Little Love*, for his Omnibus label. It sunk without a trace, as did the act itself when the draft board nabbed Bill Sleeper. 'John decided to stick around with me so I thought I'd get back into working in small clubs and bars. I should explain something before I go any further. There was a group called the New Christy Minstrels who were owned by three people – Randy Sparks, George Grife and Greg Garris. Randy Sparks, who owned a third of the band, crossed swords with Grife and he was bought out for about two and a half million bucks. So Randy took his sell-out money and decided to open a folk club called Ledbetters in Westwood, near UCLA. That became the other folk club in LA besides the Troubador, but whereas the Troubador crowd were all dope freak crazoids, the Ledbetter crowd was the funky starched jeans, clean shirt set. To give you an example, Tim Buckley came out of the Troub and John Denver came out of the Ledbetters.

'There was a lot of competition between the two clubs. Guys from each would go out onto the Hollywood streets looking for starving performers. I naturally gravitated toward the Troub and I talked John Weston into giving me a chance to try out there on a Monday night, Hoot night. I got up there with my guitar, harmonica, wool hat and blue jeans jacket, and this guy came backstage after the set and said, "that was sensational, I'd really like to talk to you about a publishing deal". Now in those days a publisher bought a song for $50 or hired a writer for $50 a week if it looked like the guy was prolific. Those days are gone now for anyone with a brain in his head. I said, "Who are you?" he said, "Randy Sparks", I said "far out" and we did a deal. I signed a publishing deal with him and got $600 which was an enormous amount for

someone who was nearly destitute. Randy told me that he also wanted me for a new project he was putting together. I'd got about $10 for my Troub spot but Sparks was offering me about $75 a week, which was the rent for sure. Coupled with my advance of $600, wherein he picked up *Different Drum*, *Some of Shelley's Blues*, *Propinquity*, *Nine Times Blue*, etc, songs which later made my yearly publishing royalty up to six figures, I was doin' all right. Sparks later sold my publishing to Screen Gems who now hold the copyrights to all my early work.'

Randy Sparks had big plans for Michael Nesmith. 'Randy decided that he wanted to put together a new folk group along the lines of the New Christy Minstrels, to use at his club. I really wasn't very interested – but the streets of Hollywood impel you to seek security, it's kind of a rough existence without dough. It didn't seem too bad, as long as I could have some kind of creative input, so I became leader of the Survivors. He put us into rehearsals and seemed to like the original songs a lot. These rehearsals went on for a long time and there were no other demands on my time, so I kept hanging out at the Troub and Doug asked me to take over running the Hoots. You see, Monday night was like local talent night . . . "Ladies and Gentlemen, here's a young man who's really good and we're sure you'll like him – Stephen Stills." The Troub was white hot then, Linda (Ronstadt) was hanging out there with the Stone Poneys and so was virtually everybody who ultimately became the Byrds, Buffalo Springfield, Association and the Eagles. The Survivors never did happen because Ledbetter's burned down and, with no place for us to play, Sparks wasn't really happy about paying our salaries. So I kept on at the Troub.'

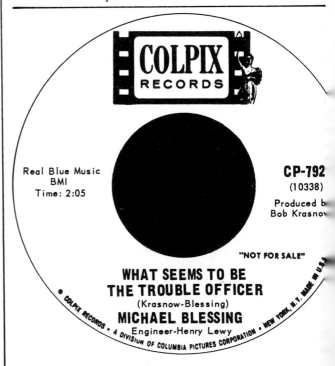

During the Ledbetter's period, Mike had run into Barry Friedman in Spark's office. Friedman, who would later become the Reverend Frazier Mohawk, began peddling Mike's appealing, well-structured songs around town. He pulled off quite a coup by placing (and producing) *Mary Mary* with the ultra-cool Paul Butterfield Blues Band. 'My songs were beginning to attract some attention in the legitimate rock community. It was happening to a lot of people in the folk community, like John Herald and The Greenbriar Boys, as part of an insemination process that was occurring. Around this time a producer called Bob Krasnow was looking for someone to sing a Tom Paxton song that he thought would be a hit. He wanted someone to record it, so he came round to Randy's place, which was a sort of talent pool. He had swung this deal with Colpix Records who were willing to fund two or three singles. Bob liked me as an artist so I was chosen.' The Paxton song was *The Willing Conscript*, which Mike cut as *A New Recruit* under the name of Michael Blessing. Krasnow went on to produce Ike and Tina Turner, Captain Beefheart and to be a house producer for Buddah Records and to later form Blue Thumb Records.

Mike was not a Variety subscriber and was thus unaware of the advertisement placed by Raybert Productions. However, everybody else at the Troubador and in the folk community heard about it within hours. Barry Friedman first brought it to his attention, followed by a regular crowd of university students who urged him to apply. 'I thought, ugh! that'll be the *worst* kind of show business . . . the kind of clowns who'd put an ad like that in the paper.' But, he decided to go along and see for himself. Kept waiting for hours, he was in an ornery Texas temper when finally summoned into the interview. Rafelson fired off his first question: 'What do you think you're doing here fella?' The light dawned on this dumb cowboy a little quicker than most. 'They were deliberately putting me on . . . just to see if I could improvise my way out of it. They were pretty ruthless, I'll say that for them. After I mumbled some pretty sarcastic reply about being there 'cos of some crazy and badly written advertisement, they just left me completely alone for a while. I was supposed to stand there and shuffle my feet around or twiddle my thumbs or something. It was a test and it was up to me to do something about it. So I fooled around with some things they had on the desk and I started asking questions of them. This fooled them and a couple of them actually started answering me. Then they realized I had switched the roles around. I saw them start to relax, then join in the spirit of the thing. I realised that these weren't bad guys. So I got the part. They cast me in the role of a guitar player named Mike Nesmith, which was a part I did pretty well. But being married and a father, I guess I felt older than other guys my age. I went down to try out because I didn't think anything would come out of it.'

In between the initial interview and the individual

personality screen tests, Mike became unavailable for duty on the set. Lester Sill had to show up at the local court house to bail him out and settle his debts before the project could continue. A number of unpaid debts had resulted in Mike's station wagon being repossessed and himself behind bars. It was an incident that Mike usually chose not to recall when later recounting the early days of the Monkees.

George Michael Dolenz was born on 8 March, 1945 in
Los Angeles, California, the firstborn of George and
Janelle Dolenz. His father was a Hollywood character
actor on the ascend, courtesy of the patronage of
Howard Hughes, his appearances including *The Four
Horsemen of the Apocalypse*, *Enter Arsene Lupin*, *My
Cousin Rachel*, *The Purple Mask* and *The Last Time I
Saw Paris*. George Michael grew up as plain Michael in
North Hollywood, the heart of the film community. He
was educated at the private Eunice Knight Saunders
School in the San Fernando Valley. 'I always liked
showbiz and wanted to make my living at it,' he recalls,
'but at the same time there was never any glory or
glamour about it. I saw it all behind the scenes and
knew how it worked. I didn't know if I would have
enough talent or determination to really make a career
out of it.'

Three sisters eventually came into his life; Coco when
he was two, Debbie when he was nine and Gina when
he was thirteen. The Dolenz family was close, happy
and secure, and Micky hero-worshipped his 'star'
father. He manifested this admiration with a passion for
fancy dress and role playing. After seeing *The Wizard of
Oz* he spent weeks trying to dress like the scarecrow. At
the age of eight he won a Halloween fancy dress
competition, dressed as a book – 'The History of
Halloween Vol. 1.' Coco recalls, 'Micky and I often
sang songs together, putting on shows at home for our
parents. We'd team up on some big song of the
moment, like Gogi Grant's *Wayward Wind*. I'd come
walking on holding a candle, with all the lights off, and
Micky would be hiding behind the couch with a piece of

cardboard, making a wind so that the candle flickered
and finally went out. Micky used to write songs too, and
some of them were pretty good. He'd come up with the
main idea and then we'd change them around to suit our
voices.'

By the age of nine, Micky Dolenz was the classic 'Dennis the Menace' kid, complete with an ear-to-ear grin, a forest of freckles, bright white teeth with a cute gap, and an Icabod Mudd crew cut. This wholesome image did not go unnoticed by his father's agent, who suggested that he audition for the lead in a new Screen Gems television series to be titled *Circus Boy*. George Dolenz agreed and briefed his son on how to handle the audition: 'be natural, that's all you gotta do. They'll ask you to read a few lines but mostly they'll be watching you to see how you behave, to see if you fit the part.' Micky fitted it perfectly and the series went into production under Herbert Leonard, who was also responsible for *Route 66* and *The Naked City*. As Micky recalls, 'it was an adventure show for kids, about an orphan boy called Corky who travelled around with a circus at the turn of the century. It was hard work for a kid but it was a lot of fun too. I loved doing it and working with the other actors and all the animals.'

By this stage George Dolenz was well established as television's *Count Of Monte Cristo*. So, at his father's suggestion, Micky used the surname Braddock, his mother's maiden name, so that he would not be seen to be capitalising on his father's fame. His hair was grown long and dyed blonde and the volume of fan mail from little girls was quite astounding. 'I could get the girls but I couldn't take them anywhere . . . I couldn't drive a car so I had to rely on the other guys in the show for lifts.'

The *Circus Boy* working schedule made scholastic pursuits difficult. 'They had pretty tough rules and regulations for kids like me. I still had to go to school and learn good English and how to add up sums. I didn't mind because I figured it would help me work out percentages on my salary and help me understand the fine print in contracts. That's the way I thought – I didn't want to be anything but an actor by then. I had to spend afternoons in the studio school and then learn my lines and study some more in the evening at home.'

The show ceased production in 1957, during its third year, and Micky returned to a normal school life. 'I don't remember being disappointed,' he says. 'I was so young I didn't understand much of what was going on. All I knew was that we weren't going to film any more.' He was enrolled in North Hollywood Junior High (now called Walter Read High) and then moved to Van Nuys High. His three years there were academically average and filled with sporting and drama activities. The sporting pursuits were short-lived after a doctor diagnosed a Perthese Disease in one of his legs, so drama took precedence. 'I loved to play in productions but I never got any leading roles because of my height. When I did finally start to grow I shot up at about three inches a month. . . . I knew that I was good at sports and really dug the open-air life, but what was the point of that when the doctors said that I could end up a cripple if I went on over-straining my bad leg.'

Music began to play an increasingly important role in

Micky's life, once the rigours of television acting had subsided. He kept on writing simple songs and singing them with Coco. 'Sometimes we got pretty close to making records,' she relates. 'One guy came and gave us the "I'll-make-you-stars" routine but nothing happened. And there was another time that a guy had the publishing rights to a song we wanted to do, but he wouldn't let us because nobody had ever heard of us.' Coco was as keen as her brother to pursue a musical career but Micky insisted that she keep on at school.

After barely graduating from high school, Micky enrolled at San Fernando College but his tertiary studies were terminated due to the sudden death of his father in 1963, at the age of fifty-five. Faced with the responsibility of his family's welfare, he left college and

worked as a mechanic for Mercedes Benz until 1964 when his mother Janelle Dolenz married Doctor Robert Scott, a minister, and moved with her three daughters to San Francisco. Micky stayed on in Los Angeles to pursue a romantic attachment. Relieved of the burden of bread-winning for his family he enrolled at the Los Angeles Trade and Technical College. 'I didn't have a major, I just took general courses with a lot of science and psychology. I liked Architectural Draftsmanship and thought about going into that. I also wanted to be an Electronics Engineer. I realised then that I should have learned more about other subjects when I had the chance at high school. It's a pity that when the most important things in your life are thrown at you, you're usually too young to want to know.'

In his late teens, Micky Dolenz wanted to know about everything. His unquenchable thirst for knowledge and artistic expression embraced reading, painting, construction, writing, movie-going, funny voices and a great deal of television viewing. Micky Braddock kept his television identity alive by occasionally answering advertisements for small part players, landing roles in *Peyton Place* (as Kitch), *Playhouse 90* and *Mr. Novak*, more for the quick cash than any career advancement.

At Trade College Micky fell in with a few young musicians and joined a rough'n'ready beat group called the Missing Links, who have been described as a 'strictly San Fernando Valley rock'n'roll outfit – comb your hair back into a pompadour and sing everybody else's songs.' Assuming the identity of Mike Swain, rhythm guitarist, he abandoned college once again and hit the Southern California dingy bar circuit. The Missing Links tried for a recording deal with any company willing to give them some studio audition time. Challenge Records ended up with two tracks in the can featuring Mr Swain's voice – *Don't Do It* and *Huff Puff* – which they were quick to release when Mike Swain became the more famous Micky Dolenz. So, when global stardom as a member of the Missing Links became a fairly remote possibility, Micky decided to quit the band and move to San Francisco to be with his family. This move was averted by Lillian Barkley, his old film-set schoolteacher, who urged him to stay in Los Angeles for the summer and try for any auditions that were going on.

When his agent alerted him to some auditions being conducted in September 1965, Micky had no reason to consider it any more important than the dozens of others he had attended since he left high school. He was a little stunned, though, when he arrived at Columbia Pictures to find hundreds of hopefuls scrambling for attention. He was equally amazed when ushered into a shabby green building with grimy walls and crumbling stairway behind the main office block. In ten years of hanging around backlots he had never come across anything quite like the second floor reception room he now found himself in; cluttered with magazines and strange posters declaring 'War Is Not Healthy For Children And Other Living Things' and 'He Who

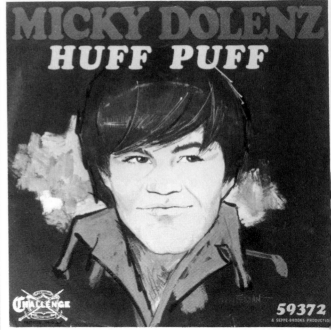

Meddles In A Quarrel Is Like One Who Takes A Passing Dog By The Ears' (printed over a shot of LBJ hoisting his pet dog in the air by its ears).

When he got out of the place he telephoned his mother and stuttered, 'Now listen, you're not gonna believe a word of this. I've been to auditions but this was like nothin' I've seen before. These two guys sat behind a desk and hardly said a word. So I figured it was up to me to do something. I started pulling crazy faces and twitching my hands. Did a coupla impressions of movie stars . . . all the time looking at these guys to see if anything was registering. Sometimes they smiled a bit so I just went on – I figured that if they wanted someone who was insane I'd do my best to give that impression. I tried to tell them about *Circus Boy* and stuff but they just kept on staring at me.'

Weeks passed and no word was forthcoming from Raybert Productions, Screen Gems, or Columbia Pictures, so Micky kept on with his preparations to move north. 'One day I was hanging around with some buddies doing nothing and one of them said he'd been reading about how I was due to go into a new television series. He said he had seen it in *Variety* so I got a copy and sure enough, there was my name. So I rang the *Variety* office and said, "Listen, I saw my name in your paper, is it true?". And they said "of course, didn't anyone tell you?" I was really happy.'

Peter Halsten Thorkelson was born on 13 February, 1944 in Washington D.C., the first of four children to Virginia and John Thorkelson, a nomadic pair of Norwegian descent. Within a year of his birth the family moved to Detroit, where another son, Nicholas, was born. In Washington John Thorkelson had been a government draftsman; in Detroit he worked as a magazine journalist. During the war he had served in the Army and in 1946 he was posted to Germany as a lieutenant to assist with mopping-up operations. The entire family moved to Berlin, where five-year-old Peter acquired a surprising command of the German language. 'We had a chauffeur,' Peter recalls, 'who couldn't speak a word of English. We became good friends and the only way I could communicate with him was to learn his language'.

Peter started school in Germany before he'd turned five and when the family returned to the United States his father refused to allow him to repeat first grade. 'From that time on, until I got to college, I was always about a year younger than the other kids. A year makes a hell of a difference in school. Kids don't like getting involved with someone they consider to be their junior. It didn't make things too easy.'

The Thorkelsons settled in Madison, Wisconsin, to facilitate John Thorkelson's graduate studies at the University of Wisconsin, and once he had achieved his Ph.D he uprooted the family yet again. He was offered an economics teaching post at the University of Connecticut, so the family headed east for what would be their final move. 'My life between then and my senior year of high school was a total disaster,' says Peter. 'In fifth grade I started going downhill because I was unhappy. I was constantly trying to make friends and trying to be funny but never succeeding because I was so much younger. I did have a small circle of friends but that was at home, it didn't have much to do with school'. . . . Within a cloistered academic community Peter began to take education very seriously. 'I just assumed that I was going to be a college English professor when I grew up.' Such an aspiration may have been achieved, had it not been for a growing fascination with music. 'When I was little I wanted to be an orchestra conductor. I remember a time when I was in Germany, I was about four-years-old, we went to a restaurant where they had an orchestra and the leader let me get up and conduct it. As I got older I began to love folk music, particularly the Weavers stuff.' Around 1956, as rock'n'roll was beginning to make its impact, Peter was pursuing rather different musical interests. Folksinger Tom Glazer (who scored a top twenty US hit seven years later with On Top Of Spaghetti) became a friend of the family and presented fourteen-year-old Peter with a ukelele, which he mastered with disarming ease. 'Then I took up the guitar and later I learned to play the five string banjo. Learning to play musical instruments always came easy to me. Other things I couldn't learn no matter how hard I studied.'

Peter's adolescence took a turn for the better around the time of his high school senior year, when he was moved to the newly-opened University of Connecticut High School. "It was much more comfortable. The age difference ceased to matter and I finally got a chance to make some real friends. This is when I guess you could say I blossomed out. There were all kinds of amateur societies I could join, like drama and rifle shooting. I even started going to football and baseball games. My father and I did a lot of target shooting together. I was very interested in drama but I was a late grower and because I was so short I never got any big romantic leads. My acting debut, at age sixteen and a half, was as a thirteen-year-old paper boy in Our Town. This was a bit degrading; it reminded me of the age problem that had dogged me all through school.' Peter also contributed to the school newspaper, submitting bizarre humour pieces illustrated by his younger brother Nick.

Buoyed by new confidence and security, Peter took a crash course in the french horn and was invited to join the University (not high school) of Connecticut Orchestra, as fourth chair french horn. 'I really began to love music, just about every kind except opera. Sometimes I liked listening to classical music better than anything. My favourites were Prokofiev, Bach, Rachmaninov and Stravinsky. Pop music seemed kinda drab around that time. The hard core rock'n'roll era had ended and most of the excitement had gone. I was hung up on the orchestral music we played at school. About the only popular stuff I used to really listen to was Ray Charles.'

While most of his friends went on to the University of Connecticut, Peter enrolled in Carleton College, a liberal-arts school in Minnesota, hoping to pursue a career as an English professor, an aspiration that met no

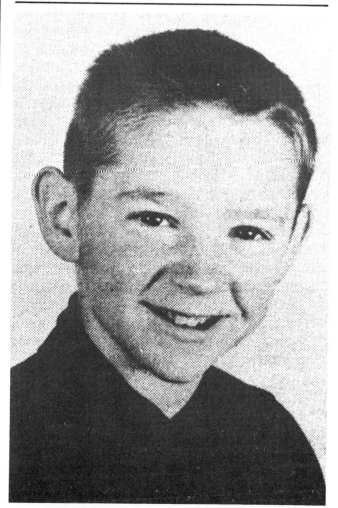

opposition whatsoever at home. The first term showed him to be a student with his mind occupied by thoughts other than those related to classical literature. 'During my second term I had a rather painful interview with the principal. He said my scholastic progress was just not good enough and so he was going to flunk me. Then I went home for another painful interview with my dad.' There followed what appears to have been a rather ferocious falling-out between father and son.

Peter took a job in a local textile factory and began to assert some independence. With a little money at his disposal and a normal obsession with most things female he began to get out and about, ready to sow his fair share of oats, wild or not. 'I guess it was a boring job but I met a lot of guys, must of them much older than me, who taught me a lot of new things. I enjoyed hanging out with them.' Details from this period are sketchy although it is known that, at the age of eighteen, he married a sixteen-year-old called Judy Babb. They separated after three months and were divorced soon after. This short-lived union became a remarkably well-kept secret, despite a number of hints dropped during the later years of media scrutiny. This new responsibility sent him back to Carleton fourteen months after he dropped out for another crack at academic honours. He managed to scrape through a year with a C+ average but was flunked at the beginning of the following year. 'It was the same problem as before, I didn't care enough. I was out doing dance dates with bands and I knew I had something inside me wanting to get out and that it was to do with music. I eventually had to level with myself and admit that I just didn't care enough about mere scholastic ability. I wanted more.'

Apparently unwilling to live near his father, Peter set off to New York City alone, to stay with his grandmother. 'We used to spend a week there two or three times a year and I loved the place. I got a job as an office boy at a theatrical agency and my grandmother wouldn't think of accepting any contribution toward the rent of the apartment whatsoever, so I managed to put aside a little money, which kept me alive later.' These savings were required when Peter began picking up small jobs around Greenwich Village as banjo picker. 'Once I got on a stage it was all over. I knew I had to be some kind of entertainer. I loved it! I got my own place in the Village with the money I'd stashed away but the beautiful thing about the Village was that it didn't take much money to live comfortably there. There was a strong community sense among the Beatniks. If you were down and out there were a half dozen people ready to take you in for a day or three or five. I was always being offered a new shirt, or a pair of boots or a meal. I was the best pampered Beatnik around!'

Peter was part of the Greenwich Village music community for about two years, through 1963 and 1964. Personable and ever-smiling, he made a better living from busking than most. He wandered into places like The Pad, dressed in a red check hunting jacket, blue T-shirt, jeans and sneakers, carrying a

bedroll and his bluegrass banjo or battered guitar and charmed the clientele with zany songs co-written with his brother Nick, such as *Under The Undertaker Gah-Goo-Gah*. Calling himself simply 'Tork' he soon earned a reputation as a talented musician and 'the friendliest guy in the Village.' Always eager to accept the lowest billing and open the show, he developed a smooth patter to extract the maximum amount of loose change from an enraptured audience. 'Ladies and Gentlemen, as you know, folk singers are very badly paid and have to rely on contributions from the audience. Here you see my bango [with the back neatly pried off]. In a minute or two I will pass it around and ask you to drop money in it. The metal money will go "clink" and the paper money will go "swish." If yours goes "swish" everyone here will know what a music lover and expert you are.' With this ploy Peter came by many more 'swishes' than 'clinks', to the disgust of the higher billed acts who scored the few meagre coins left in the pockets of these patrons of the arts. 'I learned how to put on a special kind of look which sort of reproved anyone who made no effort to contribute. It was a sad, appealing sort of look with my cheeks all hollowed out to look as if I hadn't eaten in days. In fact, most evenings we all used to earn enough for a slap-up meal between us. One night I somehow managed to collect $45 on my own account and I thought I was a millionaire. At least I did until a couple of the other guys reminded me that I owed them around $25 from the nights when I hardly collected a cent and they staked me to meals.'

One of Peter's fellow subsistence-level basket-passer was an unknown blind Puerto Rican singing guitaris called José Feliciano. Some years later he recalled th period fondly: 'I was reasonably well known in th coffee bars and some of the smaller clubs when I me Peter. He was a real nice guy, easy going, sincere and very good musician. I used him to warm the audienc up for me. I'd give him a few dollars and he'd go ou and get them laughing and smiling. When he built up name for himself we'd often perform at the same place together. We might both start early at the Bitter En and later in the night I'd make my way to the Gasligh with my dog and he'd be playing there as well. I don't know if Peter feels the same way as I do about those days but I got that much more satisfaction out of my music because I wasn't really being paid for it.'

'I suppose there really were times when we were starving,' admits Peter, 'but I was always very happy. People in those circumstances, doing what they want to do, usually are. I lived with a friend called John Hopkins in a three-room coldwater flat on Bedford Street which had bugs of every shape and variety. It was furnished in "contemporary side street" – with furniture discarded in back alleys and Salvation Army stores. That wasn't the way I wanted to live all my life but it was great for a while. The Village has always been great for people who want to write or paint or perform. It draws a lot of hopeful people to it – some who have real talent and a lot who have none. At the time the atmosphere was right for me. Nobody tried to tie me down or bug me. I didn't have to get into an office at the crack of dawn to have the coffee ready.'

Peter's first professional engagement, for a fee rather than a basket pass, was at a club called Charly Bates' on New York's East Side, where he made $50 for a week. Shortly thereafter he spent ten days as a sideman with Casey Anderson and the Realists and began jamming on stage with the Mugwumps, the folk group that was later to become known as the Mamas and the Papas. 'I had a belief that pop music could become exciting again and the Beatles came along and proved it.' At the Four Winds Cafe, an old Bob Dylan haunt, Peter ran into a young Texan guitarist and singer called Stephen Stills and the two joined with John Hopkins in an informal performance trio. Both had been aware of each other well before the meeting, due to their similar appearance. Peter's first words to Stills were 'So you're the guy who looks like me!' The pair shared an apartment for a month or so and became fast friends. The trio busked and scratched but splintered swiftly. 'Trouble was, we got bored. Not with each other but with the hard graft in the clubs for money that came only when customers were in a generous mood. So I took a job for about six months as an accompanist to the Phoenix Singers. I went out on tour with them, which was a change from the Village.'

Another change occurred late in 1964 when Peter accompanied his grandmother to Venezuela, where the Thorkelson family were temporarily relocated during a short-term academic work project. John Thorkelson was now Associate Professor of Economics at the Univeristy of Connecticut and becoming a widely recognised man. Mrs Cathering McGuire Straus, Peter's maternal grandmother recalls, 'During the six weeks Christmas holiday we spent in Caracas he went out almost every day to explore the Southern Andes Mountains, and the change of scenery and relaxation seemed to do him a lot of good.' So much good in fact that he became dissatisfied with the Greenwich Village lifestyle upon his return. 'I'd built up a circle of buddies who, in some strange way, had come to depend on me.

Don't ask me why, I was no better at finding work than they were. But I'd become a sort of unofficial leader of the gang. I really wanted to get into showbiz, make a name for myself, but I didn't want these guys to think I was planning to duck out on them. In the end I made up my mind to go to California and try my luck there. I set out in a '37 Chevvy that broke down outside Las Vegas. When it started to belch brown water out of the tail pipe I knew it was all over. I hitch-hiked the rest of the way. I had a lady friend waiting for me, I thought. Turned out I was more threatening in the flesh than at a safe distance. I managed to pull together a job playing double bass for a while for a black female vocal trio called the Apollas. I got to repay the favour later on.'

Like migratory fruit pickers in the depression years, there were hungry musicians to spare in Los Angeles. For every folk club spot there were a dozen eager strummers on hand to fill it. There was none of the communal sharing attitude of Greenwich Village; it was more a case of 'every man for himself' in the sunny west. 'Where I'd made a few cents singing in New York, the competition in California was that much greater. I just had to make the grade in showbiz or I was gonna explode inside, so I kept alive by washing dishes at the Golden Bear Hotel in Huntington Beach. Back in the village, when times got real bad, I'd worked as a kitchen boy in restaurants, and drudge-type jobs really never worried me much. You can actually learn to wash dishes with your eyes closed . . . and let your mind wander off on great flights of fancy. One day, I felt I just had to sing to keep my spirits up, so I got into a couple of hillbilly folk songs. What happened was that the other guys there liked it, so they said for me to keep on singing and they'd take care of the great piles of steak-stained plates. There was me, stuck in one corner and dressed in my overalls and just singing away like I was entertaining an audience. I didn't do the work, but I got paid – and it seemed like I was keeping the other guys' spirits up as much as my own.'

Tork was oblivious to the auditions going on over at the Columbia lot until alerted by Stephen Stills, who had also made the trek west and was playing with Richie Furay in a nine-piece folk outfit called the Au Go Go Singers. Stills had made a strong musical impression on Bob Rafelson but, as he told *Melody Maker* in 1967, 'his hair was falling out and he was losing his teeth. We figured he would need $500 worth of improvements to get him into shape so we turned him down.' When Stills was refused the part he magnanimously suggested his inquisitors track down his lookalike friend Peter Tork, who was a pretty fair musician as well. Summoned to the interview room Tork made an immediate impact. 'The first thing he did,' recalls Rafelson, 'was bump into the wall as he came in. I thought he was the funniest stupid person I had ever seen. He reminded me a lot of Harpo Marx and Charlie Chaplin.'

Peter Thorkelson in action in Greenwich Village.

take a giant step

The four chosen Monkees with acting coach/director Jim Frawley.

The four did not come together again after the filming of the pilot until March 1966, when they assembled on Sound Stage 3 of Screen Gems/Columbia Studios at 1334 Beachwood Drive, Hollywood, for two months of intensive 'polishing' at the hands of Jim Frawley. The training took place inside a windowless cubicle erected within the sound stage. A sign tacked to the padlocked door declared simply, 'Monkees – Keep Out'.

'At first they were embarrassed; they were stiff and a little raw,' recalls Frawley, whose teaching methods certainly were not from the Lee Strasberg handbook. He applied his own concept of spontaneous improvisation, closer to the style of live theatre or even television commercials than film/television acting. 'It wasn't teaching them to act at all because that wasn't what we were really looking for. We were trying to find *our* kind of humour so we improvised a lot – much the way Mike Nichols and Elaine May did. We just carried on until they began to know their own sense of humour, their own personalities and how they could interact. It was fantastic and exciting, and scary at times because I was working with four different personalities. There were fights on the set – I yelled, they yelled at me. But that kind of exchange was marvellous, it kept it alive! One of them would say, "Don't show me how to do it because I can't do it as well as you. Tell me how to do it." It was constant adjustment. I'd come to work wondering what kind of a day it was going to be. . . . They'd all contribute ideas. I'd say, "Hey guys, I'm in trouble, I'm dry today. What's funny about, ummm, archery? I don't have an idea right now." And the answers came from the Monkees, from the crew, from everywhere.'

As a widely experienced actor, Davy considered every moment of the training vital to his craft and was a model pupil. He recalls, 'we would sit around for hours watching the Marx Brothers, Three Stooges and Laurel and Hardy, learning comedy timing. We practised different accents and worked in different character roles so that when we were confronted by an unusual idea or situation in the show we had the reactions to it built in automatically. It was like putting a tape cassette into a machine. There were a lot of people depending on us, we had to know exactly what we were doing.'

During these early days, Davy was the Monkee with whom the creators felt most comfortable. He was an actor, a professional artist. Most of the early press generated for the series concerned Davy. Some bright spark at Columbia started splashing around an absurdly fabricated tale about him returning home to England after being chosen as a Monkee and riding no less than twenty-six winning horses. The proceeds from his wins were, depending on the publicist's mood on the day, either blown on big-stake racetrack gambling, or used to buy a $20,000 house for his family. Pure Hollywood puff.

When details of the project found their way into the business community of Los Angeles, hopeful sponsors were lining up at the studio door. 'Everyone wanted to get in on the deal,' recalls Mike. 'I was getting picked up by limousines in the morning and taken out to companies such as Vox where I was subjected to presentations on why I should use their amplifiers. This was about ten days away from having to worry about how I was gonna buy a $5 set of guitar strings.'

The allocation of musical roles caused slight friction. Mike and Peter were both accomplished players, so their respective lead guitar and bass duties made sense. Micky, however, was also a guitarist and wished to remain so, feeling that his face would be hidden if he was stashed away at the back of the stage on a drum stool. But he was also enthusiastic and energetic enough to tackle most challenges so, with a declaration of 'I'll try anything, I used to be Circus Boy you know!' he submitted himself to daily drum lessons – which he mastered with remarkable speed. Nobody was really sure what musical function Davy would serve, so he was relegated to tambourine banging, winsome glances and second lead vocals.

Contrary to general belief, the Monkees *were* initially given the opportunity to generate the musical content of the show but, as Peter later admitted, their own efforts were 'directionless and musically unproductive.' 'At first it was great,' explains Mike. 'There was all this

Davy Jones and Bob Rafelson

fabulous equipment suddenly laid on us, with nobody really giving two hoots about it. We had this big sound stage to practise on so we began to generate music among ourselves from the very first occasion that we had some time together. We were a real band but not a very good one, kind of a silly one because of our ridiculously disparate music tastes. In a way we were as much of a garage band as you could hope for. But we had a meeting to discuss our various interests and work out what directions the music should take and then we went into the studio and cut some rough tracks.' The tapes were left running during these early sessions, capturing goofs, snatches and complete songs. 'I can't give a specific figure on how many tracks we put down, but a hundred seems a pretty accurate estimate.'

When Bert and Bob heard the sounds being produced in the studio they were mildly impressed. 'There were many times when I thought that what the boys were doing sounded lousy,' revealed Schneider, 'but there were enough times when I heard them and got gooseflesh.' Unfortunately time was against Raybert's honest desire to have the Monkees perform their own music. Acting lessons, photo sessions, costume fittings, audition sets before major distributing record companies, and advance promotional activities left the four no time at all to rehearse as a band. 'All of a sudden the music became an area nobody wanted to talk about,' says Mike. 'It all just slipped away from our grip while we were being groomed to become big television stars.'

Boyce and Hart, having supplied the songs for the pilot, felt certain that they had the producer's job in the bag, but Schneider wasn't convinced of their ability to meet network demands. He wanted to try out producers with a better track record, so after the pilot had been sold, Schneider rang Boyce:

'Unbelievable, we've sold the pilot'. 'Fabulous', Tommy said, 'when do we start to do the records?'. 'Ah, funny you should say that. Now we need an unbelievably hot producer so how about I give you guys $500 each for what you've done and you give me the names of five producers?' 'Sure' Tommy instantly replied, 'Boyce & Hart, Hart & Boyce, Tommy & Bobby, Bobby & Tommy, TB & BH'. 'I'm very serious' snapped Schneider. 'So are we' screamed Boyce, 'we're the only guys who can produce this group'. Schneider emphasised that he needed someone who was popular and well known. So Boyce blurted out, 'Snuffy Garrett, Mickie Most, Goffin and King . . . and don't ever speak to me again!'

After a fruitless call to an uninterested Mickie Most in London, Snuffy Garrett and Leon Russell were the first 'name' producers called in. They attempted a recording of Goffin and King's *Take A Giant Step* with Davy on lead vocals but quit after half a day, apparently because Mike implied that what they were doing was 'garbage.' However, difficulties in initiating the music for the series was not Raybert's only headache. They found that they had misjudged the disrupting influence of

Mike Nesmith with Bert Schneider before the national television debut of The Monkees.

30

their radical concept on the insular and suspicious television industry. The tension on the backlot was first noted by *TV Guide* magazine: 'At Screen Gems they call it no-man's-land. It is a shabby green building, converted from a duplex apartment, its walls scuffed, its steps in a crumbling state of disrepair, crammed between buildings at the far end of the parking lot. This is GHQ for the Monkees. It's given a wide berth by the studio's Sta-Prest pants set – the TV establishment is not yet ready for the Monkees.'

Davy grimly recalls the hostility directed toward the four of them from the outset: 'We were hated on the lot at Columbia. The fifty-to-sixty-year-old sound and props men weren't ready for long haired punks coming onto the set, especially with their own TV show. They were only used to nice boys like Paul Petersen, Ricky Nelson and James Darren who knew their place and never said a word to anyone. Hollywood was supposed to be decadent and bizarre but they couldn't even handle our hair; when we walked into the studio commissary for lunch the place would empty in protest. Over at Disneyland, Walt Disney had personally banned all long haired boys from entry. It was crazy!'

Raybert shrugged off the establishment apprehension with the attitude that 'everybody over thirty is a square', which infuriated the rest of the studio. Reporters were a cause for further headaches, particularly when they got wind of the group's musical ineptitude and threatened to expose the frantic fabrication efforts being effected to get the show on the air. The most damaging incident occurred at Chasen's Restaurant in Hollywood. NBC Television was wining and dining its affiliate station executives, the men who ultimately decided which new network programmes would be run during the following season. These men were not, in the remotest sense, contemporary, enlightened or progressive; rather they were human manifestations of the lowest common denominator of taste level for which their stations catered.

Ignoring Schneider's protests, Screen Gems and NBC scheduled an appearance by the Monkees at this bloated-bellied and gold-toothed gathering. Studio writers knocked out a comedy sketch which they were to render as a surprise climax to the proceedings. The progress of the evening was chronicled by a *TV Guide* reporter: 'Things ran late. The Monkees stood outside, tired, nervous and unfed. I said "are you guys going to do the material?" "Hell, no!" they said. Somebody had dragged along a stuffed peacock and they were playing volleyball with it, stopping traffic on Hollywood Boulevard. Micky got into the restaurant switchbox and turned off all the lights. Finally they were introduced by Dick Clark. Since they had no musical instruments – everyone was afraid to let them play – they did "comedy" material. Micky shaved with a microphone. Davy pretended to be a duck. The jokes began to die. The affiliates were already hostile and what was not needed was a bunch of smart aleck kids. On the way out I heard one affiliate say "That's the Monkees?, forget

it!" The network paid dearly for this unseemly display; at least five key stations failed to pick up the show.'

The Chasen's debacle attracted the attention of the major news media and Raybert found that they could no longer hold the big guys off. So with just eight weeks to go until the start of the season, Schneider and Rafelson began to panic. They put through a call to Screen Gems Music boss Don Kirshner and, according to the *Saturday Evening Post*, pleaded, 'Donnie, we need a miracle.'

The Man With The Golden Ear

All the tapes on hand were sent to the thirty-two-year-old millionaire publishing magnate, who probably knew more about hitmaking than any other man in the industry, having been primarily responsible (with partner Al Nevins) for aligning tin pan alley with rock'n'roll back in 1958. His Aldon Music company had fostered the growth of such seminal New York Brill Building pop writers as Carole King, Gerry Goffin, Neil Sedaka, Howie Greenfield, Barry Mann, Cynthia Weil, Neil Diamond, Jack Keller, Toni Wine and Bobby Darin. He also served as musical supervisor for Screen Gems Television and had been responsible for providing the themes for *Gidget* and *Bewitched*. Kirshner promised to supply prototype records with a 'driving, exciting, frantic young sound.'

Meanwhile, Boyce and Hart were not taking their dismissal lying down. They were aware that their publisher was intending to book every hot session player available to cut the Monkees' backtracks. Boyce made peace with Schneider and Lester Sill and cajoled them into bringing Kirshner to their audition studio before he had a chance to check out anybody else. In a small room off Vine Street near Capitol Records, Boyce and Hart had put together a band comprising Jerry McGhee, Louie Shelton and Boyce on guitars, Larry

Taylor on bass, Billy Lewis on drums and Hart on organ. As the heavyweight contingent of Jackie Cooper, Don Kirshner, Lester Sill, Bert Schneider and Bob Rafelson walked around the corner, the band launched into *Last Train To Clarksville*, followed without a breathing space by *I Wanna Be Free* and *The Monkees Theme*. 'When we finished,' recalls Boyce, 'Kirshner said "that was fantastic, you guys are the producers." So we started cutting records the next day and the rest is history.'

Tommy Boyce (right) on the set with Micky and Peter, 1966

The Monkees were already familiar with Boyce and Hart, two bright guys their own age with senses of humour, so they voiced no objections to commencing serious recording work with them. On the first day, it seemed that every Screen Gems executive was in the studio offering suggestions. Boyce and Hart were not imposing enough to control the situation and the confused and irritated Monkees had no idea which master to obey. When Don Kirshner, who had not been introduced to the group, put forward his ideas Dolenz dumped a glass of ice water over his head in exasperation. 'I thought he was just some go-for, 'cause he had been out getting cokes for everyone. He yanked me out

in the corridor and said with controlled rage "Don't you *ever* embarrass me like that again." I must have apologised to him twenty times over the next few months.'

With just seven weeks to countdown, Boyce and Hart had no time for pleasantries. Each Monkee was given an audition which amounted to an assessment of rudimentary vocal talent. As Boyce explains, 'We sat them around a piano and had them sing all the songs we had written for them. It was obvious that Micky had the Paul McCartney voice, he could really sing. Davy had a passable ballad voice, Michael thought he was Merle Haggard and Peter had no voice at all. Now when you put all that together it wasn't the rock image that the show was supposed to have, so I told them that the truth of the matter was that they were hired as actors and there wasn't much we could do with all their peculiar talent.'

By this point, the four Monkees, with varying degrees of graciousness, had accepted that professional session musicians would create the backings for the records. They had been given a chance to prove their worth as a musical unit and had simply not delivered the goods. Davy and Micky conceded that they were hired as actors and that was the challenge they would meet; being studio musicians was not the job for which they were paid. But Mike who had so unnerved every producer who had tried to record the group, saw it all in an entirely different light and was not going to let Tommy Boyce stand between him and the artistic fulfilment to which he considered himself unassailably entitled. As Boyce remembers, 'Michael was trying to get his own way right from the start, so I told him that he was fabulous, his ideas were valid and that he was in the wrong gig – the kids weren't interested in country music. I did give Peter a voice audition on *Saturday's Child* but I had to finally say, "look Pete, I can't play banjo and you can't sing. If I played the banjo I'd sound like you singing, I have to erase the tape." So Peter left in a huff and came back with Michael, who pulled off his motorcycle helmet, crashed it down onto the console and demanded "why don't you let Peter sing? You guys never let us come to the sessions, it's just you two with Davy and Micky." So I said "well that's the way it should have been in the first place Michael, you know what I mean? You should have stayed with the Randy Sparks Trio." In the end we let him do a couple of tracks on his own just to calm the situation down a little.'

Apart from the obvious ruling that all recorded songs had to be Screen Gems copyright, the producers were free to slip in as many of their own songs as they could get away with. So, apart from the three tracks they had dished up at the Kirshner audition, they put forward *Gonna Buy Me A Dog*, *Let's Dance On*, *This Just Doesn't Seem To Be My Day*, and (Tommy Boyce and Steve Venet's) *Tomorrow's Gonna Be Another Day*. From the hallowed Goffin and King catalogue came *Take A Giant Step* and *I'll Be True To You* (Goffin/Titelman). Nes-

...mith came in late at night and worked on his own cornshucking *Papa Jean's Blues* and his collaboration with Gerry Goffin and Carole King, *Sweet Young Thing.*

There is no doubt that Don Kirshner had enormous influence on the creation of the Monkees sound and initial musical image. Regardless of the producer credits, which appeared on the albums recorded during his reign, his instructions to the musicians, producers and engineers carried considerable weight. He reserved the right of 'fine tuning', even to the point of altering written songs to suit his requirements. He would often have to explain to his contract writers, 'I know you are artistically correct, but this is how it will sell.'

As the four actors were getting together on the sound stage an awesome corporate machine was grinding into action. As Davy explains, 'one of the reasons Ward Sylvester left New York was to close Colpix Records down. They had asked Lester Sill to head Colpix only to shut it down a few months later, knowing full well they were about to put together the Colgems label with Don Kirshner in control and the Monkees as the only artist on the label.' Colgems (the name acknowledging the equal participation of Columbia Pictures and Screen Gems Television/Music), accepted a distribution deal from RCA, which was successfully handling the biggest teen idol of them all, Elvis Presley.

Colgems swung into action with the release of a debut single by the Monkees. The Boyce and Hart song *Last Train to Clarksville* was chosen because it had been used in the pilot episode and everyone involved with the project was busily humming it. It should be understood that this single, issued on 16 August 1966, was not intended as anything other than publicity for the television series. The themes to *Davy Crockett*, *Gidget* and *Rawhide* had all been hits so *maybe* a Monkees

This Cashbox *front cover shows the Monkees musical production unit (top right photo) – (left to right:) Bobby Hart, Don Kirshner, Tommy Boyce and Lester Sill.*

record could also pick up some spin-off sales. Don Kirshner felt he had a good chance of going beyond the standard 'novelty' penetration of television soundtrack songs. So from his chauffeured Cadillac with an eleven channel radiophone, Kirshner, "The Man With The Golden Ear", helped to conceive a saturation campaign which cost RCA $100,000, exactly double what Capitol had spent on launching the Beatles in the American market a little more than two years previously. A task force of seventy-six advance 'Monkeemen' criss-crossed the country to announce the impending arrival. Six thousand disc jockeys were furnished with preview records and thousands of bumper stickers proclaiming 'Everybody Is Going Ape For The Monkees' and 'Monkee Business Is Big Business' were strewn from coast to coast. Actual interviews with the four unknown pop sensations were strictly forbidden by Jackie Cooper, wary of defusing the impact of the television debut.

Colgems/RCA's advance promotion for the records was exceeded only by Screen Gems' advance promotion for the series. And when the two met on a common project the effect was extraordinary, as demonstrated by the San Juan Capistrano exercise on 11 September: Rafelson and Schneider, advised by Colgems of nega-

Launching Last Train To Clarksville *in San Juan Capistrano.*

tive reaction from radio to *Last Train To Clarksville*, cooked up a brilliant deal with Radio KHJ in Los Angeles. In August they offered a station executive a guest spot on the TV series if he played the single on the hour, twenty-four hours a day for a month. The day before the show went on air, a sixteen-coach train was hired, stocked with station listeners and sent down to the coastal town of San Juan Capistrano, which had been renamed Clarksville for the day. The Monkees flew there by helicopter, descended a rope ladder to the beach, to the accompaniment of a seventeen piece brass band and the tumult of more than 15,000 kids, sang one song, climbed back up the ladder and flew back to Los Angeles. So, by the time the series debut was imminent the song was a smash Californian hit and radio claims of 'a rip-off of the Beatles' ceased to matter.

The newly formed Monkees were flown to San Juan Capistrano by helicopter. The Californian coastal town was renamed Clarksville for the day.

Two days before, at 3.45pm on Friday, 9 September, at the Broadway Theatre in downtown New York, the Monkees had been presented to 2,000 (mostly female) teens, described by the *New York Times* as 'too old for Barbie dolls and too young for mini skirts.' The four told jokes, showed film clips and casually sang some songs. The select audience were then sent back to their neighbourhoods to tell all their friends to watch NBC TV on Monday night at 7.30pm. Those who tuned in on the night of 12 September saw four shaggy cherubs save the Princess of the Duchy of Harmonica from the clutches of the evil Archduke Otto.

Initial reaction to the show's irreverent, unorthodox production style was encouraging. 'Progress can turn up in the strangest places,' commented the *New York Times*. But the ratings were not so encouraging. Neilsen's figures placed it at number 70 in the overall TV market, but it was soon to move up into the top twenty and capture an estimated ten million viewers weekly.

Apart from the network stations who had rejected the programme after the Chasen's fiasco, other (predominantly rural) stations were taking it off the air following a loud backlash from redneck America, incensed at 'sissy longhairs' being given such prominence on the airwaves. As innocuous as it appeared, the show was threatening the values of middle America, as Micky recalls: 'At that time long hair meant gays, dope addicts or Jesus freaks. Kids would bring home Rolling Stones records and hide them under the bed. But we were right in the living room, we brought long hair and youth spontaneity to the dining room table. Now there were four long haired kids who didn't do anything evil, who didn't molest children, who worked and were happy

An early publicity still.

and healthy looking, so all these kids say to their parents "hey, why can't I grow my hair long?" and the parents can't find any convincing reason to say no.'

Newsweek noted that '*The Monkees* is fresh stuff for TV' but cautioned, 'Its freshness could conceivably be its downfall.' Several rural NBC affiliates refused to carry the show. 'There is a giant resistance to kids with long hair,' says Rafelson. 'The TV reviewer on the Portland, Oregon paper won't even look at the show. There's also a conservative resistance by adults to the music.'

On top of the conservative backlash came accusations of plagiarism. A *Newsweek* review observed, 'Such cinematic kinetics are really the property of Richard Lester but television is a medium which thrives on thievery, and there, Beatlemania has been exchanged for Monkeeshines.' There was always, within the camp, a niggling fear that the origin of the species would come crashing down on the million dollar clone and, perhaps as a defence, the four always spoke of the Beatles in terms of adoring reverence. 'If we could only be a quarter as good as the Beatles' said Davy, 'or even a tenth.' Raybert's worst nightmares were realised when two young television producers filed a suit demanding $6,850,000 in damages for plagiarism. Dave Yarnell and David Gordon claimed that their pilot television programme *Liverpool USA* had been transposed into *The Monkees* without them receiving due credit or reward. The case was eventually settled out of court with an undisclosed payment.

Last Train To Clarksville hit number one in America

As part of the greatest media campaign that has ever taken place in rock music, records of the Monkees songs were pressed onto the back of breakfast cereal boxes. Tracks such as Valleri *and* Teardrop City *were made available in this form up to two years before their official release.*

on 29 October, displacing The Four Tops' *Reach Out I'll Be There* and The Mysterians' *96 Tears*. By the time it reached the top ten at the beginning of October it had already sold half a million copies. At the same time, the debut 'soundtrack' album was at number one and the

biggest musical phenomenon since the Beatles was sweeping America.

The power of television made the make-believe Beatles quite irresistible. America was still reeling from the social impact of the British Invasion. After the initial shock had subsided, the national preoccupation with the flash and flurry of pop music was seeping into the creaking bones of a basically conservative people who had still not shaken off the trauma of President Kennedy's assassination. The message which the Monkees transmitted from their opening song was optimistic, positive and *very* American.

> Hey hey we're the Monkees
> And people say we monkey around
> But we're too busy singing
> To put anybody down . . .
> We're just trying to be friendly
> Come and watch us sing and play
> We're the young generation and
> We've got something to say.

'What do the Monkees want?' insisted the publicity blurbs. 'To be free, to make every day Saturday night, to climb impossible mountains, to take a trolley car to the moon, to deflate the stuffed shirts of the world, to do everything and anything . . . Their unrepressed happiness is the best answer available for an unusually grim world. It certainly is *the* answer to television's need for a wacky, wonderful, fast-moving comedy series set in the frugging, Watusi-ing discotheque sound of the sixties.' The kids soon tapped into the wholesome message. Asked by *Tiger Beat* to finish off the sentence 'I like the Monkees because . . .', a fourteen-year-old from South Pasadena offered: 'they don't protest life, they celebrate it,' while another fourteen-year-old in Minnetonka, Minnesota gushed 'they have tried so hard to give of themselves for others to make our world a *much, much* better place to live in.'

Below: The Monkeemobile

The first Monkees album had been put together in an atmosphere of chaos, disagreement and enforced spontaneity. Asked why there is no bass guitar on *Let's Dance On*, Boyce shrugs, 'we didn't have time to think about it; we had to cut it real quick, like in about seven minutes. By the time the bass player got to the studio, we'd done it.' Yet, almost in spite of itself, the album possessed a charm and exuberance that exemplified the very image that Raybert were creating on celluloid. In Britain *New Musical Express* described the album as 'Mid-Beatles . . . probably the most pleasant, tuneful, catchy and occasionally funny LP I've heard since "Rubber Soul" . . . Good, unpretentious pop.' The Monkees themselves were far from dissatisfied with the quality and success of their first record releases. To show their gratitude the four presented Don Kirshner with a huge mounted photograph of themselves, bearing the inscription 'To the man who made it all possible.' Kirshner would have cause to find the dedication very amusing within just a few months.

The huge success of the Monkees, if not initially as a television show then certainly as a chart pop act, offered a precedent as regards the side-stepping of time-honoured procedures in the music industry. Colgems had a free, half-hour, national television advertisement for their product so their strategy did not require the involvement of the radio business or the conferral of the rock press. Micky, who confesses that at the time he didn't even know what *Cashbox* or *Billboard* were calls the initial assault 'the first time that television and music industries combined forces in a concerted attack against the American consumer.'

With the fiascos of the Beatles' Saltaeb Inc. marketing well noted, Raybert, Screen Gems and Colgems expertly maximised on their sudden windfall. Franchises were allotted for fifty Monkee products, including bracelets, lunch pails, pencil cases, shirts, wristwatches, chewing gum and dolls electronically wired to reproduce each member's voice. Mike's familiar green wool hat was rolled out of the mills at $1.98, 48c more than he paid for the original. By the end of 1966, Monkee merchandising had earned $20 million. The Monkeemobile car used in the series (a Pontiac GTO redesigned by Dean Jefferies in the manner of Batman and Robin's Batmobile) was earning $3,000 for each appearance at supermarkets. One thousand, six hundred 'Monkeewear' sections and 'Monkee Nightclubs' (selling soft drinks only) were opening in department stores across the country. As Screen Gems' Ed Justin so succintly remarked 'These boys are not only in show business, they're in the advertising business.' Or, as Jackie Cooper admitted, 'You can fool some of the kids some of the time.'

shades of gray

From the very first episode of *The Monkees* it was apparent to even the most casual viewer that this was not standard situation comedy. If the Beatles and those they spawned had toppled the established order of the music industry, then Schneider and Rafelson were hell bent on shaking up the inflexible, intolerant world of corporate telvision. The show had an inbuilt mockery of traditional popular culture that was nothing less than radical in 1966. Technically, it horrified the highly standardised Hollywood film community. It was a testament to Rafelson's declaration, 'I do not regard film as a sacred parchment but as a pliable canvas.'

Rafelson must be seen as the prime creative force behind the non-musical success of the Monkees concept. In the summer of 1976 issue of *Sight and Sound* he explained. 'The tempo was of paramount importance, the shows were very fast moving. The boys had little, if any, acting experience so the whole show was created in the editing room. The average number of set-ups for a television show was about twenty-five a day. I brought the production team together and said "Look we will not travel in the customary teamster vans with all the equipment – we'll do this on the run." The first day that I shot I made one hundred and twenty-five set-ups. I said "Don't light the background, nobody will see it on the tube anyway." So we just didn't light anything, and once that was established as a concept we could travel much faster.'

Rafelson encouraged the principals to improvise dialogue and movement whenever they felt like it. Complete scenes were sometimes discarded in favour of ad-lib conversations conceived on the set, often captured when actors presumed that the cameras had stopped rolling. 'The idea of using new directors perhaps not too encumbered by traditional ways of thinking was initiated on the Monkees series and continued in the movies I made later.' Of the first thirty-two episodes, twenty-nine were directed by individuals who had not previously directed television

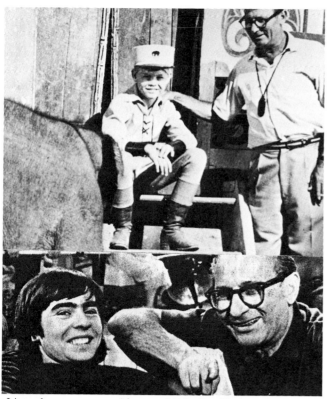

Lippy the cameraman with young Micky Braddock working on Circus Boy *and Lippy the cameraman with Davy Jones working on* The Monkees.

(Rafelson included). Jim Frawley had a crack at the early episodes, allowing his charges total freedom. In true *cinema verité* style he had hand-held cameras follow them as they romped in the surf, fought bulls, lifted weights, scrimmaged with gypsies, walked into cream pies, rode motorbikes over sand dunes, duelled like musketeers and slid down spiral staircases. Frawley's 'romps' were cut up and used as rapid cutaways in the finished print, many snatches appearing over the opening credits.

Some of the hired directors wanted no part of such an approach. Barry Shear left the set in disgust, angrily saying, 'If you don't care about your focus and lighting and if you're going to let four idiots ad-lib your dialogue, you don't need a director.' He may have been right, as there were more than enough creative people on hand to ensure consistently fresh input. As Davy recalls, 'There were people pulling cables who weren't meant to be. There were ideas from the soundman, the boom man; we had the prop man playing a part, a real family situation.' One cameraman, known affectionately as Lippy, a veteran of forty-five years who had worked on the *Circus Boy* series with Micky, became a father figure to the Monkees, regularly taking Davy home for dinner. 'It's a very unconventional set,' commented Jim Frawley at the time. 'People who walk on the set just

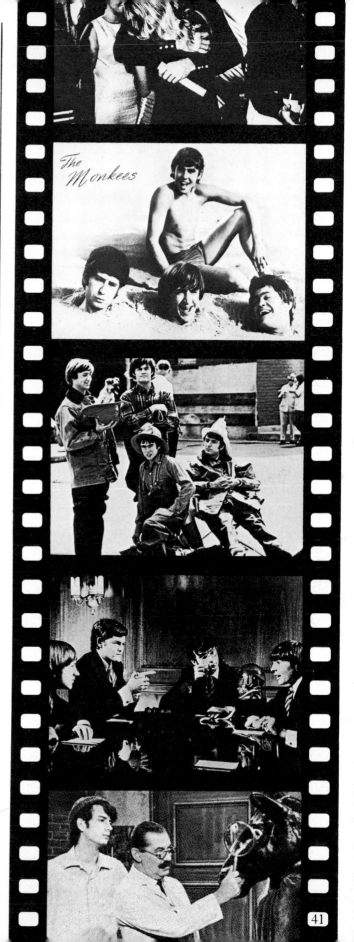

can't imagine that anyone could shoot this way. Guest actors are amazed! They find themselves doing things they never did on any other show because the atmosphere was very set – like a huge dinosaur taking it step by step, grinding and pushing it out. We're willing to make mistakes, to take a chance. We work extremely fast and shoot probably three times as much film as other TV shows. Everybody on the show really cares about it.'

An unprecedented amount of creative control was afforded the four Monkees, enabling Mike to casually state, 'We never try to fool the kids' He later observed 'There was a feeling generated by the producers that we were in the driver's seat, which was mythical. Their attitude seemed to be: "We know how to make the film and do the deals and maybe we can trust the sense these twenty-year-olds have about what's hip. Let's let them do their own clothes, pick their own instruments and sort of ad-lib along." What they really wanted was a show that mirrored the times without actually being part of it.'

Raybert was certainly not alone in its progressive application of contemporary music to intelligent celluloid concepts. During 1967, the Lovin' Spoonful fell in with Roger Corman protégé Francis Ford Coppola, who was manifesting *his* Richard Lester fixation with *You're A Big Boy Now*. 'It was actually the first film of it's kind that used a so-called hard rock score' he claims, and although he doesn't acknowledge any influence from *The Monkees* series, the style of the film, with visual absurdities like a girl glimpsed reading in a fountain, free-wheeling treks across Central Park as decoration for conversations, abrupt transitions, and cutting to a beat music soundtrack, suggests such a likelihood. Recently described by rock writer Ken Barnes as: 'The most bizarre comedy series since the

truly surreal *Burns and Allen Show*,' *The Monkees* became the most widely circulated television show in Screen Gems' history, seen in thirty-five countries with episodes dubbed into some twenty languages. The humour and appeal proved to be universal.

As long as the studio regime gave Sound Stage 7 a wide berth, all the rules continued to be broken. 'They wear hip-hugger corduroys, patent leather skirts, vinyl boots and the haunted stares of a Keane painting,' said the *Saturday Evening Post* of the after-school horde gathered by Rafelson in the set's conference room each day to send out postcards soliciting fan club members. They stood in groups inside and outside the studio, quietly following their favourite Monkee, unwilling to speak a word. 'When girls work on the show we ask 'em to drop back after shooting because it's cool to have them around,' drawled Mike. One regular visitor was

Coco Dolenz on the set with Peter Tork.

Mickey's nineteen-year-old sister, Coco. She was crawling the set on her hands and knees one day when showbiz reporter Jane Marshall was trying to conduct an interview. Asked the nature of her foraging she informed Marshall, 'I'm collecting all the dud bullets for Micky. He's going to make peace symbols out of them.' The schoolgirl brigade was eventually marshalled into a highly efficient workforce, overlorded by Marilyn Schlossberg, head of Monkee publicity, and assistant Charlene Novak. Frew Smallwood, one of Mickey's old girlfriends, was given a position as the head of Monkees fan mail (which was coming in at a rate of 65,000 letters a week). These three had the exhausting task of keeping the volunteers behind their desks and off the sound stage, a task assisted somewhat by the Monkees habit of dropping in to the press office to collect gifts, sign autographs and generally goof around.

Volunteer Lee Sellers spent many hours in the three-room publicity office over Christmas 1966. She recalls that Micky was once presented with a model castle, made out of plaster of paris, plywood, marbles, cork, cardboard and plastic. It had a photo of each Monkee set in the windows and both American and English flags flying from the turrets. Two girls had taken more than a month to construct this 'Monkee Manor' and were rewarded with Bert Schneider's decision to use it as a prop in the show. 'After I finished work one day,' relates Lee, 'I was outside the studio gate with some girls who had been waiting for six hours to see Davy. When Peter came out and told us that Davy had gone to England for his sister's wedding, a few days before, the girls started crying uncontrollably.' Girls cried from one end of America to the other; they blubbered and bawled over their homegrown Fab Four. They plastered their walls with pin-ups and reassigned their proposals of marriage from Paulie and Herman to little Davy.

In Hollywood the relative proximity of the new Valentinos was sometimes too great a burden for fans to bear. Those who couldn't wrangle their way onto the set took to seeking out Monkee domiciles. Davy, then living with Mike and Phyllis, would sometimes have to drive his free Pontiac GTO (all four had been given one, along with a Honda 450cc motorbike) around the block eight times to ensure that he was not being followed by fans. One enterprising girl conducted a cash pool among her friends and hired a helicopter to follow him home from the studio. Another fan started writing up to five letters a day from the beginning of the series and maintained the flow for more than three years.

Hilda Kubernick worked as a senior secretary for Raybert Productions and often helped out with the overloaded Monkees fan club. Her young teenage son, Harvey spent most of his spare time hanging around the backlot. At the Monkees debut party, held at Columbia's Burbank Ranch, Harvey met and befriended failed auditionee Rodney Bingenheimer, and the pair attached themselves to the floating Monkee community which followed the four new stars around. 'Males were not allowed on the set after school,' he relates, 'it had to be girls, on order from the Monkees. Sometimes I had to sneak in with a bunch of them when one of the guards didn't know me. I used to get put to work licking stamps on the fan club kits – I think I did a million of them. I knew Micky from when he lived with the Missing Links down on Normandy Avenue, so he let me stick around when they were filming. Jack Nicholson was always hanging around the set so Rodney and I asked him all these questions about Roger Corman films. He just loved talking about Corman. For a high school kid it was a really neat place to hang out. There were all these girls in mini-skirts everywhere, so Rodney always came dressed better than the Monkees! There were buzzers and lights and zany things going on, and everybody was breaking union rules. I often helped Micky set up his own props. Cher's mum often worked on the show as an extra. After shooting, all the Raybert people like Frawley, Rafelson, Nicholson and Schneider, would go to the Black Rabbit Inn, and the Monkees John London, me and Rodney, Frank Zappa, and all the girls would go to Norm's Eatery. There was this great waiter there called Miles Ciletti who had gone to Fairfax High with the Reverend Fraser Mohawk.'

The dramatic and certainly unexpected chart success of Monkee records presented a situation for which no allowance had been made – massive demands for live concert appearances. The fabricated foursome were, in the eyes of teenage America, a bona fide pop group who would, of course, visit their respective home towns. From the outset, Screen Gems dreaded the thought of the Monkees competing with professionals like the Beach Boys and Paul Revere and the Raiders. One executive realised the profit potential but privately cautioned, 'The kids don't mind buying an image but they like an image that can sing.' The Monkees themselves forced Screen Gems' hand, demanding that

Paul Revere and the Raiders also had their own television series Where The Action Is. *One Saturday morning Davy Jones and Boyce and Hart dropped by.*

they be allowed to go out on the road. Thus began an exhausting programme of rehearsal and almost theatrical production. From this point the work pressure on the four increased dramatically. Each morning they would be at the studio by 7.30 and, apart from a brief lunch break at the local greasy spoon, would remain there until around 11pm. Each episode was taking three or four days to shoot, with whatever time left over being devoted to concert rehearsal. It would have been convenient and quite acceptable to send the Monkees out to sing thirty minute sets of their hit television songs to either backing tapes or a hidden backing group, in typical American 'supporting a hit single tour' tradition. Certainly this is what the show's critics were expecting. Instead, the Monkees' earnest ambition and Screen

Gems powerful resources worked together to create a diverse and polished concert act. Choreographed by David Winters, the shows were opened by The Apollas (the Supremes-style trio that had once employed Peter), Jewel Akens and Bobby Hart's Candy Store Prophets (basically the musicians on the first album). Each of the Monkees was individually showcased with lead vocal assignments and elaborate solo spots. They were placed on the stage in classic rock band formation, with Davy flogging a mean tambourine at the front. The four dispended their own musical backing for most of the set, and Micky took the lead vocal on *Take A Giant Step*, *Last Train To Clarksville*, *She's So Far Out She's In* and Nesmith's *Mary Mary*. Mike sang *You Just May Be The One*, and Jones warbled *I Can't Get Her Off My Mind* and a Byrdsish *I Wanna Be Free*. No means had yet been discovered to make Peter's voice sound anything less than painful so he was kept silent.

Davy took over on drums towards the end of Mary, Mary *on the early live dates.*

Towards the end of *Mary Mary*, Davy replaced Micky on the drums and the song was reprised at high speed. This commenced the solo sequences, which invariably drew the most rapturous response from the female-dominated audiences. With musical backing by the Candy Store Prophets, Peter performed *Cripple Creek* on five string banjo, Mike dabbled in blues with Willie Dixon's *You Can't Judge A Book By The Cover* and Davy serenaded weepy teenybops with Anthony Newley's *Gonna Build A Mountain*. One vignette would be segued into another with cute mocking introductions

The Monkees on stage in Hawaii December 3, 1966 – their first concert appearance.

like, 'Ladies and Gentlemen, the world's hottest looking midget, Davy Jones!' On a cue of 'Please welcome the hardest working man in show business, Micky "James Brown" Dolenz!', the drummer would launch into a screaming rendition of Ray Charles' *I Got A Woman*, complete with a steal of Brown's famous stage routine of mock collapse. Mike would come on stage to drape a velvet cloak around Micky's convulsing shoulders and then assist him off stage. A blatant blueprint certainly, but presented before middle-class white children who had probably never heard of James Brown, it went down an absolute storm.

Two try-out concerts in Hawaii on 3 December, 1966 almost erupted into violent riots, with fifty club-wielding cops storming into the hysterical crowd. From the moment the four leapt through *papier mâché* speakers onto the stage, Beatlemania was resurrected. It was exactly three months and four days after the Beatles had played their final concert at San Francisco's Candlestick Park. However, what was not acknowledged from the midst of this mad orgy of moneymaking was that the whole project had actually backfired. From the outset, the Monkees were intended to be solely an acting unit, and it was only the necessity of having two songs per show seemingly performed by the protagonists which resulted in tracks being recorded, and eventually, discs being released. The debut album and single took off before the show went on the air and had already reached

number one before the series had taken a firm hold. Accordingly, as bitter a pill as it was for the other principals to swallow, the high profile of the Monkees was as much a victory for Don Kirshner's expert musical manipulation as for Raybert's celluloid brain-child.

This situation was a crimson flag to the bullish Mike Nesmith. He had come to mistrust, dislike and publicly malign Don Kirshner, whom he saw as a barrier in his path to musical creativity and credibility. During December, with the Monkees radiating an innocent, cheeky charm over mass America, a bitter and resentful Mike Nesmith told the *Saturday Evening Post*: 'The music has nothing to do with us. It is totally dishonest. Do you know how debilitating it is to sit up and have to duplicate somebody else's records? That's really what we are doing. The music happens in spite of the Monkees. It's what Kirshner wants to do. Our records are not our forté. I don't care if we never sell another record.' This statement was the first public acknowledgement of an escalating war between the Monkees and their musical director. 'The Monkees' album had sold over three million units, higher than the sales of any Beatles' album, and there were a million advance orders for the second LP again higher than for any Beatles album. With dollar signs flashing in their eyes, every songwriter or producer associated in any way with Screen Gems made a mad scramble for a piece of the

Monkees action, vigorously elbowing Boyce and Hart aside as they threw themselves at 'daddy' Kirshner's feet. The eager contributors were undoubtedly well credentialled. They were the hottest young white professional pop songwriters in the country. Among those who secured instant wealth on the Monkees' second album were Carole Bayer (*Groovy Kind Of Love*), Roger Atkins (*It's My Life*), Ben Raleigh (*She's A Fool*), Neil Diamond (*Cherry Cherry*), Jack Keller (*Run To Him*), Jeff Barry (*River Deep Mountain High*), Sandy Linzer and Denny Randell (*A Lovers Concerto*), Neil Sedaka, Gerry Goffin and Carole King, The Tokens' team of Mitch and Phil Margo, Hank Medress and Jay Siegel, and Diane Hilderbrand. Each had a song and most wanted to produce the track themselves, resulting in no less than 9 producers being listed on the 'More Of The Monkees' album. Boyce and Hart, yelling from the back of the room, managed to include *(I'm Not Your) Stepping Stone* and *She*. Kirshner decided against using Bobby's Candy Store Prophets on this album and filled the studio with the likes of Hal Blaine, James Burton, Glen Campbell, David Gates, Leon Russell and Eddie Hoe.

Mike was once more allowed to contribute two of his own compositions and productions on the album –*The Kind Of Girl I Could Love* (co-written with Roger

Atkins) and *Mary Mary*, featuring dynamic Glen Campbell guitar and uninterested Dolenz vocals. The release of *Mary Mary* saw Elektra Records president Jac Holtzman showered with angry letters. As Mike explains, 'Jac got all this mail from irate hard core blues freaks saying, "do you know what that jerk, sell-out freak Mike Nesmith of the Monkees is doing? He's claiming he wrote the Butterfield Blues Band's *Mary Mary*, the creep!" Jac wrote back to them all saying "sorry pal, you lose, he did".'

Released on 10 January 1967 (three months after the first LP) 'More Of The Monkees' was a pot-pourri of slickly manufactured pop songs, highlighted by Neil Diamond's two offerings, *I'm A Believer* and *Look Out (Here Comes Tomorrow)*, ably produced by the multi-talented Jeff Barry; and Goffin and King's elegant, sensitive, powerful ballad *Sometime In The Morning*, sung exceptionally well by Micky. There was a clumsy piece of Token's tedium called *Laugh*, on which Davy's vocalising made Peter's squawking on *Your Auntie Grizelda* sound positively operatic. It was quite a jumble, a jumble that sold some five million copies. 'We

Monkee songwriters (left to right) Carole Bayer, Bobby Hart, Toni Wine, Tommy Boyce and Wes Farrell.

lowered the age at which kids bought records,' insists Davy, 'no kids ever bought Sinatra records but fourteen-year-olds bought the Beatles. We lowered the age to twelve.'

The all-important second single, drawn in advance from 'More of the Monkees', stands as one of the greatest double-sided blockbusters in rock. *I'm A Believer* was perfect pop – taut, crisp, percussive and

Italian picture sleeve

insidiously melodic. Diamond's lyrics were wide-eyed and innocent, a classic celebration of popular music's cornerstone subject – love. Then, lurking on the other side of the vinyl was Boyce and Hart's pure punk snarl *(I'm Not Your) Stepping Stone*, an angry, vindictive, threatening song. Micky's vocal work was just edgy enough to give both tracks vitality and bite. In December, *I'm A Believer* reached number one in sixteen countries – America, Canada, Australia, England, Mexico, Eire, Japan, Sweden, Germany, Holland, Denmark, Philippines, Singapore, Finland, Norway and New Zealand. In most markets it was an official double A-side, while in America *Stepping Stone* charted independently at number 20.

During the second album's chaotic sessions Mike began to rebel openly, changing his occasional tantrums and caustic moments to outright hostility. During one studio screaming match, Carole King apparently burst into tears under Nesmith's stinging criticism. As Mike recalls, 'I would say "hey fellas, don't you realise this is crap? This is not good music, *this* is" and pointed out what was happening on the street. Generally I told them that the music they were producing was garbage, patently designed to sell, with no redeeming social value at all. Peter and I cared critically about the quality of the music, and our standard line was that we had this phenomenal and wonderful opportunity to create some-

thing of meaning and lasting value but we were proffering junk on the people. And they all looked at me as if I had a bug on my nose. Maybe it was because I was screaming and yelling and saying things that by and large were not very coherent. I was young, I was frustrated and unable to make my position understood. The usual response was "what do you mean it's no good. It's selling millions".'

Peter may have also cared critically about his contribution to the music but his actions did not approach Mike's arrogant presumptuousness. 'Kirshner has to be given all the credit in the world,' he later conceded: 'He certainly knew what hit tunes were and how to make them hits. The thing is, we did not have any need to challenge Donny personally, but he took it as a direct affront. All I wanted was to be allowed to play instruments on the records – given the same producers, the same arrangements, the same writers, the same studio. I didn't want to produce the records, Boyce and Hart did that fine. I didn't want to pick the songs, Donny had that all together. What I really needed was to be an instrumentalist so that when the press said "you guys don't play on your records" I could say "we do too!". I mean, I could play, you know.'

Don Kirshner and his wife Sheila visited producer/writers Boyce and Hart at the RCA studios during the recording of Valleri.

Micky was of a similar, but more practical point of view: 'I didn't want to be there when they decided which record to release. I wouldn't have known what to say and I would have had very little advice to give. As far as I am concerned they knew what they were doing and they made very few mistakes, the proof is in the pudding. With Tommy and Bobby the chemistry just worked, they got along with us, we got along with them. But after we'd worked seven to seven on the TV show and we were asked to go and do the vocals for the records we'd all go urrgghh! There were times when I thought that the show would only last a year because we'd all be dead by then. I wasn't exactly jumping up and down about adding playing music to our work load.'

Inevitably, the running skirmish was laid before Raybert, who managed to successfully distance themselves from problems pertaining to music, publicity and promotion. Mike invited Bert Schneider to hear the band perform as a unit and when Schneider commented: 'Hey that's not bad at all' Nesmith delivered his demand. 'Bert, the time has come, we wanna play on the records, we wanna do it now. We don't want Kirshner involved anymore. We'll go out on the road, we'll do all kinds of stuff that you want us to, but we've got to be able to have some form of musical integrity.' Schneider said, 'Well, I go for it, but Donny's sure not gonna let go that easy.' 'Now I had realised very early the kind of power I could exercise by just refusing to show up so I told Bert, "Kirshner *will* let go of it or I won't be around anymore, it's as simple as that. You gotta call him up and tell him to bail out and leave the thing alone or you'll have to recast one of the Monkees." Bert sort of understood what I was talking about, he liked the fact that it was feisty.'

In a way, Schneider did want to see his puppets become real live boys. He realised the possibility of contributing to the overall quality of contemporary music and having his creation compete on the same level as Buffalo Springfield, Byrds, Turtles, Lovin' Spoonful and other credible outfits. After all, it did parallel the idealistic concept of the television series. But, as he warned Mike, Kirshner was not exactly joyous at the suggestion of stepping down from one of the most powerful and lucrative positions in the music industry. Rafelson also sided with the Monkees. Talking about the first album to a fan magazine, he offered, 'There's something barren about the sound. Something cold. Mike's a great singer and I think his songs deserve better treatment.'

Viewing the scenario in retrospect, Mike concedes: 'It was an arrogant and ridiculous thing for me to have done and it was probably terribly offensive to Bert. I mean here was this guy who had worked real hard on this great idea, putting it all together when people were telling him he was crazy. He made it tremendously successful, made me an eventual millionaire and I come along and say, "Well, that's it, now it's all gonna be done my way." But I was not impelled by a feeling of self aggrandisement or a play for more cookies, it was an artistic impulse. I felt I was forced into a position where I had to risk my job security and a very large amount of money. You have to understand the nature of the times. This was *our* generation. Spiritually we were involved with Vietnam, the street riots, the challenge of racism, and I think that most of the people involved with the show realised the very unique position of power we were in. But the Monkees got so caught up in the musical part of it that we really didn't care much about trying for any sort of control over the show itself, which is where we could have had some fun and some real power.'

The Christian Scientist Nesmiths.

The battlefield just got bloodier. When it was revealed that Mike would be receiving $30,000 in songwriting royalties for his songs on the first album, he was rained upon with caustic snipes to the general effect of, 'If you hate the music so much why do you accept the cheques, why do you take the money?' In fact, Mike and Phyllis were the first to truly indulge in mansions, furnishings and gadgets. Their expenditure came complete with a delightful disclaimer that was dutifully carried by the fan magazines. 'Mike's longing for something better,' explained *Tiger Beat*, 'is greatly influenced by his religion, Christian Science. He and Phyllis believe that if you desire material things and you have them, then they become less important. So they spared no expense in building their beautiful home.' The house was high on Mulholland Drive, with twenty miles of uninterrupted views.

Peter relaxing between takes with Leah Cohen, Mama Cass' sister.

Peter lived in the smallest Monkee mansion but was swiftly gathering a reputation as a young Errol Flynn. He was regularly seen in the company of lovely Leah Cohen, younger sister of Mama Cass, but his lifestyle was by no means monogamous. Davy was a little more discreet but just as ravenous in his appetite for all things female. 'I like blondes mainly,' he informed one reporter. 'I like to be seen out with tall pretty girls and I like to hear people say "look at that little guy over there with that girl" – it really gives me a giggle . . . I like to go out with girls who are six feet tall.' Micky's amorous pursuits were much more subdued and confined to the occasional dating of Randy Creadrick, a young actress who appeared in an early episode.

When Davy returned from Christmas holidays in England (he had been written out of an episode to allow him some time with his family), the first Monkees concert tour commenced. Kicking off in Denver on 26 December it made its way through Memphis, Louisvil-

le, Winston-Salem, Pittsburg, Phoenix, Cleveland, Cincinatti, Nashville (where the four became star guests at Brenda Lee's New Year's Eve party), Tulsa, Detroit and San Francisco, where the final concert was performed at the Cow Palace on 22 January before a capacity audience of 18,000.

One review of the final date read: 'Bounding on stage in navy suede jackets and grey pin-striped pants, the four whipped through most of the tracks on their first album. Their act was long and exhausting but they gave their all. The only disturbing factor was the violent crowd – the four were, at times, frankly scared, Davy in particular. The primarily eight to fourteen-year-old crowd has learned well the techniques of mobbing from their older sisters, but somehow they lack the honest emotion and passion that their predecessors lavished on the Beatles and Stones. All "pre-packaging" aside, The Monkees, musicians or no, put on an impressive and entertaining show. They've earned the right to be called a real "group".'

By the end of their month jaunt, the Monkees were jubilant actors indeed. Each had competently displayed a sense of style and musical ability which had surprised even themselves. Buoyed with a feeling of being 'a real band' the Monkees ceased to be just the cast of a television show, whether Screen Gems liked it or not. The overall commitment to Nesmith's cause had increased and the showdown with Kirshner that had been delayed by the tour now loomed as inevitable.

Financially, Screen Gems had little cause for immediate concern. The twelve mainland dates grossed $542,960.00, with the highest gate ($74,707) coming from the Detroit Olympia Stadium. The $54,375 gate in Phoenix broke the house record. The Monkees were not excluded from the windfall. They received thirty per cent of the net profits from live performances, which was somewhat more substantial than their ten per cent share of Raybert's merchandising profits (the same percentage which the Beatles got from Seltaeb, before Brian Epstein realised that he was being fleeced mercilessly). 'We made very little from the TV series,' explains Davy, 'but we each collected record royalties of over a million dollars before it was all over. I remember that Micky didn't think our first LP would sell at all and Don Kirshner said to him, "OK, if you feel that way, I'll give you $50,000 for your royalty payments." None of us knew that we would do so well out of the things on the side.'

The lid finally blew off late in January at Kirshner's private bungalow at the Beverley Hills Hotel. The four Monkees were attending a gold record and royalty cheque presentation ceremony, posing for trade photographs with their musical puppeteer. When the formalities were over, the Monkees were presented with acetates of four new songs, from which the third single was to be chosen. Mike exploded in anger and told Kirshner in short, blunt blurts that he was no longer prepared to have his name put on other people's music. When Kirshner, flanked by Lester Sill and Screen

Gems executive Herb Moelis insisted that he had every right to select whatever song he considered would be the most successful, Mike bellowed, 'Donny we could sing *Happy Birthday* with a beat and it would sell a million records. Your argument is no longer valid because *we* are the Monkees, we have incredible TV exposure and now we have all this power. Either we play or I quit.' Herb Moelis curtly growled, 'You'd better read your contract' and any restraint Mike had left disappeared. White and trembling with rage he smashed his fist through the wall screaming 'that could have been your head' and stormed out. Kirshner caught up with him in the lobby and sheepishly thrust a gold plaque upon him, leaving an embarrassed Lester Sill to drive him home and try to calm the situation. Peter Tork has said of the incident: 'There was never any need for a confrontation. If Kirshner had said "We can work something out, come into the studio with Tommy and Bobby and we'll spend a bit of time and involve you guys" everything would have gone on as before. But Don didn't reason in those days.'

Don Kirshner left no doubts about his role in the Monkees project on this jukebox EP disc.

The next day Mike faced his 'angel of peace', the ever-conciliatory Schneider, who had been bombarded with everybody's version of the incident. 'I blew it,' he admitted, 'I shouldn't have lost my temper, but it's horrible to be the number one group in the country and not be allowed to play your own records.' Faced with losing a Monkee or a musical director, Schneider closed ranks behind Nesmith, telling him. 'Well, it's reward-ing to see you guys act as a group rather than four egotists who don't pull together.' Schneider was becom-ing increasingly alarmed at the profits Kirshner was deriving from the project. While the Monkees shared a standard five per cent artist's royalty between them (not unfair in light of their vocals-only contribution) their musical director was scooping up fifteen per cent of Colgem's pre-tax profit. With six million singles and eight million albums sold by mid-season, Kirshner's personal profit was well over $350,000, with a projected five year figure of $5 million. Raybert was incensed that someone whom they had called upon to work on *their* brainchild was making more money out of it than them.

By siding with the group, Schneider mortified Screen Gems, Columbia and NBC executives, who had no precedent for the problem of contracted actors demand-ing to become musicians and so blatantly flaunting the suspension clauses which normally quelled disputes. They had a tough Musician's Union agreement to abide by which made no provision for the dilemma which they now had to face. Events rushed on as Nesmith, after brooding in a hotel room one afternoon, struck upon the idea of holding his own unofficial press conference. He called up all the magazines in town and asked them to send reporters down. Only *Look* and *Time* despatched writers but that was enough. 'There comes a time when you draw the line as a man,' he told them. 'We're being passed off as something we aren't. We all play instruments but we haven't on any of our records. Furthermore, our company doesn't want us to and won't let us.'

When news of this action came to light, Columbia Pictures and Screen Gems held an emergency joint meeting to decide the future of *The Monkees*, which was then twenty episodes old. Apart from the last resort of invoking Nesmith's suspension clause, the executives could reach no decision on how best to handle one of the most serious rebellions by a contracted actor in televi-sion history.

While the stalemate, and Mike's future, was being debated at high levels, he approached young musician and producer Chip Douglas at the Whisky Au Go Go, where he was playing bass with the Turtles. Douglas Farthing Hatlelid, as he chose to credit himself on album jackets, was a former member of the Modern Folk Quartet. Asked outright if he wanted to become the Monkees' new producer, he agreed on the spot and quit the Turtles. Apart from having played bass on the smash hit *Happy Together*, Douglas had few credentials. The invitation was like one free wish from Aladdin's lamp; in fact as Mike recalls: 'Chip's first cheque was for about $50,000!'

Chip's first task was to re-record *The Girl I Knew Somewhere*, a Nesmith song which the group had recorded during their first rehearsals prior to filming the television series. Enhanced to a quite attractive state, with a harpsichord solo contributed by Peter, the tape was handed over to Colgems for use on one side of the third single. However, Kirshner would not even enter-tain the idea. He publicly announced that the third

Above: The photograph of the bearded Monkees with Chip Douglas and Hank Cicalo (seated) was deleted from the rear jacket of 'Headquarters' after the initial run.
Right: Announcing the Monkees in England, late '66.

single would be *A Little Bit Me, A Little Bit You/She Hangs Out.* When Schneider told him that such a release was unacceptable the two locked horns. The Monkees themselves, by this point incidental to the upper-echelon feud, were not able to monitor the developments first hand, their presence being required across the Atlantic, where Monkeemania was forming a second front.

Introduced to the British public by the single *Last Train to Clarksville*, the Monkees had achieved a respectable 23 chart placing late in December. Davy had subjected himself to a press conference at the Westbury Hotel during his Christmas visit to generate advance interest in the television series, due to debut on BBC television on 30 December. A retinue of publicists and assorted officials then escorted him around London's music press offices where he was greeted with indifference. The exception was *New Music Express*, where young writer Jeremy Pascall took an instant liking to Jones, the group and its music. Davy told Pascall, 'We get a lot of stick from other groups who've had to gig around for years, paying for PA's and climbing the ladder. They don't like it that we've had it made. But we're not a group, we're an act. Whereas they do a twenty-five minute stand we do over an hour.'

Pascall gave a good half page to Jones' utterances, concluding: 'There's a certain something that makes me say the Monkees could be the biggest thing in Britain in 1967.'

By the end of January he was proved right. The series was viewed in an unprecedented five million British homes, igniting Monkeemania overnight. RCA pressed 120,000 copies of *I'm A Believer* and sold them within two days. Another 150,000 were snapped up by the end of the week, with a total of 500,000 singles sold within two weeks. The song was unchallenged in the number one position. The Monkees were dumbstruck when a British friend of Mike's rang through to the sound stage with the news. 'We nearly tore the set apart,' admitted Micky. 'We just freaked out completely. We never thought we'd make it in England. They didn't like our first record much and there was so much talk about us copying the Beatles that I had given up hope.'

To fan the flames, three of the Monkees flew into England at staggered intervals during early February on what were officially designated as 'holidays.' The pop press had become absolutely effusive in its treatment of the group by this point. But then, after three frantic years of bulk shipping Anglo beat groups over to the lucrative American market, the English could hardly object to the first stateside act seeking to reverse the process. *New Musical Express*, with Pascall at the helm, went completely overboard, devoting saturation coverage to every aspect of the visits. However, Fleet Street was not quite so supportive. News of Nesmith's unauthorised American press disclosures had filtered through to England and reporters from the daily papers were sent along to extract some scandalous headlines from this new teenage sensation. Micky experienced the full brunt of their muck raking. Rushed from the airport to the Grosvenor House Hotel in Park Lane, bleary eyed and needing a shave, he tumbled head-first into a well-baited trap. He guilelessly told the gathered press corp that, because of the pressures of filming schedules, they did not actually play the backings on their records. With distinct echoes of John Lennon's 'bigger than Jesus' comment to Maureen Cleave, Micky's words were translated by Jack Bentley of the *Sunday Mirror* into howling banner headlines which proclaimed 'A Disgrace To The Pop World! Here are a bunch of kids trading on other people's talents and cashing in on millions.' Asked why his hair had changed from blonde to brown between *Circus Boy* and *The Monkees*, Micky explained that different producers desired different images. 'I guess you could say I'm a Hollywood phony from way back,' he foolishly quipped, leaving himself wide open for the inevitable headline, 'I'm A Hollywood Phony Admits Monkee.'

As the storm in the rock press broke, Mike dived for cover leaving Micky and Davy to handle the flak. 'I'm an actor and I have never pretended to be anything else,' defended Jones, 'The public have made me into a rock'n'roll singer. No one is trying to fool anybody.' Micky added, 'I don't know why everybody's screaming – do Sinatra, Sonny and Cher or the Beatles play all the instruments we hear on their records? We're fed up with the rumours that we can't play at all – so we've decided to make the time to play everything.'

It soon became apparent that much of the vitriol

Police were called in to protect Micky when he flew into London on 6 February 1967.

being directed at the shellshocked Monkees found its source in thinly veiled jealousy. When other rock artists were polled on their opinions of the Monkees, almost all the upper echelon (Beatles, Rollings Stones, Hendrix etc.) offered comments along the lines of, 'It's obvious what's happening, there's talent there. They're doing a TV show, it's a difficult chore and I wouldn't be in their shoes for the world.' When Mike was introduced to John Lennon, he reportedly asked him, 'Do you think we're a cheap imitation of the Beatles, your movies and your records?', to which Lennon replied, 'I think you're the greatest comic talent since the Marx Brothers. I've never missed one of your programmes.'

The furore merely underlined the immaturity of the rock music culture. In 1977 rock writer Ken Barnes highlighted the absurdity of the incident with his comment: 'Nowadays when the hipness of a record is generally measured by its lineup of sidemen, when it's known that a group as forbiddingly cool as the Byrds didn't all play on *Mr. Tambourine Man*, and when considerable doubt had been cast on Ringo's percussive role, it's hard to get excited about the Monkees' peccadillos.' Over in California, Brian Wilson must have been amused at this storm in a teacup, having just presented the Beach Boys upon their return from a concert tour with completed backtracks for the 'Pet Sounds' album, which required just their vocals.

When Davy paid a return visit to Coronation Street, Ena Sharples (actress Violet Carson) was unimpressed with his long locks.

Despite the press, the visits were fantastically successful. Davy's arrival was treated as the return of a conquering hero by thousands of hysterical girls at Heathrow Airport, who managed to cause so much property damage that the matter was raised in Parliament the following day. A chant of 'Davy, Davy', to the tune of *Daisy Bell*, was heard at deafening volume twenty-four hours a day outside Grosvenor House, prompting an official missive from a furious Princess Margaret demanding that the din be quelled. When he arrived at the BBC Lime Grove studios to appear on *The Rolf Harris Show*, frantic fans nearly demolished the limousine, eliciting a shaken response of, 'If they can do that to a car, imagine what they could do to me.' Scared

of a repeat scene, he cancelled a visit to his father in Manchester. Meanwhile, Mike flew in quietly with Phyllis, making no attempt to hide his wife. Peter's absence occasioned the startling *New Musical Express'* explanation that he had gone to Connecticut to visit his ex-wife – one of the very few times this matter was raised in print. Amazingly, none of the scandal-mongers seemed to pick up on it.

Micky and Mike were interviewed on *Top Of The Pops* and *Pop Inn* and were guest adjudicators on *Juke Box Jury*. They were introduced to members of the British rock élite including Paul McCartney, Spencer Davis, members of the Kinks and Hermans Hermits. McCartney invited them to Abbey Road studios to watch the recording of a track for the 'Sgt. Pepper' album and then invited Micky to visit him at his St. John's Wood home. Mike gravitated towards John Lennon, given the fact that both were married teen idols with a male offspring. Mike recalls, 'I was with John at a club one night and he had this little tape recorder on which he played me this fantastic song. He said, "Isn't this incredible?" and I said "Yeah, it's fantastic, who is it?" It was Jimi Hendrix doing *Hey Joe*. At the same time, I found out later, Micky was out seeing him play in some little dive. He went to see him play again in New York a few months later. Both of us were just amazed by him.' Acceptance into the Beatles' private domain came as an enormous shock to the Monkees, who were still very unsure of their position in the pop world. They did not know whether the Beatles would consider them a joke or as something approaching peers.

Micky Dolenz with Paul McCartney in London, February 1967.

Micky with Samantha Juste who escorted him around London.

Not even time spent with John Lennon could lift the spirits of Mike, who continued to take himself unbelievably seriously. His profound proclamations included, 'Money in itself is a useless commodity . . . All I need is clothes to cover my nudity, a roof to give me shelter and food to keep my body going.' He finished off with a discussion on the plight of the American negro, by which time the interviewer had undoubtedly nodded off. Micky had no time for heavy philosophies as he was being dragged around London tourist spots by Jeremy Pascall with a photographer in tow, to capture every thrilling moment. Pascall was not Micky's sole companion in London, however. During the filming of *Top Of The Pops* he was smitten by the beautiful Samantha Juste, a popular young model who appeared regularly on the show as casual interviewer, fashion expert and hostess. She asked Micky and Ric Klein if they would like a guided tour around London and was inseparable from the Monkee for the rest of the trip. They were seen together in Carnaby Street, at the Cromwellian Club, at the *Valentine* magazine pop awards staged at the London Hilton, and at Heathrow Airport when the blitzkrieg had ended. The transatlantic phone ran hot for weeks after, followed by an unexpected visit to California by Sammy (as she was universally known) to attend Klein's wedding.

Kim Fowley remembers Juste as 'a real princess.' He was producing records in England at the time for Soft Machine, Rockin' Berries, the In Betweens (Slade), the Hellions (Traffic) and others, and was part of a clique of industry-ites that hung out at the Cromwellian, a club regularly frequented, by various Beatles, Rolling Stones, Whos and Yardbirds. 'I took Samantha out a couple of times and we were part of the floating crowd that went dancing at the Cromwellian most nights. We hung out with people like Keith Moon, Olivia Newton-John, George Young (Easybeats), Paul and Barry Ryan and Bruce Johnston, who was in town then flogging "Pet Sounds" to the press. I think that Samantha was the fiancée of one of the Ryans, but she dragged Dolenz down to meet us anyway.'

One startling indication of just how Monkee-obsessed Britain was in February 1967, was the debut edition of *Monkees Monthly* magazine, published by Beat Publications Ltd, in the same format as the *Beatles Book* and *Rolling Stones Book*. The first of thirty-two issues sold an unbelievable 200,000 copies in the UK and managed to maintain that level for most of the year. In England rock music really was the predominant popular culture whereas in American it was still viewed as a juvenile novelty. The Monkees were well aware of that when they made their successful play for British acceptance.

Irish television (believe it or not) had beaten the English to the punch by screening the series a good two months ahead of its neighbours. A great many English kids were able to pick up the signal from across the border and their initial record purchasing surge contributed strongly to the overall British Monkees explosion.

Though the promotional visits were confined to England, European reaction to the Monkees was on a par with the rest of the western world. A February 1967 *Billboard* headline screamed, 'Europe's gripped by Monkeesteria' and described the group as, '. . . The biggest and fastest selling commodity since the Beatles came out of the Star Club and the Liverpool Cavern,' noting: 'Their rapid ascent to international fame and fortune marks another phase in the renaissance of American talent in the world's hit parades, so long dominated by Liverpool and then London. The Screen Gems quartet has joined the pioneering Beach Boys in restoring the balance.'

In Holland, *Last Train to Clarksville* entered the top ten before the series was ever screened – the only European territory where that occurred. *I'm A Believer* then stormed to number one remaining there for a month. An EP entitled 'Monkees Themes' shot high into the single charts as well. The achievements were even more impressive in the light of the unique Dutch method of allocating television air time which resulted in the series being seen infrequently. Scandinavia was similarly affected. With the screening of the series still more than a month away, the Swedish chart had *I'm A Believer* firmly lodged at number one, as did Norway and Denmark. France and Belgium took a little longer to ignite. The series had not begun screening although

Above: In the streets of London the larger Monkee was haunted by press photographers.

Monkees Monthly: based upon the successful format of The Beatles Book *and* The Rolling Stones Book.

some residents were picking up Dutch telecasts. For some peculiar reason, the French were offered *I'm A Believer* as an EP rather than a single, which delayed chart-topping somewhat.

Meanwhile, back in Hollywood, Don Kirshner decided to break the stalemate by issuing Colgems' single number 1003 – *A Little Bit Me, A Little Bit You/She Hangs Out*. Within hours of the move, Bert Schneider persuaded his father, Abraham Schneider, President of Columbia Pictures, to dismiss Kirshner as head of Colgems Records on the grounds that he had issued an unauthorised disc. Less than a month later Kirshner resigned as chief executive of Screen Gems Music. In a public statement, Kirshner claimed that Columbia Pictures had instituted a programme of harassment designed to force him out of the music division, by destroying the rights which, he claimed, were explicitly defined under his contract. The March 8 issue of *Variety* stated: 'Bert Schneider wants Kirshner to keep clear of all future Monkees recordings, this feeling is intensified by the discontent of the group members.' In the staff shuffle that followed, Emil La Viola was moved up to head of Screen Gems Columbia Music; Lester Sill was promoted as the new head of Colgems Records, and single number 1003 was withdrawn. It was replaced on 8 March by 1004 – *A Little Bit Me, A Little Bit You/The Girl I Knew Somewhere*. By this time the Monkees were back in Hollywood, initially unaware of the recent events. Mike recalls sitting in a car waiting for his wife and brother-in-law Bruce to come out of a supermarket. 'I turned on the radio and the guy said "that was one side of the brand new Monkee single, I'll be back in just a moment to play the other side." So I told Phyllis to hurry back to the car to witness a moment in history. I said to her, "if this ain't my song, I'm out of a job. I'm gonna be on the streets looking for work." So we

Neil Diamond, 1967.

twiddled our thumbs until the opening chords came on and I realised it was my song. It felt like such a tremendous victory after all that fighting.'

A Little Bit Me, A Little Bit You was Neil Diamond's offering after *I'm A Believer*, sung rather thinly by Davy after Mike's voice was tried and rejected. It streaked up the charts in the manner of its predecessor but was kept out of the number one position by Frank and Nancy Sinatra's *Something Stupid*. Bronx-born Neil Diamond was a discovery of Ellie Greenwich and Jeff Barry, who had signed him to Bert Berns' Bang label in 1965 and begun placing his songs. He made the American top ten himself in October, 1966 with *Cherry Cherry*, but it was *I'm A Believer* three months later which established him as a hot hitwriter. After success with the Monkees, he wrote hits for Lulu, Vic Dana, Deep Purple and Elvis Presley, before becoming a successful solo artist in his own right.

When the dust had settled, the Monkees and Chip Douglas set about creating a credible third album which would silence the critics. Squeezing in sessions between filming commitments, they spent $25,000 of Screen Gems money to produce 'Headquarters', an ambitious country, folk/pop, garage band album. Coming after

Japanese picture sleeve

'Pet Sounds' and just before 'Sgt. Pepper', its self-indulgence had little musical significance, notwithstanding that the Monkees themselves hail it as a masterpiece to this day. The jacket made it absolutely clear: 'We aren't the only musicians on this album but the occasional bass or horn player played under our direction so that this is all ours.' The 'outsiders' were Vince DaRosa (french horn), Fred Seykora (cello) and Chip Douglas on occasional bass. The Monkees were credited with an array of instruments, from jawbone to banjo. Noticeably lacking Kirshner's expert commercial polishing, the album was unnecessarily overladen with Mike's twangy and not terribly adept pedal steel guitar work. The repertoire was split between originals and stock Screen Gems copyrights (from Jack Keller, Diane Hilderbrand, Boyce and Hart, Mann and Weil) as a concession to Lester Sill, with Micky's *Randy Scouse Git (Alternate Title)*, Peter's *For Pete's Sake* and Mann and Weil's *Shades of Gray* standing out. The four Monkees penned *No Time* and gave the credit to engineer Hank Cicalo as a gesture of appreciation, enabling him to buy a house with the royalties. One of the most appealing tracks was *Early Morning Blues And Greens*, written by Diane Hilderbrand with veteran Jack Keller (also responsible for *Your Aunty Grizelda* which had caught Peter's interest when tendered for the second album) and featuring impressive percussion effects. Peter gave Diane a call and Lester Sill took her into the recording studio to meet the group while they were working on the song.

Diane Hildebrand's album of her own songs.

Peter was enchanted by this young Ellie Greenwich-the-making. He began spending time with her, often dropping by her Screen Gems office after work to co-write songs. The pair were primarily responsible for the stunning *Goin' Down* (apparently one of Lou Reed's all-time favourite tracks), which bore an eventual writing credit of Hilderbrand-Tork-Nesmith-Dolenz-Jones. Diane later established a friendship with Mike to the point of being present in the studio during some of his Nashville escapades. She never got close to Davy, who was far more interested in another young songwriter called Carole Bayer (*When Love Comes Knockin'*, *The Girl I Left Behind Me*, *We Were Made For Each Other*).

Though the album did not yield one track suitable for release as an American single, in June 1967 it did reach number one in the album charts within three weeks, to be displaced by 'Sgt. Pepper' two weeks later. But when the sales sheets were tallied it ended up selling just 2½ million units, half the sales of its predecessor. 'As soon as we took over, the record sales plummeted,' Mike cheerfully admits today. 'They just kept going down, right to rock bottom, because we weren't that good, we didn't make very good records. I can't deny that everything that the Schneider/Mazursky/Rafelson/Kirshner regime concocted to work worked perfectly and was immensely successful on a monetary level. Everything that the Monkees can account for, the four of us in cahoots with whoever, didn't work at all as far as selling. So these guys all stood around shaking their fingers and saying "we told you guys and you wouldn't listen" and they were right. The Hollywood bottom line is the dollar and you can't argue with it.'

Nesmith and Schneider's victory over Kirshner had given Boyce and Hart little cause for joy. Having been virtually stripped of their producer's role on the second album, they were now well and truly on the outside looking in. Lester Sill's influence ensured that they were well represented as songwriters (*I'll Spend My Life With You*, *I Can't Get Her Off My Mind*, *Mr. Webster*)

Serious music making during the 'Headquarters' sessions.

but Chip Douglas' name had definitely replaced their own on the production credit. Tommy Boyce claims that, despite the lack of credit, his and Hart's creative input was not entirely absent from 'Headquarters'. 'The Monkees brought Chip in as a front man so they could have someone to play bass for them and so that they could do what they wanted in the studio. We'd been fired from the project so many times that we weren't upset anymore, so we went along to watch Chip work. We wanted to show that we really didn't care. I guess they all thought they were great musicians and songwriters but as far as I'm concerned the only reason they began writing songs is that they saw Nesmith's publishing cheque for the first album and wanted to make a lot of money. They couldn't write hit songs but their stuff was good for album tracks. They had really changed since we worked with them in the beginning. I don't think they particularly liked each other at all by then. They used to argue about the script – "you have more lines than I do, I'm going on strike!" that sort of thing. Micky used to bribe the cameraman, slip him $25 to make sure he got the most closeups. But Davy gave the guy $35 and, because Micky would *never* go that high, Davy would get them all. Most of it was laughed off as a joke but there was an underlying resentment there that wasn't very pleasant at all.'

Boyce and Hart were imbued with a self-preservation instinct strong enough to preclude any self-pitying lethargy. When Douglas and the Monkees rejected their song *Out and About* as the follow-up to *A Little Bit Me, A Little Bit You*, they decided to turn it into a hit themselves. 'I had gone up to the Cow Palace in San Francisco in December to watch Bobby and the Candy Store Prophets open for the Monkees' explains Boyce. 'I watched the Monkees from backstage and saw all those little girls go crazy while they played our songs, so I said to Bobby "forget being the opening act, here's the deal; all we have to do is write a couple of smashes and within a year we can dash out on stage with a band behind us and have all those kids go crazy for us." So then Bobby went off to Canada and when we got together again he'd written *Out and About* and I'd written *I Wonder What She's Doing Tonight*. The Monkees could have had both of them but when they told us to get lost we went to A & M, got our own deal, and had a top forty hit by August and a top ten hit six months later. That didn't sit too well with some of them. One night we were in Miami and they were doing a big auditorium concert so we stopped by backstage. Davy was singing *I Wanna Be Free* when he looked over and spotted us. So he stopped the show and told the audience "They're here everybody, the guys who wrote our big hits ... Tommy & Bobby!!!" We ran out on stage and the place went totally mad. We hugged each

Given the shaft by the Monkees project, Tommy Boyce and Bobby Hart turned their talents to performing and emerged as a hit duo. During 1967 they appeared on the Soupy Sales Show.

other and ran around in circles – that's what we did in those days – and then ran right off again. Well Michael was just so pissed off that he had to remove his hat because his head was exploding!'

Meanwhile, over in London, another explosion was taking place. Advance tapes and tracking disclosures of the forthcoming third album had stirred up a controversy concerning the track *Randy Scouse Git*, the title of which happened to be crude English slang for a sex-crazed Liverpool layabout. A *New Musical Express* news item stated: 'The controversial Micky Dolenz track *Randy S* is likely to be cut out of 'Headquarters' when the album is released in this country in about a month's time. NME understands that RCA plans to substitute a previously unissued title.' Micky didn't know whether to laugh or cry when he was advised of the furore. The idea for the song, one of the first he had ever written, had come to him during his British visit in February and simply reflected a series of images of London. 'I got the title from the television show *Till Death Us Do Part*. It was what Alf Garnett always called his son-in-law.' When Micky was told he would have to come up with an alternate title to get the track issued in Britain he

The top teen magazine editors vied with each other for Monkee 'exclusives'. Tiger Beat *editor, Anne Moses, usually came out best.*

impulsively said, 'That's it, we'll call the song *Alternate Title*.' A little wary of the uproar his earlier innocent ramblings had caused, he explained carefully to a British journalist, 'Believe me, I didn't know that "randy scouse git" was rough language. It just sounded funny and rolled off the tongue easy. I liked the phonetic sound of it, that's all. I'm looking forward to my second visit to England and I don't want anything to spoil it.'

The release and top three charting of the song in England did anything but spoil Micky's standing in the United Kingdom, at least within the rock community. It impressed musicians and songwriters considerably; they realised that it was not the work of any cardboard cut-out pop fabrication. Six years later, British rock magazine *Let It Rock* heaped long overdue praise upon it, 'The lyric of random and unconnected images brilliantly conveyed just what it was like to be in England during that crazy winter and summer of 1967, dominated as it was by rumours about a new Beatles LP and by reports trickling back from America about flower power, very soon to be taken up by the London in-crowd. Critics smugly described it as gimmicky and nonsensical, but now it stands out as one of the very best Monkee tracks.'

. . . ON STAGE MINUTES LATER . . .
THE MONKE
WE'LL START WITH A LOCAL SONG, FELLERS, PUT THE AUDIENCE IN A GOOD MOOD!
THEN SOME OF OUR OLDIES... AND FINISH WITH OUR CURRENT NUMBER THREE!

As the Monkees developed into a hot commercial commodity the exploitation began in earnest. If the four actors had not been so preoccupied with the fight to play instruments they would have noticed the cheap'n'nasty products flooding the market with full authority from Screen Gems. Not just trinkets, but comic strips, paperbacks, teen annuals and the like, carrying quotes, captions and dialogue which were purported to have come from their own mouths. Generated by hack writers, these parasitical printings completely perverted the carefully crafted image and influence of the television characters. These were not the sharp, aware profiles created by Rafelson, Schneider, Mazursky, Tucker and Frawley, but tired, inane clichés.

Into the fray came the hangers-on, roadies, stand-ins and 'friends' who sold 'intimate' and 'exclusive' stories to teen magazines like *16*, *Tiger Beat*, *Movie Teen Illustrated*, *Teen Life*, *Flip*, *Teen World*, *Teen Pin Ups*, *Teen Scoop*, *Hullabaloo*, *Screen and TV Albums*, *Teens Top Ten*, *Teenbeat* and *16 Spec*. Rushed into print were *My Best Friend Mike Nesmith* by John London, *Come Along As I Travel With The Monkees* by Ric Klein, *The Secret Side Of The Monkees* by Bill Chadwick, *How I Got To Know The Monkees* by David Price and even *How Peter Has Changed* by His Banjo (!). Of course, what the magazines couldn't buy they fabricated, dazzling pubescent senses with such thrusting headlines as: 'What They Really Think Of Each Other!', 'Monkees Confess All', 'Micky's 5 Temptations', 'Mike – When He Hates His Wife', 'Peter's Private Party', 'Why Is Davy Ashamed', 'Davy's Intimate Love Letters', 'Peter – My Torrid Night' and 'Our Sizzling Life Story Secrets'. On the pages between these breathtaking revelations could be found innumerable advertisements offering Original Monkee Portraits by Roy Eberhardt, New Monkee Portraits by Frank Morton, Monkees '67 Concerts Photo Album, Monkeeland Giant Illustrated Wall Map, Monkees Love Beads, Monkees Paint By Numbers Set, The Monkees Party Book, Monkees 4-Ever Stickers and Flip's Monkee Wallet Photos.

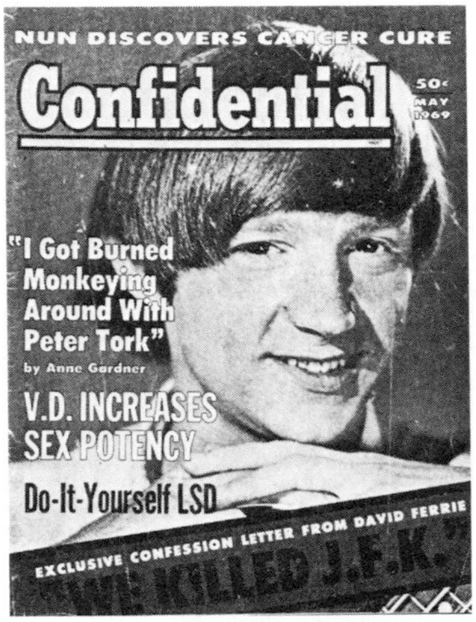
NUN DISCOVERS CANCER CURE
Confidential
50¢
MAY 1969
"I Got Burned Monkeying Around With Peter Tork"
by Anne Gardner
V.D. INCREASES SEX POTENCY
Do-It-Yourself LSD
EXCLUSIVE CONFESSION LETTER FROM DAVID FERRIE
"WE KILLED J.F.K."

do like the Monkees do...
wear Thom McAn Monkee Boot
Official Monkee Boo
only by Thom McAn
Ankle high, the Monkee Boot feels just right. Hugs your foot
real soft leather. And the flexible sole moves when you move.
Thom McAn has trimmed the toe to give you a neat look.
style is frill-free and clean-cut.
The Monkees wear Monkee Boots exclusively. They like them
wear no others. And you can swing it—Monkee Boots are

PETER TORK
MY GRANDSON
A MONKEE
by Mrs. Catherine "Grams" McGuire Straus
The true, in-depth life story of Peter that only Peter's beloved "Grams" is equipped to tell!

Inevitably, those small record labels which had recorded demos or issued singles featuring members of the Monkees before they became famous began rummaging through their back rooms to dig up the tapes. Davy's Colpix album was reissued with a new Monkees-era jacket, prompting him to warn his fans, 'Don't buy it. The whole thing is terrible and I really resent the fact that when I first recorded those songs people didn't want to know.' Despite his misgivings, fans did buy the material in fairly large numbers. 'I don't feel as strongly about the practice as Davy does,' said Micky, as an old Missing Links demo *Don't Do It* (featuring Glen Campbell on guitar) was issued by Challenge in March 1967. When it reached seventy-five on *Billboard*, he conceded, 'it sure doesn't sound the way I do now, so in a way the fans are being misled. Still, I suppose that people who paid out good money for recording sessions are entitled to try and cash in on it if the circumstances change.' Challenge then, without a conscience, issued a second single, *Huff Puff*, which did not chart.

Possibly the strangest records that appeared in the wake of Monkeemania, were a number of singles on the Davy Jones Presents label. On Don Kirshner's advice, Davy had taken on the services of business manager Hal Cone, who helped him form a record company (Davy Jones Presents), a music publishing company (Syncro Music) and a management firm (Jon-Con) in March 1967. Executive Vice President of the combined enterprises was former Ember Records head, Jack Angel,

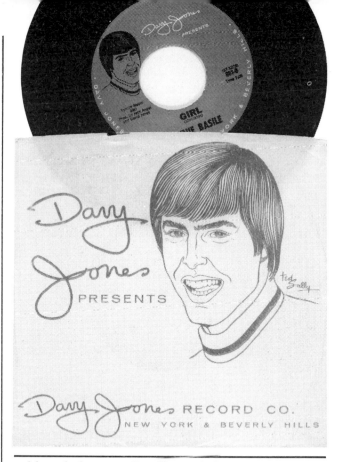

with rock drummer Lee Young as Beverley Hills office manager. The label released four singles, by artists Vinnie Basile, The Relations, Randy Johnson and Dickie 'Flying Saucer' Goodman, each with an Angel/Jones production credit. All of them disappeared without a trace, and by December Davy was suing Cone for $150,000, claiming mismanagement of his funds.

April 1967 was a hectic month, kicking off on April Fool's Day itself with a brief Canadian tour that commenced in Toronto, where 17,000 tickets were sold in just four hours. When Davy returned home he was advised by the United States Army that he had been passed by an Army Medical Board and he could expect to be drafted before the end of the year. The news was leaked to the press within hours, probably by the army, the public relations arm of which was obviously looking forward to another Elvis Presley-type PR boost. Hal Cone, who by this point was banned from the Columbia lot, freely admitted 'I spoke to Davy on the phone this morning and he was surprised at rumours about his call-up. He still has to undergo various educational and psychological tests and could not be drafted until these are complete. We think it is probable that he will be deferred under the hardship case, as his father is a dependent relative. Davy's appeal is certain to take several weeks. Even if it fails, the draft board will probably allow him to complete his existing commitments. If the army insists on drafting Davy we shall make every effort to ensure it does not take place until 1968.'

Such seemingly blithe acceptance of the possibility of the most cuddlesome Monkee being called-up by a decidedly un-hip army sent shivers down the collective spine of Monkee fandom. In London, an estimated 500 weeping female fans besieged the American Embassy, brandishing lipstick-scrawled placards declaring 'Davy Deserves To Live, Not Die' and 'Singer Not Soldier, Monkee Not Guerrilla.' Embassy staff permitted leader Linda Harris to enter the building and present a petition of signatures, the covering letter of which read in part, 'Dear President Johnson. We are very much against writing you this letter but it seems necessary because you plan to draft Davy Jones. We know Davy won't protest, but if you don't draft him, he won't have to.' One eleven-year-old petitioner at the Embassy gates told a reporter, 'It's all very well to say get out there and fight, but he's too small. He's only 5'3" you know!'

Rumours soon began to circulate that Screen Gems had already chosen Davy's replacement who was standing by to take over at short notice. The nominated substitute was twenty-year-old Tim Rooney, son of actor Mickey Rooney and brother of guitarist Mickey Rooney Jnr. of the MGM group Song. Within weeks the issue was defused by the announcement that Davy's appeal, on the grounds of being his father's only means of support, had been upheld.

British fans took to the street when the American Army made noises about drafting wee Davy Jones.

While Davy's future was generating copious Monkee headlines, Peter Tork quietly admitted that he had already been before his friendly neighbourhood draft board. 'I was unacceptable. I didn't like the army, so we came to an agreement. To put it bluntly, they thought I was crazy,' he revealed backstage at the Troubadour. He had called by his old haunt during April and was persuaded to deliver an impromptu fifteen minute acoustic set for the 200 patrons. To an announcement of 'someone who is no stranger to any of us,' he shyly walked on stage and enthralled the crowd with jokes, finger picking and songs ranging from the 1920's chestnut *I Wish I Could Shimmy Like My Sister Kate* to some unreleased Monkee tracks, encoring with a Michael Murphy ballad. According to one review, 'His

humour was a bit more sophisticated than the Monkee show brand. His lines often proved to be a bit faster than the audience.'

Just like Elvis, the Monkees had to suffer celebrity visitors to their sound stage. During April the Yardbirds and Jonathan King dropped by to check out the suspicious American group that was cutting such a swathe through the British charts. King was furiously swotting up on D. H. Lawrence's *Sons and Lovers* during a song-plugging tour, in preparation for his Cambridge finals. He decided that Micky was 'a big phony' but that Peter was 'very creative and very talented.' Yardbirds drummer Jim McCarty echoed King's impressions: 'Peter was definitely the most friendly and talkative. He seemed to be very modest; he said that the acting wasn't that hard because it consisted of quick cuts. He showed us a script and told us that there wasn't much ad-libbing.'

Along with celebrities and an endless stream of giggling Miss Teenage Seattles and Miss Monterey Parks, the set was forever invaded by journalists, many of whom had flown in from England. All accumulated full note pads of thoughts, philosophies and sometimes controversial comments. Davy shook the Monkees boat a little when he declared that he still wanted to make 'fake records' for the good of the show because the others were becoming too heavily involved in recording. The other three countered with suggestions that Davy's mounting business interests would inevitably detract from his acting efficiency. Tracked down by a British reporter, Micky said, 'I really don't know that much about Davy's opinion on the matter. I believe he wanted to continue as we had been, but the rest of us are determined to do all our own work in future. There is no split in the group, we will stay together. Chip Douglas is our producer and we are *all* very happy with our new recordings.'

Thirty-one of the thirty-two episodes for the first series of *The Monkees* were finished off in April and the early episodes were repeated as soon as the last one went on the air at the end of the year. However, the re-runs were not exactly the same shows that had been seen since September 1966. To give the show a more current feel, a large number of songs from the first two albums had been removed from the dream sequences, and replaced by songs from the 'Headquarters' album. Weaker pieces like *Laugh* and *Hold On Girl* were replaced by tracks like *Randy Scouse Git* and *Forget That Girl*.

The large demand for songs – at least two a show – actually resulted in a surplus of material which was not absorbed by record releases. A considerable number of high quality tracks either stayed in the can or were not issued on vinyl until many years later. Some of the more notable songs which escaped early release were Mike Nesmith's *All The King's Horses*, Neil Diamond's *Love To Love*, Boyce and Hart's *Apples Peaches Bananas and Pears*, Chip Douglas' *Steam Engine 99* and Peter Tork's *Tear The Top Off My Head*. One of the richest sources of rare material was the final episode of the first series, *Monkees On Tour*. This fascinating edition of the show was a dramatic departure from style after thirty-one doses of madcap comedy. With a serious documentary approach, it presented the Monkees in real life, touring the midwest. Filmed in Phoenix, Arizona during the first concert tour late in 1966, the show offered a rare glimpse of the group appearing as guest disc jockeys on the local radio station, riding horses, signing autographs and arriving at a concert venue. The second half of the episode was rapid cutaways of the Monkees, in concert, with tantilising snatches of *Sweet Young Thing*, *Mary Mary*, *Last Train to Clarksville* and the four solo sequences. These were intercut with philosophical raves from the four about the road and personal aspirations.

Lynne Randell and Davy Jones at New York's Sherry Netherlands Hotel.

On 27 May the Monkees played Wichita, Kansas, supported by the Fifth Dimension and a young Australian singer called Lynne Randell, and on 9 and 10 June made their long overdue debut at the vast Hollywood Bowl. These shows were not part of a tour, but one-off dates fitted into filming and recording schedules as dress rehearsals for the upcoming London appearances and full-scale American tour. The Hollywood Bowl shows were the Monkees' Shea Stadium equivalent, complete with screaming, stage dashes, faintings and a ludicrous distancing from the fevered audience. Dressed to kill in double-breasted burgundy velvet suits, lace cuffed shirts, floral ties and dress leather boots, the four multi-media heroes bounded onto the stage after the moderately received sets from Lynne Randell and Ike and Tina Turner and The Ikettes, oozing unlimited energy and implied sexuality.

The repertoire from the first tour was basically retained, fleshed out with most of the 'Headquarters' album. Davy took over on drums on two occasions, while Peter alternated regularly between bass and keyboards and sang *Auntie Grizelda*. Mike played rudimentary pedal steel guitar on *Shades Of Gray* and Micky attacked a giant kettle drum throughout *Randy Scouse Git*. The screen projections pioneered on the first tour had become much more sophisticated, beaming

slides, film sequences and lighting effects to a dazzled audience. At one of the shows Micky actually took a dive into the Bowl moat. The two concerts were screaming, roaring, surging, exploding sell-outs, carried by the national and international media as prime news. The concerts also provided undreamed-of exposure for the seventeen-year-old blonde nymphette, Lynne Randell, who became a modern-day Alice in Wonderland. Her involvement with the Monkees began in late 1966, during a brief American promotional tour. In Australia she had scored five substantial hits in just over a year and was about to sign a recording deal with Epic records in New York. 'I got to America just as the Monkees were breaking out, and that's all everybody in the music industry was talking about. My manager and a couple of guys from the William Morris Agency took me along to the Basin Street East club to see Dusty Springfield, and Davy was there. When Davy found out that I was a singer he got really excited and asked me to come to the Sherry Netherlands Hotel the next morning to meet Gloria Stavers, the editor of *16* magazine and the most powerful person in the whole teen idol business. Gloria pulled out a camera at the meeting and took a shot of Davy with my head on his shoulders, which found its way all over the world and had me labelled as a "Monkee girlfriend" forever. At Davy's request, Gloria gave me a lot of exposure. She portrayed me as a friend and buddy of the Monkees rather than a serious girlfriend and thus an enemy, which really became important a few months later.'

The Monkees with influential 16 Magazine *editor, Gloria Stavers.*

Early June also saw the Academy of Television Arts and Sciences bestow an Emmy Award on the Monkees for 'Best Comedy Series of 1966–67.' Unashamedly proud, they donned tuxedos to attend the glittering television presentation ceremony with Bert, Bob and most of the creative nucleus of the show. However at the same time as the overblown television industry was patting itself on the back, a quorum of heavyweights in contemporary music were putting the finishing touches to an ambitious co-operative concept that would have dramatic and far-reaching consequences upon rock music, youth lifestyle *and* the Monkees.

good clean fun

The Beatles 'Sgt. Pepper' album was described by Micky as 'The greatest musical achievement of our generation'.

In 1955, when rock'n'roll music was uprooted and transplanted from dingy black dives and 'race' labels to network television and the popular press, it *threatened* more change to the social fabric of the western world than it actually delivered. But the generation transfixed by beat'n'bravado still held firm to the general moral principles of their parents. The years from 1964 to 1967 witnessed greater changes in music, morals, attitudes and art than any comparable period in this century. The youth power that arose and exercised itself provoked frightening adult retaliations, born from fear and confusion. Rock music became an intellectual experience rather than a simple joyous celebration. Rock'n'roll performers were hankering for recognition as intellectual influences and as artists who play the music of peaceful protest and mass liberation. Their musical concepts were being contorted by mind-expanding drugs, and the underground media was heralding a 'New Age Of Freedom', a counter-culture of peace, flowers and free love.

The first international festival of rock at Monterey in June 1967 set the scene for the 'Summer of Love.'

It was the beginning and the beginning-of-the-end of hippies, flower power, human be-ins and mind expansion, the gathering of the tribes. Organised as a non-profit making celebration by Lou Adler, the manager of the Mamas and the Papas, John Phillips and a board of directors comprised of the great names of pop music of the time. Monterey Pop gave a focus to the dramatic new identity which rock had assumed. Adler recalls, 'I think it was Paul McCartney – said it was

The Monterey International Pop Festival.

Above right: Micky in the garb he wore at Monterey.
Below right: Peter and his errant wallet
Over page: Peter Tork and Janis Joplin were part of the elite Monterey audience.

about time that rock'n'roll became recognised as an art form instead of just a musical phase. Rock had in fact grown up; we had experienced the Beatles, the Stones, and Dylan going electric. . . . Those three days at Monterey seemed like a great idea – it could be a celebration, a festival that would show the evolution of contemporary music and demonstrate where it might be heading.'

The organisers never for a moment considered booking the Monkees; after all, this was a 'serious' music festival. 'L.A. music was street music, like the Seeds, the Leaves, the Doors and Love,' explains Kim Fowley. 'The Monkees weren't particularly scorned or held in contempt, they were just totally overlooked. We all thought of them as actors, and the movie and TV world walked on different sides of the street in Hollywood.'

They were there though, or at least two of them. Neither Mike nor Davy cared much about flower children and expanded consciousness, but Peter and Micky hungered for acceptance and recognition within the new 'aware community.' They eagerly accepted Stephen Still's suggestion that they attend as VIPs, complete with backstage passes. This was their big chance to 'belong,' to shake off the ridicule and prove that they were not dumb schmucks from the idiot box but cosmically conscious citizens of the new order. Micky's offering to this credibility campaign was to stride around the fairgrounds dressed as an American Indian brave, squatting occasionally to lecture groups of pre-pubescents on philosophy. Cornered in the cafeteria he solemnly assured one reporter, 'We were the first group formed for the sole purpose of entertaining little kids. The Beatles have progressed and left all the little eleven and twelve-year-olds behind. We are trying to give them something which is their own. We have our market and naturally we must play to it.'

Peter wisely kept his mouth shut and managed to assimilate himself into the performing community without much difficulty. Mama Cass introduced him to Janis Joplin and he sat backstage swapping acoustic guitar licks with Paul Simon. He was heard rehearsing an acoustic version of *Take A Giant Step* on Simon's guitar but a rumoured surprise solo spot did not come about. However, he was persuaded to take the stage to calm down the audience when rumours about the Beatles being on the Fairground in disguise got too strong. He also introduced short sets by some folkie friends from his Village days. Some reporters noted that he was often to be seen toting an infant in a papoose sling, a young lady slinking quietly behind him, vanishing whenever the word 'press' was uttered. The girl was Karen Harvey and Tork was not the father of her child.

As Rolling Stones Brian Jones and Nico strode ceremoniously through the crowd unmolested, D. A. Pennebaker's film crew in tow, Peter was vying for camera angles, almost as if it were a Monkees episode being filmed. When Brian Jones draped himself over a wooden chair in the press enclosure to sip a Budweiser, Peter made his move. Tom Nolan, in Johnathan Eisen's *The Age Of Rock*, recounted the incident: 'The beer made everything hazily pleasant, even Monkee Peter Tork conspicuously walking up, conspicuously presenting his conspicuous hand. "It's a great honour sir, a great *honour*" he beams, shaking Monkee bashful. Then, Monkee cute, "You know there's about a hundred photographers just dying to get that shot; would you mind again?" "Oh," said Brian, taken aback, "Oh well, if you really *want* to." They shake again and Monkee Peter beams, clowning for cameras, a

65

puppet on a string. "Eceeeaaaah" says Brian softly. "How embarrassing".' Comedian Robert Baker, observing the incident, was heard to remark, 'Peter is probably one of the most honest people I know but . . . he gets a mental block, the shutter comes down and he starts playing at being Peter Monkee. When that happens no one can reach him. I believe, above all else, he really wants to be accepted as a folk singer.'

Peter got a second chance at pinning his star on flesh'n'blood rock credibility with Jimi Hendrix. Four hours after coming off stage at Monterey, Micky invited the Jimi Hendrix Experience to become the support act for the Monkees American tour commencing in Atlanta, Georgia, three weeks later. Negotiations were conducted at Stephen Stills' Malibu house, where many of the festival's performing roster had retired that night. Stills, Hendrix, Hugh Masekela, Buddy Miles and others jammed for fourteen hours, while Tork, using his friendship with Stills to observe and participate, was in a euphoric state.

After Hendrix's Monterey set, the black guitarist was celebrity of the month in Los Angeles, showered with invitations to play, partake, reside and officiate. Peter Tork's persistence paid off and Hendrix moved into his mansion in the fashionable musicians' ghetto of Laurel Canyon. The mansion was open house to the 'serious' rock community of which Peter so much wanted to be part. Hendrix described the place as, 'About a thousand rooms, a couple of baths, two balconies which overlooked the world, and Piccadilly Circus. There is a carport in which there is a Mercedes, a GTO and something that looks like an old copper stove. In the house there is a stereo that makes you feel you are in a recording emporium. There is an old electric piano, amplifier and guitars all over the place.'

In June 1967, the Monkees managed to find nine days to record their fourth album, 'Pisces, Aquarius, Capricorn and Jones Ltd,' which was urgently required before the US and UK tour commenced on 30 June. Though they were still playing together in the studio, the novelty of being a self-contained group was fast wearing off. So divergent were their individual tastes and directions that the entire recording process was a frustrating exercise in compromise. By the time the album was finished, it was clear to each of them that it would be impractical to continue recording as a unit. Producer Chip Douglas did not have the experience to apply firm direction and control where it was so obviously needed. In truth, the Monkees had fought a bloody battle for a freedom for which they were not yet equipped.

In a revealing interview with Keith Altham from *New Musical Express* on completion of the album, Mike sounded off about the pressures he and his partners were under. 'Everyone would like us to be something we're not. I'm convinced that our TV series is a comedy classic and will be regarded as such in years to come. But everybody expects us to be as creative as the Beatles. We would like to spend more time on our records but we just don't have it. I regard 'More Of The Monkees' as probably the worst album in the history of the world. We are now putting more time into our records but it's still not enough. This album was completed in just nine days. It was cut in our own time, between TV rehearsals, concerts and everything else. How creative can you be in that amount of time? We have to be content to produce music that makes people happy while the Beatles create music to make people think. It's impossible to continue at the present pace; by the end of the year we will have to stop.'

England was eagerly awaiting the arrival of the Monkees: 'Monkees Filming Here All June?' conjectured *New Musical Express*, suggesting that the group would be spending all month in the British Isles filming two or three episodes of their series. 'Two big name British pop stars will be invited to guest in the shows filmed here' the journal assured. Daily press bulletins advised on the state of ticket availability, which Wembley Pool officials were controlling carefully through a postmark priority system. British Rail announced provisions for a number of 'Monkee Express' trains to bring fans in from outlying areas for the five concerts on 30 June and 1 and 2 July. *New Musical Express* came back with: 'An unconfirmed report suggests that one of the Monkees will go to each of the four home countries for individual filming – so that England, Scotland, Wales and Ireland will be represented in the television series. Davy Jones will travel to his home in Manchester and probably film sequences at a nearby racetrack.' This report prompted the Marquis of Bath to offer the use of his stately home, Longleat House, as a filming location.

When the recording of 'Pisces, Aquarius, Capricorn, and Jones Ltd,' was finalised on 23 June, the Monkees flew to Paris to meet up with a vacationing Bert Schneider. They were accompanied by Ward Sylvester, tour manager David Pearl, Jim Edmundsen the head of security and publicist Marilyn Schlossberg. After a few days rest and sightseeing, they devoted Tuesday 27 June to the filming of silent slapstick sequences around Paris (incorporated into episode twenty-two of the second series). They cavorted through fruit markets,

A scene from the Monkees In Paris *episode.*

around the Eiffel Tower and along busy streets, revelling in being virtually unrecognised and therefore unhampered in the process of efficient film-making; something that was even becoming a problem in Hollywood, where a posting to Sound Stage 10 outside the main studio gates could mean a mad dash through crowds of waiting fans.

When the Monkees arrived in London on Wednesday night it was apparent that more than a year of intense pressure and heavy workload was beginning to take its toll on the normally effervescent stars. Mike and Peter both admitted to suffering from strain and fatigue; Micky had a heavy cold, and Davy had cut his hand and hurt his ankle. 'I feel terrible,' he complained, 'I've been tired since December. My voice is all shot to pieces and if I lie down I'll sleep for three days.' Micky told Jeremy Pascall, 'Man I'm beat, I hardly know where I am, we've been working so hard recently.' Asked how long he felt he could maintain the pace he quipped, half seriously, 'I don't know. Some day I'm just gonna stop dead. Stick around, it just may be tonight!' 'The guys are working so hard I'm just amazed they haven't cracked up already,' admitted Bob Rafelson in his hotel suite. He went on to apologise for not doing any filming for the television series in England. 'If it could be guaranteed that they could work unham-

Rehearsing Randy Scouse Git *in London.*

pered it would be different. But there's so much excitement building up here that the boys would never be able to get on with their work if they wanted to film on location . . . I know, having looked around London and fought off hordes of writers and photographers myself, that it would be impossible. The Monkees really are *too* popular!'

Rafelson's observations were quite valid. Sitting at number two in the British charts as the Monkees arrived was *Alternate Title (Randy Scouse Git)*, issued as a single by RCA in England to take advantage of the controversy surrounding the title. It was also a hit in Australia,

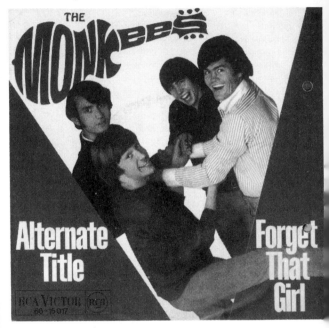

German picture sleeve

where it reached number five, but it was never issued as a single in America. Apart from the British connotations, the song was a smash because it deserved to be. It was fresh, imaginative and rather startling for what was virtually Dolenz's first serious songwriting attempt. The short time that the Monkees had free before the concerns began was put to furious use by all four, as they caught up with old friends and made some new ones. Micky locked himself away with Samantha Juste, for whom he arranged a front row seat in the VIP box for every show. Jonathan King came by to show Peter his Cambridge honours degree and warned, 'Get out and go your own way. Split up now before it's too late.'

The noon press reception on Friday was kept short and sweet, owing to the Monkees' intense mistrust of certain sections of the British press. Mike was sullen from the outset and consequently attracted questions like 'Why are you so rude?,' to which he responded, 'Perhaps it's because I have set high standards for myself and I tend to react to anyone who falls short of my ideals.' This announcement was treated with the contempt it deserved and the attention swung back to Master of Ceremonies Davy. Asked how much the group earned he quipped, 'Three and a tanner or four bob . . . the others don't know what I'm talking about.' Micky admitted, 'Davy is beside himself with delight at being able to show us your country. He's very upset because we can't fit a date in for Manchester. The city has turned over to being a big personal fan club for him.' To the subtle probe 'Do you take drugs?' Peter angelically offered, 'I took aspirin once.' Off on the side Bert Rafelson was explaining 'We didn't manufacture the Monkees – we arranged them. Rather like arranging a Japanese wedding. What we should all remember is that there is a very low divorce rate in Japan.' The function ended with an assurance that the Monkees had every intention of making their first feature film on location in England early in 1968, providing a suitable story line could be found.

For Brian Epstein's NEMS Enterprises the Monkees played five concerts before houses of 10,000 at Wembley Pool Arena – three evening shows and two matinees. Those who witnessed them, regardless of musical tastes, were overwhelmed by the sheer power of a spectacle which rivalled the cacophonic insanity of Beatlemania. The Monkees had the advantage of being actors as well as musicians, a dual talent which gave them the rare capacity to present a multi-tiered piece of entertainment.

For a time, it seemed likely that the concerts would be filmed by the BBC and shown as a special thirty minute edition of *Top Of The Pops*. Unfortunately negotiations between the BBC, NEMS Enterprises, Screen Gems and Raybert failed to overcome the basic obstacle of the 'no outside television' edict instituted by the project's creators at the very beginning. Over-exposure was already becoming a worry so more coverage of the Monkees on the tube was not that desirable anyway.

The repertoire for the London shows was based upon the set from the first American tour. The specialist solo spots were exactly the same, with current hit material added around them. *I'm A Believer* and *Last Train To Clarksville* got proceedings off to a fairly raucous start and were followed with *You Just May Be The One*,

Lulu was chief support at the Monkees' five London concerts.

Sunny Girl Friend, Your Auntie Grizelda, I Wanna Be Free, Sweet Young Thing, Girl I Knew Somewhere and *Mary Mary*. After the solo pieces, the pitch reached hysterical heights with *Alternate Title (Randy Scouse Git)* and *Stepping Stone*. The first half hour of the bill had a BBC Radio 1 disc jockey (a different one at each concert) making tonsil-bursting introductions, an adequate soul outfit called Epifocal Phringe (merely The Echoes some weeks before), delivering the likes of *Knock On Wood* and *Sweet Soul Music*, and Scottish pop belter Lulu who managed to overcome the chants of 'We Want The Monkees' with a storming set that impressed the Monkees. *New Musical Express* reviewer Alan Smith described her as 'absolutely fantastic' in a critique that is worth recording here.

'The interval was over when the whole building seemed to reverberate with the screaming. A twenty yard queue outside the ladies lavatory suddenly disappeared entirely as its members rushed back to their seats. It was a false alarm. Keith Moon of The Who was in the audience standing up and shouting "We Want The Who." Then it happened, the lights dropped and on to the stage bounced the Monkees, clad in wine coloured suits and white sweaters. Mike and Micky were wearing black arm bands in sympathy with the jail sentences on Keith Richards and Mick Jagger . . . First number was *I'm A Believer* and Davy looked surprisingly aggressive as he thrust his bass guitar toward the audience . . . Mr Nesmith looked suitably weary of it

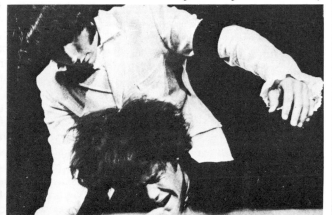

The Monkees wore black armbands while in London to protest against the outrageous jail sentences handed out to the Rolling Stones.

all, as usual. His famous green wool hat turned out to be a vivid blue. Peter Tork didn't seem to make much impact although he did look highly proficient as he flicked through his banjo solo with great dexterity . . . During Davy's *I Wanna Be Free* we got a shot of Mick Jagger projected onto the screen . . . The closing number *Stepping Stone* was magnificent. I hesitate to use the word psychedelic but the entire production and dizzy whirls of light seemed to crash at the senses and send the mind reeling. When it was finally, breathtakingly over, the Monkees ran off the stage and we all stood for *God Save The Queen*. It didn't seem the same somehow.'

Reviews were almost all positive. 'They worked non-stop for well over an hour, which makes it the longest bill-topping performance I've yet seen. The Monkees give, in every way, absolute value for money. An unforgettable evening,' *Record Mirror*'s Peter Jones enthused. He did not mention that Mike had collapsed from exhaustion after the first show and was revived by the administration of pure oxygen.

Using the National Anthem as a cover, the Monkees were rushed directly from the stage to a catering van and whisked back to their hotel each night. As an added precaution, Ward Sylvester stationed a Davy Jones lookalike by the stage door to draw off any girls so delinquent as to have split during the Queen's spot in the show. After the Friday night concert, Mike was distraught over the fact that much of the audience had booed when Jagger's face was shown, 'I can't tell you how miserable that made me. I can only hope that they were booing authority and not the Stones.' Mike buried his sorrow at around 4 am by taking a crowd of party guests over to Radfords (a car dealership) in Hammersmith to see his seventh vehicle acquisition – a custom-built Morris Mini with unlistable accessories and modifications. Costing £3,750 (US $9,100), it was the most expensive Mini ever built.

When Mike took delivery of his custom-built Mini at Radfords, the beast refused to function.

Davy was keeping in close contact with his father in Manchester, who was prevented from attending the concerts by ill health. Davy went to the extraordinary step of setting up a phone link at the side of the stage for a whole show so that he could catch every vital moment. However, as his father himself explained in a telephone interview with America's *Hullabaloo* magazine, 'Even though Davy kept rushing over to tell me what was happening, I couldn't hear too well because his voice was drowned out by the screaming.'

On Monday the Monkees departed independently. Davy went to Manchester, Micky flew back to Paris with Samantha, and Mike called into Radfords to take formal possession of his masterpiece Mini. He sank into the aircraft seats, turned up the stereo tape deck, wound up the perspex tinted windows, switched on the illuminated 'No Smoking' sign, waved to the press photographers and had barely uttered 'This goes like a scalded cat . . . Holymotheragod was that 7,000 revs? . . . this is the greatest moment in my life' when the machine came to an abrupt stop in the middle of the road and refused to continue. For some strange reason (a slow news day?) the incident was carried around the world by news wire services.

One full year into Monkeemania, Jackie Cooper, made wary by the John Lennon furore and generally terrified by the unpredictable Mike Nesmith, was still jealously guarding the Monkees from the American press. As Dolenz recalls, 'He was afraid we'd say "Well, we're bigger than the Beatles, which means we're bigger than Jesus, and we shoot Drano!".' As the tour in England went relatively smoothly, the policy was relaxed to allow maximum promotion of the American tour. A formal press conference was staged in the same New York hotel room that the Beatles had used for interviews a year earlier. Playing it safe, Cooper filled the room at the Warwick with Screen Gems staff journalists. He also gave the four Monkees a strict set of rules regarding taboo subjects and responses. Nesmith was told, 'if they ask you about drugs, talk about asthma.' Micky and Davy had no objections at all to the carefully controlled conditions, still regarding themselves as actors before musicians. They wanted to transfer the fantasy of the television series to real life, with loony lines and cheeky cavorting. Peter didn't care much one way or another and Mike grudgingly agreed to curb his tongue.

From their dramatic entrance in psychedelic Carnaby Street garb hoisting a giant garbage can aloft, the Monkees proved themselves to be every bit as promotionally adept as the Fab Four. Did they plan to put their music into the pyschedelic bag, asked a sixteen year old girl reporter: 'Yes, we're going to give the tape recorder LSD' earnestly assured Micky. What did they think of the Rolling Stones drug bust? 'It's a tragedy,' offered Mike. When Peter explained, 'We're well dressed because we all have girl friends who are tailors,' Micky broke into a high feminine voice and began to describe each other's dress. 'Is it true that the group is breaking up?' 'Sure,' they chimed in unison, walking away from each other. Expectant silence descended when the questions switched to drugs. 'Have any of you ever taken LSD?' asked one keen young writer. 'I haven't,' said Davy, 'Have you?' 'Yes,' he shot back. 'Would you recommend it?,' returned Davy, receiving no reply. After emphatically asserting that they played all their own music, on records and stage, the four merry pranksters left the room, having greatly impressed the Big Apple's wizened press corps.

The second American tour opened on 7 July at Braves Stadium in Atlanta, with Lynne Randell, the Sundowners and the Jimi Hendrix Experience in support, and threaded its way through Jacksonville, Miami, Charlotte and Greensboro. After five shows crisis struck. Halfway through his performance in Greensboro, Jimi Hendrix gave the audience the finger, issued an expletive and stormed off stage, announcing that he was quitting the tour. This came as no surprise to those who had watched the psychedelic purveyor die a death at every show. The surprise was that he had actually been booked in the first place, particularly to play in southern cities where integrated shows were still relatively rare.

Above: Jimi Hendrix and Peter Tork on tour.
Right: Davy taunts fans from a window of the Warwick Hotel.

The Monkees had hoped to use Hendrix to break out of the sub-teen market, appeal to older teenagers and gain acceptance in the rock establishment. It was also, as Tommy Boyce points out, 'A personal trip. They wanted to watch Jimi Hendrix every night, they didn't care if he didn't fit.' Hendrix and Chandler had their own reasons for accepting the dates. They had achieved three top ten hits in England (*Hey Joe*, *Purple Haze*, *The Wind Cries Mary*) but they were yet to chart in America. The scorching set at Monterey was a start, but it needed to be capitalised upon immediately, and Dick Clark's offer of playing before hundreds of thousands of record-buying American kids, was hard to refuse. However, after the first few concerts, it was becoming painfully obvious to all concerned that an awful mistake

had been made. 'His was the type of music and guitar playing that was inextricably interwoven with the drug culture and the whole Haight-Ashbury thing,' explains Mike, 'and the Monkees had nothing whatsoever to do with any of that. We may have looked similar but we were two very different animals. When Jimi was on the same stage as the Monkees it was like having your mouth all set for pineapple and getting lemon.'

The Monkee fans were not shocked, but puzzled by the heavily sexual act that confronted them after the innocuous Lynne Randell and Sundowners opening, but their outraged parents and assorted theatre managers made formal complaints about the erotic nature of the act and it was this that provided a timely explanation

The Monkees were so impressed by Lynne Randell at Wichita and the Hollywood Bowl that she was asked to join them on the second American tour in July 1967.

for the quitting. Dick Clark had no choice but to agree to letting Hendrix go. He turned a blind eye when Lillian Roxon, accompanying her friend Lynne Randell on the road, concocted a wonderful press release which insisted that pressure from a right wing group called the Daughters of the American Revolution, who claimed that Hendrix was corrupting the morals of America's youth, had been responsible for him being removed from the tour. Such publicity was absolutely perfect for Hendrix. He went on to play Fillmore West with the Jefferson Airplane, score his first American hit with *Purple Haze* and storm through Sweden, Holland, France, Denmark and Great Britain, on a tour culminating in his appearance at the Windsor Jazz Festival, staged on 11 to 13 August, alongside Cream, the Move and the Jeff Beck Group.

The severance of the Jimi Hendrix Experience from the tour may have been mutually agreed by both acts but at least one Monkee was infuriated by the brutal realisation that his group had no place in the new rock movement. According to Hendrix biographer David Henderson, 'Hendrix's leaving confirmed for Peter Tork the artistic conflict he felt with the Monkees clown-pop image. He was more at home with the serious music coming out of the Laurel Canyon musician-writer colony. He let it be known that this could be his last tour.' However, the problems with Jimi Hendrix had absolutely no effect on the success of the tour, which was exceeding all expectations.

They arrived in New York on 15 July for their first Big Apple concerts, at the prestigious Forest Hills Stadium, as part of the city's 1967 Music Festival staged by Leonard Ruskin. The conservative *New York Times*, not accustomed to offering critiques on rock'n'roll performances, sent Murray Schumach to review one of the three shows and devoted a prominent half page to his evaluation.

'The setting on Saturday night was almost perfect. The rain had stopped and almost all of the 14,000 seats were filled mainly with girls in their early teens. A half moon rose in the twilight, giving a romantic touch to the audience's adoration, expressed in hanging bedsheets painted with such slogans as "Monkee Power" and "We Love The Monkees".

'As it turned out, no one profiting from the millions being brought in on television, radio, gadgets and costume manufacture need have worried about the investment in the Monkees. The audience protected them beautifully. From the moment the four personable young men bounced out on the stage at 9.15, until they left an hour later, amid a psychedelic display on a screen and swinging giant spotlights on the audience, a shrill, ear-shattering scream of adulation pierced the air.

'The Monkees wore a variety of suits, shirts and shoes, and they had enormous energy as they jumped up and down like human pogo sticks or threw themselves in amusing dance steps that allowed their collar length hair to flap like wings.

'One could also see them putting fingers to guitar or banjo, sticks to drums or mouth to mic. There was an unquestionable strong rock beat that vibrated steadily through the stadium and periodic sounds that were identifiable as country music.

'All of this was complicated by an impulsive electronic system. In fact, in one of the few lulls, when the audience stopped for breath, a voice, presumably belonging to one of the Monkees, was heard to say, "a little bit of sabotage." And shortly after that all four of the Monkees went into a prolonged period of tuning up, while some other people tinkered with machinery on stage.

'None of this bothered the audience. It shrilled steadily and piercingly. At the same time, what seemed like thousands of flash bulbs kept popping. The Monkees spoofed the audience, taking pictures of one another in weird poses, waving, jumping and feigning screams of ecstasy. Periodically, while the Monkees went through the motions of singing and playing, colour photos of them were thrown on the screen over the stage, showing them in close-up or disporting at the beach or in their television shows.

'This of course, only made the bedlam more intense. At one point a few other musicians were used. This seemed to make no difference. One mystery was solved toward the end. Frequently during the performance a sound that resembled the bellowing of a sick cow hovered over the stadium. This turned out to be one of those horns, often heard at Shea Stadium during baseball games. It didn't seem to hurt the musical evening. In fact, it was soothing, a sort of poultice for the eardrums.'

After New York, the Monkees played twenty-two more cities finishing up in Spokane on 27 August. Throughout the two month jaunt the Monkees immersed themselves in a feast of real live musicianship, both on and off stage. Extended jams were a regular occurrence, featuring all four Monkees, the Jimi Hendrix Experience (whilst on the tour), the Sundowners, John London, Stephen Stills, David Crosby and whoever else was able to drop by after a show including, according to legend and bootleg tapes, the Animals.

Lynne Randell travelled on the private jet during the entire tour and has difficulty separating one outrageous incident from another on what was essentially an airborne orgy. 'Because I was kind of straight, nobody tried to force me into what was going on, but they didn't try to hide it from me either... Famous people would join the plane at one city and get off a few days later at another city. All of the Buffalo Springfield were on board for a while, I think they were making a connection to go to India. Peter Fonda was hyping everybody

about *The Trip* and David Crosby was getting high with Peter. For a while Davy had Jan Berry on the plane. It wasn't that long after his car accident and he was still really a vegetable. I got lumbered with reading him the John and Betty books and feeding him occasionally. I really got close to him because I'd never seen such determination. He managed to say to me, "I was always the smart one and Dean was the dummy . . . but now I'm the dummy." I don't know why they had him on the plane, maybe they thought it would do him some good. I doubt it did.'

Peter has his own recollections of the airborne madness. 'We had a lot of fun on the plane and between shows with Jimi. He taught me how to play guitar vibrato one day. We used to smoke together up the back because the front was full of press people. But the pilot would announce that he couldn't make up the weight difference so could we please come back up to the front. Everybody knew, nobody said anything. I was the only head in the group to begin with. The damage I did to those poor boys' minds!' However, once the novelty of airborne drugs, sex and lunacy had abated, philosophy became the number. Peter was rarely without his copy of *I Ching – The Chinese Book Of Changes* and would regularly chair discussion groups which included Hendrix, assorted Monkees, Lynne Randell and Lillian Roxon.

These American dates saw Davy Jones emerge as quite a reasonable concert musician. Gretch had customised a three quarter sized bass guitar for him, with which he was able to regularly release Peter for keyboard duties. Peter was his staunchest supporter, and has been quoted as saying, 'Of course Davy is a musician, he's musically very solid. He can pick up an instrument quickly through his physical co-ordination, singing ability and plain positive attitude. Some people you can never teach about music, but Davy is a musician at heart. He has the heart and mind for music with the will to want to know more.' Such expressions of support were never heard from Mike, who basically considered all three to be musically inferior to himself. He came off the road complaining about a loss of hearing. 'My hearing has gone off twelve per cent in one ear and eight per cent in the other because of all the racket the fans make.'

'The road was just a blur, I don't remember much of what happened,' claims Micky. 'We were shoved from the back of a limo, into a garbage entrance, into a hotel room, into another garbage entrance, into a meat wagon that deposited us behind the stage. Then we did the whole thing in reverse an hour later. I realised that I was really a rock star when I started getting paternity suits from places I'd never been. I showed them to other rock groups who said "Oh yeah, you got one from the Carlisles in Ohio too, how about that!" Some guy and his mutant daughter would send identical letters to every performer they could think of on the off chance that just one of them would be stupid enough to want to avoid litigation by sending them $5,000. It was like chain paternity letters!'

Italian picture sleeve

During their American tour *Pleasant Valley Sunday*, their fourth single, reached number three. It was a rather heavy handed swipe at conformity and suburban values, written by Gerry Goffin and Carole King, who seemed to be trying just a bit too hard. 'The opening line "the local rock group down the street is trying hard to learn their song" is maybe a touch too bitter,' suggests Carole King's biographer Mitchell S. Cohen. 'A lot of local rock groups were riding high (with original material) and encroaching on Goffin and King's territory.' Nonetheless it was a bright spacious production from Chip Douglas and the B-side, *Words*, was Tommy Boyce and Bobby Hart at their best – brilliantly structured, powerful pop. Douglas produced it with

style, using a whispered opening vocal from Micky and an effective answer vocal from Peter. The song was so powerful that it charted in its own right on Billboard at position 11. The release of this Goffin and King/Boyce and Hart single made it apparent that the Monkees had not gained complete control of their recordings. Screen Gems contract writers were still indispensable when it came to pulling in the big publishing money. The only A-side written by a member of the group was *Alternate Title (Randy Scouse Git)*, and that had been released as a result of an independent decision by RCA in England. In America the situation would not change until the release of *Good Clean Fun*, almost two years later. Notwithstanding the continuing iron hand of Screen Gems and Mike's complaints about lack of recording time, 'Pisces, Aquarius, Capricorn and Jones Ltd.', proved to be a creative and artistic victory when issued in November. Although sales were just one fifth of 'More Than The Monkees' (a bare million), it still made number one and reinforced the Monkees' capacity for introducing and launching exceptional new talent.

At least nine months before John Lennon, Paul McCartney and Derek Taylor got around to ringing singer/songwriter Harry Nilsson at the Security First National Bank Computer Centre in California to tell him how great he was, the Monkees had discovered the fact for themselves. Harry was neatly juggling two careers at the time; computer supervisor and pop songwriter of promising proportions. Taken under the wing of Phil Spector he had penned (with Phil) *Paradise* and *Here I Sit* for the Ronettes and *This Could Be the Night* for The Modern Folk Quartet.

Mike contemplates the source of Cuddly Toy.

Early in 1967, not long before RCA signed him to a $75,000 recording contract, Harry asked Chip Douglas to play the Monkees his demo of *Cuddly Toy* and they were exceedingly impressed. Its' appearance on 'Pisces, Aquarius, Capricorn and Jones Ltd.', on 1 November, 1967, coincided with the release of Harry's debut album 'Pandemonium Shadow Show' which featured his own version of the song. With heavy LP/EP airplay of the Monkees version, the patronage of the Fab Four (Fab Two anyway) and a Yardbirds cover version of *Ten Little Indians*, Harry was able to quit his day job and begin his ascent to the realms of superstardom.

A second great undiscovered talent was lurking within the ranks of the Monkees' 'sister' act, the Lewis and Clarke Expedition, who were also produced by Jack Keller and supervised by Lester Sill. Lurking as Travis Lewis was Texas singer/songwriter Michael Murphy, who gave the Monkees the exceptional *What Am I Doing Hangin' Round?* which was tailor made for fellow-Texan Mike Nesmith's plainsman voice. Murphy's bandmate John London collaborated with Mike on the captivating *Don't Call On Me*, which Nesmith sang with anything but a plainsman's voice. Douglas coached him in singing soft and close on the microphone and he turned in a vocal performance that was more like Johnny Mathis than Cowboy Pete.

1967 was a truly extraordinary year for rock music, which was being propelled to dizzying new heights by every major album release. No one knew this better than the Monkees and, even with only nine rushed days of recording, they managed to contribute to the rapid evolution with some important innovations. A more practical approach to the question of session musicians had been adopted and a sensible complement of session players were used and duly credited, among them were drummers Eddie Hoe and Kim Kopli, supreme banjo picker Doug Dillard, pianists Bill Martin and Chip Douglas and Moog synthesizer pioneer, the late Paul Beaver. 'I had the first Moog on the West Coast,' explains Micky. 'It was only the third one ever made. The first one Robert Moog himself had and Paul Beaver had the second.' Micky played his Moog on Goffin and King's *Star Collector* and Nesmith's *Daily Nightly*. The flying saucer effects on the latter inspired some critics to compare it to Beatle studio innovations.

Italian picture sleeve

Micky playing his Moog Synthesizer – the first used for rock recording.

As a producer (and bassist) Chip Douglas had outlived his usefulness after two albums. His parting effort with the group resulted in their fifth American single and their second biggest hit. *Daydream Believer* was written by John Stewart, a former member of the Cumberland Three and the Kingston Trio, and one of the finest singer/songwriters in America. Douglas chose the song for a single over Neil Sedaka's *Rainy Jane* (which Davy stuck in his pocket and recorded solo four years later), despite out-of-character opposition from Davy. 'We'd done twelve songs and the thirteenth was *Daydream Believer*. I said, "that's terrible." I was a baritone and it was in the wrong key for my voice. I'd been in the studio all day, I was tired and I'm singing these words about twelve times, "cheer up sleepy Jean, oh what can it mean to a daydream believer and a homecoming queen." I kept asking Chip what the words meant and he said "don't worry, just sing them." I said O.K. . . . I'll sing it until I get it right. So Chip says, "all right one more time, *Daydream Believer*" and I started it and I failed and I failed and I failed. Hank Cicalo, the engineer, had his own way of numbering takes so he could find them, he'd call them 1A or 2A, like that. Anyway, all of a sudden he says "7A" over the talkback and I wasn't listening so I said "what number is this?" and they said "7A!" in unison. That kicked me on a bit and I got it down but you can tell from the vocal that I was pissed off.'

Peter cites *Daydream Believer* as one of the few tracks that features playing that he is proud of. 'I'd play fourth chair guitar on one of Michael's cuts on the first album, probably *Papa Jean's Blues*, and of course "Headquarters", and to a lesser extent, the fourth album featured us all. But one of the Monkees' songs I still really like is *Daydream Believer*. I can identify with it because I played the piano lick on it and I feel like I made my mark because on Anne Murray's version her pianist plays my lick.'

Released in November, *Daydream Believer* gave the Monkees a Christmas number one (number two in the UK). On the flip was a real gem, the dizzying, brassy *Goin' Down. Steam Engine 99*, a similar style of song, written by Chip Douglas and recorded at the same time, was inserted in the television show but was not issued on disc until 1979. Another Douglas production which remains unissued is *Riu Chiu*, a fifteenth century Spanish chant from the Modern Folk Quartet songbook which was used in the Christmas 1967 episode of the television series. Performed as *a cappella*, it was one of the most impressive musical sequences in the show.

By the fourth album, the Monkees enterprise had grown from a small creative core to a battalion of assistants, attendants, advisors and hangers-on. Each Monkee, taking a lead from Mike, had taken on paid friends, be they body-guards, travel companions or stand-ins. Mike's Texas troupe was headed by his 'shadow', John London, of whom Davy says, 'Mike

Davy with David Pearl.

wanted John to be the bass player in the beginning but he was a six foot guy with a fat face. A nice man but he wasn't right for the TV show. He didn't do comedy or anything like that.' When London had to devote most of his time to the Lewis and Clarke Expedition, Phyllis' brother, Bruce Barbour, who bore a startling resemblance to his brother-in-law, took over as stand-in. Mike and John London's progress in Hollywood had been monitored carefully at San Antonio College in Texas and when it appeared that there really was gold lying on the streets, the exodus north began. From Texas Michael Murphy, Owen Castleman and Johnny Raines joined London in the Lewis and Clarke Expedition, and David Price became a stand-in for both Peter and Davy, and head roadie. Though born in New York, David Pearl was also a part of the 'San Antonio Mafia'. Pearl was the Joe Esposito or Red West of the Monkees Community. As Davy's closest friend, and dubbed the fifth Monkee, he became the group's tour manager and, eventually, personal co-manager. Good looking and

A rare snapshot of the original Monkee stand-ins: (left to right) David Pearl (Peter), Ric Klein (Micky), David Price (Davy) and John London (Mike).

obsessively fashion conscious, Pearl often fared better with women on the road than a couple of the Monkees. Fan magazines devoted full page stories to him.

Californian Ric Klein was Micky's best friend and stand-in. Like Pearl and Jones, the pair were inseparable, each serving as Best Man at the other's wedding. Bill Chadwick, with his fuzzy afro, also came in handy as Micky's stand-in. He had remained with the group since the auditions, eventually becoming the concert sound engineer and prolific songwriter. Musically talented, there was talk at one stage of his being a replacement for Peter. Brendon Cahill began his association with the Monkees as a chauffeur, a bodyguard and a road attendant and eventually became personal co-manager with David Pearl and album co-ordinator. Gene Ashman, the costume designer on the series, spent a lot of time with Davy. The two drew up ambitious plans for a clothing design and manufacture partnership that would flood American stores with Davy Jones brand products. Like so many of the ambitious private projects by the individual Monkees, it got lost in the rush.

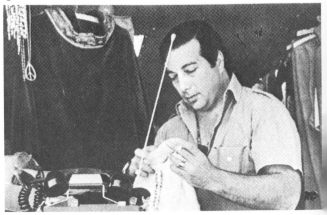

Monkees costume designer Gene Ashman.

looking for the good times

The 'new look' Monkees from the second television series. No more wool hats, matching button-patch shirts or well-groomed hair.

The second series of television shows (just twenty-six episodes, as opposed to thirty-two in the first series), got underway on a high note after the American tour in July. Of its own volition, Screen Gems increased the Monkees' salaries from $450 to $750 per week. Controls began to loosen, the budget was more flexible, uniforms were scrapped in favour of personal choice of clothes, hair was allowed to grow freely, Micky and Peter were allowed to direct some episodes, and the hated *Monkees Theme* was replaced as the show's closer by Peter's *For Pete's Sake* (sung by Micky), which declared 'love is understanding, it's in everything we do.' As Davy recalls, 'When we got that incredible raise, it was obvious that more was expected of us, we had to become more professional.'

His attitude was not necessarily shared by his comrades. Scripts became notepaper for Peter's stream-of-consciousness essays and Mike drily admitted, 'We don't learn scripts . . . hell, we don't even read them.' The four had been appalled at being presented with leftover scripts from the first series when they began the second season. Not willing to keep on beating up the same bad guys and go through the same tired routines, they voiced loud objections, which were met with such threatening responses as: 'Don't you guys want to do a third series?' When they retorted: 'Not with scripts like these we don't,' they were furnished with fresher storylines.

Towards the end of the first series, the concept of brief 'guest stops' had been introduced when one episode ran one minute short. Instead of recutting and padding, Rafelson staged a spontaneous interview during which Davy announced that the thing he wanted most in the world was Ursula Andress. To an off-camera probe of, 'You've reached a certain amount of success, if it was suddenly taken away, wiped out, where would you be tomorrow?,' Peter replied, 'I'd go back to the Village and be a folk singer.' 'I'd go back to the Village and watch him be a folk singer,' offered Davy. 'I'd probably go burn down the Village,' concluded Mike, who then launched into a diatribe about how people should 'learn to dig something ugly because it takes no special talent to dig things that are beautiful.'

These informal spots became a regular feature of the second series. Davy introduced his friend Charlie Smalls (later to write *The Wiz*), and they discussed soul music while Peter gave his thoughts on the hippie movement. 'We just have to show up on the set, act natural, not use bad language and not be drunk,' explained Mike at the time. The four were also involved in the selection of episode guests. One show opened with Mike and Frank Zappa impersonating each other, Nesmith's false nose continually falling off and Zappa wearing a wool hat and Monkee shirt. If getting Frank Zappa into prime-time television was a coup for Mike, then Micky was equally excited at his opportunity to showcase progressive singer/songwriter Tim Buckley, whom he had been plugging in fan magazines for months.

Scenes from the second series of The Monkees.

Meeting and hanging out with Brian Jones and Paul McCartney, ligging at Monterey, touring and jamming with Hendrix, experimenting with Moog synthesizers, injecting cosmic philosophies into their 'all my own work' recordings – all these experiences inspired the four Monkees with a strong proselytizing spirit, rendering them evangelists for the new order of conciousness. Their sacred duty was to spread the word, open the doors for Prophet Zappa and Pastor Buckley, make their followers aware of peace, love, understanding, self-expression and other vital tenets of the counter culture. Of course, not every young viewer caught on, or even cared about the subtle and not-so-subtle messages and meanings. Zany humour, catchy music, bright wit, flamboyant clothes and peer group dialogue seemed to satisfy the majority of the millions who tuned in each week. It was, in fact, radical academics who seemed to derive the most spiritual uplift from the proceedings. In *The Politics Of Ecstasy*, Dr Timothy Leary devoted considerable space to his impressions of the Monkees:

'Hollywood executives decide to invent and market an American version of the Beatles – the early, pre-prophetic cute, yeh-yeh Beatles. Got It? They auditioned a hallful of candidates and type-cast four cute kids. What do the screaming teenyboppers want? Crank out the production and promote it. Feed the great consumer monster what it thinks it wants: plastic, syrupy, tasty, marshmallow-filled, chocolate-coated, Saran-wrapped, and sell it. No controversy, no protest. No thinking strange, unique thoughts. No offending Mom and Dad and the advertisers. Make it silly, suntanned, grinning NBC-TV.

And what happened? The same thing that happened to the Beatles. The four young Monkees weren't fooled for a moment. They went along with the system but didn't buy it. Like all the beautiful young sons of the new age – Peter Fonda and Robert Walker and young John Barrymore and young Steinbeck and the wise young Hitchcocks – the Monkees use the new energies to sing the new songs and pass on the new message.

The Monkees' television show, for example. Oh, you thought that it was silly teenage entertainment? Don't be fooled. While it lasted, it was a classic Sci-Fi put-on. An early-Christian electronic satire. A mystic-magic show. A jolly Buddha laugh at hypocrisy. At early evening kiddie-time on Monday the Monkees would rush through a parody drama, burlesquing the very shows that glue Mom and Dad to the set during prime time. Spoofing the movies and the violence and the down-heavy-conflict-emotion themes that fascinate the middle-aged.

And woven into the fast-moving psychedelic stream of action were the prophetic, holy, challenging words. Micky was rapping quickly, dropping literary names, making scholarly references; then the sudden psychedelic switch of the reality channel. He looked straight at the camera, right into your living room, and up-levelled the comedy by saying: "Pretty good talking for a long-haired weirdo, huh, Mr and Mrs America?"

And then – zap. Flash. Back to the innocuous comedy.

Why it all happened so fast, LBJ, you didn't ever see it. Suddenly a whole generation disappeared right from view. Flick. They're gone! They won't vote and they won't listen to the good old promises and threats, and they won't answer Gallup polls, and they just smile when we arrest them, and they won't be clean-cut, hard-working, sincere, frightened, ambitious boys like Khrushchev and I were. Hey! Where did they go?'

Under the cold blue light of analysis it's hard to pinpoint any positively seditious dialogue or activity but there is no arguing that the lines were somewhat hipper than those in *Gilligan's Island*, as these examples illustrate:

GIRL (*pointing to Peter*): How did he get in here?
DAVY: Well he left home, caught a cab, walked through the studio gate and right onto this set.

DAVY (*on phone*): Hello, you've got to help us; we're being held captive by some crooks in a ghost town
COUNTRY BUMPKIN: I'd better call Mr Dillon.
DAVY: Matt Dillon?
COUNTRY BUMPKIN: No, Bob Dylan, he'll write a song about your problems.

MICKY: Hold it. (*He stops a gangster shoot-out scene and leads a pretty secretary on to the set*). The director said we should have a pretty girl in the show. (*Leads girl off set.*) O.K. now get on with your shooting.

MICKY (*on desert island*): Oh my goodness we're lost, our footsteps have gone round in circles.
DAVY: Nonsense, we're just using a small set, like the Lone Ranger Show.
FRIDAY: There's only one safe place to hide.
DAVY: Where?
FRIDAY: I can't tell you, it's in the next scene.

MICKY (*as television ratings surveyor*): Well Davy, what show did she say she was watching?
PETER: Ours, I hope!

MICKY: (*to postman*): Listen buddy, you've been late with the mail for the last four days. I want you to be here on time or I'll beat the hell out of you! Now let me see that letter. (*He snatches it, tears it open and suddenly adopts' shrill, strangled voice*) Ohhh! it's from the see-lective ser-vice people?

DAVY (*to the wolfman*): After all, what has Dracula ever done for you? Look at all those pictures you've done together; *Dracula Leaves*, *Dracula Returns*, you know you've made over thirty movies with him and you haven't even got second billing.
WOLFMAN: Urgh, Urgh!
DAVY: What you need is a good agent. These people are exploiting you.
WOLFMAN: Urgh, Urgh! (*His pretty niece enters*).
NIECE: What do you want Wolfman?
DAVY: He wants a better share of the profits; he wants time off at the weekends and he wants to play his own music.

The show was at its best when satirising and lampooning sacred cows of the mass media – dopey sit-coms, beach party movies, advertisements, the advertising industry, the James Bond cult, horror and western movies, quiz shows, traditional fairy tales, fast-talking hot-shot disc jockeys, veteran movie stars and, of course, themselves. Their send-up of beach party movies was truly inspired. The hero was Frankie Catalina (read Avalon), a hapless, hopeless narcissistic deadbeat who couldn't swim or sing, broke out in a rash when he got near girls and had to read his lines from cue cards. The Monkees, as extras, devastate this imitation Adonis by switching his cue cards and speeding up the record he mimes to.

In the *I've Got A Little Song Here* episode, Mike took a swipe at the exploitation of starving musicians by greedy publishers, touching on experiences from his own early career. Similarly, in another episode, AM radio stations were lampooned for their obsession with far-out groovy nothingness. The powerful teen magazine empire also came in for some sharp barbs in *Monkees A La Mode*, which concerned the publication of fabricated stories about the group.

Yet for all its unsubtle taunts and teases there was never any illusion that the situation of this comedy was real. References to the sound stage, crew and plot development were commonplace. Micky could be heard to remark that, 'We usually have a fantasy sequence in this part of the show.' In the Paris episode, director Jim Frawley was seen to telephone Bob Rafelson complaining that the Monkees had not shown up on the set to begin filming and were believed to be heading for France to make their own episode. Even the props were hip. One scene showed the cover of the 'Sgt. Pepper' album being used as a dartboard. A life sized manikin in the Monkees house, which issued forth quotes from famous philosophers when its string was pulled, was fondly referred to as Mr Schneider. Script overlord Paul Mazursky was even enticed before the camera, to portray Captain Crocodile's goofball producer.

Towards the end of the second series, Peter and Micky were each allowed to direct an episode, as part of an arrangement made during preliminary meetings for the upcoming feature film. Peter's effort, *Monkees Mind The Manor*, was barely distinguishable from the standard episodes but Micky displayed a more noticeable flair. *The Frodis Caper*, the last episode of the season, was an engaging half hour with cute subtleties and technical effects. It concerned an evil scientist who jams television shows with a test pattern planted with subliminal triggers designed to turn the nation's youth into zombies. Peter recalls, 'We would get spontaneous during rehearsals and if something worked, we would keep it. But once the camera angles and lighting were set up, it was hard to change things. The studio was lit very carefully with film values, if we moved more than six inches we'd flare out. Most current television shows have "flat lighting" so that you can walk anywhere on the set and still be lit the same way. By the time you saw our show on the screen it wasn't spontaneous. The pilot took eight days but when we started to get hot we could do an episode in three days.'

Just how revolutionary the words and images of *The Monkees* were remains unclear. One school of thought sees them as 'moles' for the counter culture, an arm of dissemination for progressive attitudes of the period. However, it was certainly not regarded in that way at the time. The newly-emerged serious rock media despised the Monkees and everything they represented. Tom Nolan characterised the prevailing attitude with his ridicule-ridden account of Peter and Micky's Monterey visit. In the same feature, entitled *Groupies – A Story Of Our Time*, Nolan took another swipe: 'Sherry, overdue library book in hand, is parked in her pink Mustang high in the Hollywood Hills, the city all a-twinkle below her. She watches the house she is about to enter, the house of the drummer of America's number one money-making group. She watches through the window of his den as he, unaware, flails away at his drums. His group is often being accused of being blatant bogus-Beatles, and so it is somewhat ironic (and Sherry, cynical-sharp, is not unaware of this) that the record he is practising to is the Beatles' *Lucy In The Sky With Diamonds*; and even though it is a fairly slow song, he can't . . . quite . . . keep the beat . . . and just before going in, she smiles slightly around the corners of her mouth and mind; she keeps her sense of perspective.'

Hullabaloo magazine, in a state of menopause as it shook off its *16* magazine trappings in favour of an 'underground' identity, bestowed upon the Monkees its 'Bummer of the Year' award, appending it with this justification: 'Because, as others have said, they are not worthy of their success. We can't help but think of all the unknown, not-yet-discovered talent – *real* talent – that exists in the pop music world; talent that works long and hard. Such people sacrifice, struggle, sweat and even starve trying to make it. These are the people who are the most worthy in this often corrupt music business, not the Monkees. Let's put success where it belongs.'

Lillian Roxon in *Rock Encyclopedia*, expressed the prevailing attitude: 'The cynicism with which it was done was incredible and created a lot of resentment. Nobody really minded that the Monkees were manufactured entirely in cold blood and for bluntly commercial

Waiting for Sherry to arrive?

really upset a lot of people around the studio.'

During the first series, Davy had infuriated official-dom with one incident that seems to have passed into legend. He arrived at the Columbia Studios front gate on a Monday morning, bleary-eyed and irritable, having come directly from an all-weekend party at Tommy Boyce's house. When the security officer asked who he was, Davy snapped back, 'I'm Davy Jones, I'm doing *The Monkees* and I'm late for the show.' When the guard insisted, 'You're not Davy Jones' and refused to lift the boom gate, Jones snarled, 'Fuck off, man,' and drove right through it, showering the driveway with debris. Carpeted before Jackie Cooper, his resignation offer was rejected and he was sternly warned never again to act in such a manner.

This flare up on Davy's part was certainly rare but not necessarily isolated. Professional to the depths of his tiny frame, he was never reticent about defending what he saw to be in the best interests of his career. During the first series he almost walked out on the biggest rock group in America when Screen Gems executives apparently refused to allow him to appear in the film version of *Oliver*, even in cameo. 'It choked me up it really did,' he admitted. 'When something like that happens I don't walk away from it, I come back and meet the challenge. I had to realise that in America they have different ideas about groups, the way they should behave and the things they should do.'

The establishment's answer to the uncomfortable problems caused by the Monkee's presence on the lot was to knock a hole through the back wall of the set to accommodate a giant soundproof black box, fitted with a meat freezer door and handle. Inside the structure were pillows, bunks, musical instruments, telephones, amps, refreshments and in each corner, a different coloured light to indicate which Monkee was required before the cameras. Although the corporation initially

reasons. But when, never having played together before, their records hit the top of the charts on the strength of what seemed like nothing more than TV exposure and a good sound financial push, the bitterness from other struggling groups was overwhelming.'

Not just from struggling groups. Chris Hillman asserts that he and Jim McGuinn wrote the Byrds hit *So You Wanna Be A Rock'n'Roll Star* as a protest against the emergence of manufactured pop groups like the Monkees. David Crosby introduced the song at the Monterey Pop Festival as an expression of the disillusionment his partners felt over the state of the rock business. 'The amusing thing about all this,' taunted *Crawdaddy* magazine, 'is its supreme unimportance. After it's all over and they've outsold everyone else in history, the Monkees will still leave absolutely no mark on American music.'

Back on the set, corporate attitude to the Monkees had not been softened by the success of their efforts. The actual sighting of a long-haired youth on the backlot may still have induced a heart attack for the users of the executive washroom. 'The directors tried to inspire within us an attitude of improvisation and spontaneity,' explains Micky, 'but that is not something you can shut off as soon as the cameras stop. So when we broke for lunch or went home at night we were still quite bozo – "hey!, wah!, blah!, wow!, hey what's happening?!, zap!, pow!," all over the place. And that

took steps to protect their property from such corruptive influences as drugs, women and political enlightenment, a blind eye was turned toward the black box. 'A few packets made it through the lines,' admits Davy, though Peter insists that, after a few disastrous attempts, they all opted against doing the show stoned.

Groupies were consumed more readily, smuggled in by stand-ins and roadies. Davy had the most voracious appetite, but Mike seemed to get all his pleasure from executive baiting. 'Of course there were Monkee groupies,' admits Peter, 'but I don't know, the events of the day seem so harmless in retrospect. I mean we really were innocent guys. I'm sure there wasn't half a homosexual among the whole crew and if there was it was evenly distributed. Nobody was into receiving or inflicting pain as far as I knew and there were no wild orgies in the night.'

'They used the box, which was actually a room about 12′ × 16′, to keep us out of the way, which was fine by us,' explains Davy. 'I'd be kissing one girl, going to another, saying "wait a minute I'll be with you in a second." Mike was on the phone making business calls and yelling at everyone; Peter was saying "more brown rice please, all over my nose so I can't breathe but can still read the Maharishi;" Micky was doing his "aar ghbrryesnowhyhowcomegozapwowupdownmorelessaaargh" thing, burning off energy.'

The granting of more creative control to the Monkees themselves was as much a result of Raybert's expanding outside activities as of any desire to liberate the four as individuals. For Schneider and Rafelson the success of the Monkees was a timely boost to cinematic aspirations. Bob had formed a close friendship with a young actor called Jack Nicholson, who was attracting attention in Hollywood for his portrayals of demented, unstable characters in B-movies such as *The Raven*, *Cry Baby Killer* and *The Terror*. Nicholson began hanging around the Monkees' camp in 1967 (the same year in which he wrote the screenplay for *The Trip*), and was used as a cameraman when the live concert episode of the television series was filmed in Phoenix. Relatively reticent at that point in his career, he was attracted, but also a little unsettled by the rock'n'roll industry, which was doing considerably more to live up to Hollywood's decadent image than the film world.

As Tommy Boyce recalls, 'I went over to Bob Rafelson's place one Sunday to go swimming. I was standing around the pool dressed in my Nehru suit, the medallion, the whole 60's thing, with some gorgeous blonde attached to me. Bob called me over and said, "Jack, I'd like you to meet Tommy Boyce" I said, "It's very nice to meet you Jack, what do you do?" He told me, "Well I'm an actor", but I interrupted him and said, "I'd love to continue this but I have to go swimming, would you excuse me?" Then this blonde – some rent-a-date, as I was too busy writing songs to find my own – and I stripped off all our clothes and dived into the pool naked, just for fun. . . . So I got out of the pool, asked for a towel, walked back to Nicholson and

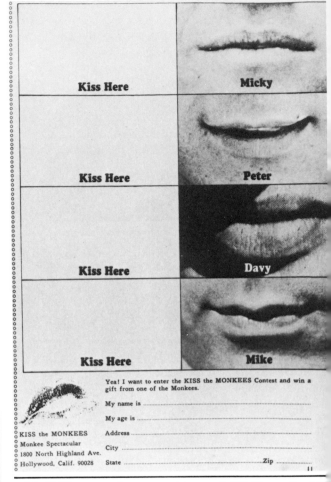

Kiss Here — Micky

Kiss Here — Peter

Kiss Here — Davy

Kiss Here — Mike

Yea! I want to enter the KISS the MONKEES Contest and win a gift from one of the Monkees.

My name is ....

My age is ....

Address ....

City ....

State .... Zip ....

KISS the MONKEES
Monkee Spectacular
1800 North Highland Ave.
Hollywood, Calif. 90028

11

said, "What was that you said you did?" He really fell apart, "Well, I as . . . I ah . . . could you do that again?". The next year he was doing *Easy Rider* and a year later he was a big star.

'You see the way he got that role was like this, Dennis Hopper and Peter Fonda came to Bert Schneider with this loose script idea for a rock'n'roll road movie about bikers. Bert took on the project and Bob Rafelson said to him, "I'd really like you to put my friend, Jack Nicholson, in this movie." Bert told him, "Sorry man, there's just no part for him," but Bob insisted. "He's gotta be in this film, it'll be a great stepping stone in his career, you've got to slip him in for at least ten minutes." "Sorry, can't go for it." So finally Bob said "Well, how many Monkee shows do we have to do for this season?" "Oh, about ten." "Hmm, well I guess I won't be directing any of them." Bert broke down and said, "All right you sonofabitch, I'll give him twelve minutes" and Jack Nicholson got to be in *Easy Rider*. There was also about $300,000 of Monkee profit invested in the film. That's where they got most of their bankroll.'

While Micky and Peter were relieving their creative frustrations by directing an episode of the series, Mike was careering off on a tangent so strange that in retrospect it probably puzzled him. On 18 and 1

November, at the RCA studios in Hollywood, he assembled no less than fifty-four seasoned professional session musicians, including guitarists James Burton, Tommy Tedesco and Howard Roberts, drummers and percussionists Hal Blaine, Frank De Vito, Earl Plamer, Cary Coleman and Emil Richards, banjoist Doug Dillard, pianists Larry Knetchtel and Don Randi, pedal steel guitarist Orville 'Red' Rhodes, and Jim Horn on woodwinds. The object was to create a contemporary big band treatment of ten Nesmith compositions, under the project name of 'The Wichita Train Whistle Sings.' Mike was the producer of the sessions, as well as co-arranger with the famous Shorty Rogers. Hank Cicalo, whom he liked and trusted, was engineer.

Screen Gems-Columbia owned his acting, singing and songwriting but had overlooked Mike's talents as a producer. 'Nobody had my production rights' he growled. 'It was the only freedom I could enjoy. The idea was to not only put together a different sort of picture of tunes I'd written for the Monkees and give them vent in my own way, rather than have them highly manipulated, but also have a record that would document a coalescence of the finest session men in L.A. at the time. One of the great stupid mistakes I made in my life was not including a personal listing with the album. I just can't imagine that I didn't do that because it was such an important part.'

Mike personally shelled out $60,000 for the project and placed it with Dot Records, who took it on as a Monkee-related item. Even so, the album was issued in a dark, obscure jacket, with small lettering and no photographs. Commercially it was the first turkey for Christmas, a bomb of immense proportions. It is unlikely that even Gordon Jenkins could have taken ten

Rare photograph from the recording sessions for the 'Wichita Train Whistle Sings' album.

simple folk songs written on guitar and rendered them successfully in a big band arrangement. The concept was ludicrous, the execution rudimentary and cacophonic. There were some moments of interest, however, notably Doug Dillard's fine banjo-picking refrain of *Cripple Creek* on *Don't Cry Now* and the opening to *Nine Times Blue*, which was a passage from Bach's Toccata in D minor.

The few reviews dismissed the album out of hand. *High Fidelity* magazine described it as: 'One of the all-time clumsy attempts at combining the big band brass with rock'n'roll rhythms . . . One has the depressing suspicion that Nesmith is proud of this catastrophe and that Rogers wishes it never happened.' The reviewer's suspicion was correct: Nesmith reissued the album on his Pacific Arts label ten years later – with complete musician credits. In what was probably the only serious appraisal of the album, John Tobler in *Zig Zag* in 1974 observed, 'the big mistake on this record is the quantity of musicians, which at times makes the sound a little unwieldy. Some fiercely competitive blowing takes place, particularly from a trumpeter attempting to play notes only dogs can hear. More than one track ends up in what sounds like nothing more or less than chaos . . . I can imagine that this album could be described as a "grower." But please don't think I'm sneering. There's something far more significant in this album than the sum total of the black plastic. I should imagine that Dot didn't really listen when Michael told them that the record wasn't likely to sell in the same quantities as a Monkees record.'

By the end of 1967 the tally of Monkee achievements was overpowering. They had collected six American Gold Discs for the year, where the Beatles and Rolling Stones had five each. Their singles had been 1, 1, 2, 3, 1 in America; 23, 1, 3, 2, 11, 5 in England and 10, 1, 4, 4, 5, 1, 10, 33, 2, 4 in Australia. American sales on their four albums were three million, five million, two and a half million and one million. Collective global disc sales were thirty million and fan mail was now running at 80,000 letters a week. Total Monkee industry earnings were estimated to be in excess of $200 million. *Rolling Stone* magazine once suggested that the timely infusion of funds from the huge success of the Monkees project actually pulled Columbia Pictures back from the brink of bankruptcy. The 3 May issue of *Variety* reported, 'over the past four years, Screen Gems-Columbia music has emerged as one of the key publishing outfits on the contemporary pop music scene. It has grown into the top money earner in Broadcast Music Inc. (BMI), with performance revenue in the area of $5 million.'

'We only want what is due to us,' Davy was once heard to say. 'Our last tour grossed two million but we only made a tiny percentage of that. Something has to change.' However, money was far from Davy's main concern as the group entered the final stages of the second television series which they knew would be their last. He was well and truly fed up with the obsessive attention paid to recording, music and hits. 'We are a film-making group that has got into a music groove,' he complained. 'What I'd really like to do with the boys is a Broadway musical. With the acting and musical experience between us we could have a smash and be the first group to do it. Or we could do a whole show at the London Palladium.'

The four Monkees had grown apart personally, musically and ideologically, and the rifts were irreparable. With the pretence of unity shattered, each pursued his own interests. Peter had taken up Mike's commitment to the protection of the group's musical integrity and was refusing to acknowledge the existence of the first two albums. In interviews he referred to 'Headquarters' as 'the first album.' He let it be known that the honeymoon with Chip Douglas was over, when he told a fan magazine, 'I like Chip Douglas on the first album. The second was a Monkees album but it was a Chip Douglas album more. I don't think it was as groovy to listen to as 'Headquarters', though technically it's much better – I think it suffers for that reason. It didn't have as much life, not nearly as much tension.'

Although Mike was cast as the aware, intelligent philosopher and Peter as the harmless and misguided clown, the perspective of time has done much to reverse those images. As a poor white Texan good ol' boy, Nesmith was socially no match for the professor's son from New England who had learned his smarts on the streets of New York. In *Up And Down With The Rolling Stones*, Tony Sanchez described the sort of rigid upper-echelon rock community in London, which never really socially accepted the Beatles because of their provincial origins. The Christian Scientist Nesmiths eschewed the drugs, the debauchery, the parties and everything else that constituted membership of the super-hip L.A. rock star community. They were simply uncool. Peter Tork, on the other hand, was the party giver, the experimenter, the cultural barometer. Peter could always be counted on to pontificate on the state of youth and the world, as *Datebook* magazine once found out: 'There's a social revolution going on and the young people are into it. I don't mean to say it's a prerogative of youth to be revolutionary but the young more automatically agree to change. When they grow up they'll be just as reaction-

Peter at a folk festival during 1967.

ary as their parents but about different things. Dogmatism is leaving the scene. Youth is examining all the old premises that used to be taken totally for granted, such as sexual and artistic mores. If the renaissance mean throwing off feudal culture, we're doing the same with pop culture now, but its more broadly based. I think there's a genuinely democratic society just over the horizon. Telepathy is the coming phenomenon. Non verbal extra-sensory communication is at hand.'

The immature finger-pointing of the critics did no stop the Monkees' social whirl. During the second half of 1967 they lived the sort of glittering, highly public lifestyle that their status demanded. When Cream finally arrived in Los Angeles, the four were in the front row at the Whisky with members of the Jefferson Airplane, Buffalo Springfield and the Cake. Late night were usually spent at The Factory, where Davy escorted Sally Field on her birthday. Early in the new year the action switched to the Red Velvet Club on Sunset near Screen Gems, a place so cool even Elvis was known to drop by.

One critic who did take the Monkees seriously was Derek Taylor, who wrote in December 1967: 'Next year, I hope the Monkees are more generously recognised as attractive, gifted, versatile, honest and sophisticated performers who didn't ever, themselves, claim comparison with the Beatles.' Derek also wrote, 'I know that the only people who use the word "psychedelic" i

Two of the un-cool Nesmiths – Christian du val and Phyllis.

Davy escorts actress Sally Field to The Factory on her birthday.

1968 will be television comedians and retarded disc jockeys.'

The Monkees enjoyed saturation media coverage during 1967, which seemed to concentrate on Davy's love life. *People* magazine dubbed him as 'the most popular young male in America today . . . irresistible to women, young and not so young.' This media preoccupation began during 1966 when Sally Field would cycle over to the backlot from *The Flying Nun* set, in her convent garb, to help the lad make it through the day with a little overt affection. Then came Lynne Randell, Lulu (who, according to the British press, was in a 'love triangle' with Davy and Maurice Gibb), and Dean Martin's daughter, Deana. The latter liaison provided perfect material for gossip columnists and women's magazines.

Deana had landed an acting role in one episode of *The Monkees* at the suggestion of Davy who, during a separation from Sally Field, escorted her to her brother Dino's sixteenth birthday party. Apparently Dean Martin had decided that the hairy British pop star was acceptable and personally arranged the date. After a string of Sunday night dinners at the Martin mansion, Davy made his exit, heading for the welcome arms of Linda Haines, to whom he had been introduced by David Pearl in Hawaii back in December 1966, where the group played their first live concerts. A tall, brunette clothes designer, Linda had so captivated the young Jones that he was reported to have bawled his way onto the plane in Honolulu when he was prised away from her. From that point she was never far out of his sight.

Davy secretly married Linda Haines just ten days after production of the second television series was completed on 22 December, 1967. They then embarked upon a harrowing campaign of deception that would last some eighteen months and be recognised as one of the best kept secrets in showbiz history. Unable to enjoy a standard honeymoon, Davy made his traditional trip home to England for Christmas, apparently accompanied by no one except Peter Tork, Peter's girlfriend Karen Harvey and an infant called Justin. The arrival in England was kept a strict secret at Davy's request. 'I don't want to be a drag but I'd like to have as much time to myself as possible and I don't think it's right that the fans should spend part of the Christmas holidays away from their families, hanging about some draughty airport.'

After family festivities were taken care of in Manchester, Davy joined Peter in London for New Year's Eve celebrations at the Speakeasy Club with Jimi Hendrix, Eric Burdon and Tommy Steele, among others. Davy ran into *Oliver* creator Lionel Bart which kept him occupied for most of the night, while Peter introduced himself to singer and actress Adrienne Posta, who had recently finished working on the film *Here We Go Round The Mulberry Bush*.

When Davy flew out to St Moritz for a few days of skiing, Peter accepted an invitation to appear on the 400th special episode of *Top Of The Pops*. Tork pulled gorilla faces, looned around with Jimmy Savile and

Davy and Linda Jones

signed an autograph for everyone who asked him. The show bubbled with such good humour and genial atmosphere that more than 600 viewers rang to offer their congratulations. After escaping from the Shepherds Bush Studio, Peter was whisked away in a black limousine to Clive Donner's world première party for *Here We Go Round The Mulberry Bush*, where he made himself known to the likes of Michael Caine and witnessed an early live performance by Traffic.

Peter was now beginning to really enjoy the PR routine. He allowed RCA to stage a press conference in his honour at the Decca offices in Great Marlborough Street, and found it somewhat less well attended than the one in June. Though he could not have known at the time, Monkeemania in England was swiftly abating. *Daydream Believer*, a top five hit in the previous month, was in fact the last top ten UK hit the group would have. *New Musical Express* was still keenly reporting every move they made, but their competitors were not quite so supportive. Under a bold headline, 'The Tailend of Monkeemania?' *Disc And Music Echo* reported 'Is the year of Monkeemania over? This winter, Monkeemania has staggered to a hideous halt. What flourished in the beginning of the year as a repeat of the Beatles has sagged into nothing. At the BBC there is talk of ending the current Monkees series. Their records are no more sure of reaching number one than anybody else's. . . . They're not a major force on the pop scene and never were.'

A few hundred thousand British fans may not have agreed with this pronouncement. Just prior to Christmas, three Lancashire girls who had missed out on a competition to meet the Monkees at their June press conference sent 10lbs of paper to NME bearing some 61,309 lines of 'Please let us meet the Monkees.'

Peter Tork and Davy Jones arrived back in Hollywood in January, 1968, to begin work on a feature film of an uncertain nature. The press followed Peter right to the airport, where he was quizzed about the woman and child by his side. Asked if they were related to him, he merely smiled and offered, 'All God's children are my relatives.' Were they married? 'Marriage has many definitions.' Asked the same question, Karen answered, 'I don't believe in marriage but this is as close as anything can be.'

Before returning home Peter had visited George Harrison while he was recording his soundtrack music for the film *Wonderwall* at De Lane Lea Studio. Peter contributed some five string banjo work at the same time that Eric Clapton was playing guitar parts. Harrison, like all four Beatles, held the Monkees in considerably higher regard than the rest of the big league rock community: 'The Monkees are still finding out who they are and they seem to be improving as performers each time I see them. When they've got it all sorted out, they may be the greatest.' Paul McCartney once said, 'I'm sure the Monkees are going to live up to a lot of things many people didn't expect' and John Lennon added, 'They've got their own scene and I

won't send them down for it. You try a weekly television show and see if you can manage one half as good!'

Most of January was spent in the studio, continuing work on 'The Birds And The Bees And The Monkees' LP. With a prominent 'Produced By The Monkees' credit, this was a sparse and unsatisfying album. It was recorded in the same way that the Beatles would do the 'White Album' a few months later; each member conceiving and executing his own work independently, often with no participation from the others. This seemed to be the only practical means of reconciling the widely diverse talents and directions of the four Monkees.

The process was a disaster, however, and the album an abomination. There was no *Glass Onion* or *While My Guitar Gently Weeps* on this miserable morass of disjointed indulgence. Psychedelic stupidity at its worst, it lurched from one ill-conceived and incomplete idea to another, any worthwhile moments buried under pointless orchestration commanded by Lester Sill and arranged by Shorty Rogers and Don McGinnis. Where, it was rightly asked, was the creative progression from the impressive likes of *Daily Nightly*, *Star Collector*, *What Am I Doing Hangin' Round?* and *Cuddly Toy*? More to the point, what had become of quality writers like Michael Murphy, Harry Nilsson, Goffin and King, and

Encouraged by George Harrison Peter began to take his banjo playing more seriously.

Mann and Weil? John Stewart and Boyce and Hart were represented but only on previous hit singles which were included on the LP by Colgems.

Two primary camps emerged under this new system of recorded production. On one hand was Mike, writing his increasingly inaccessible cosmic mind therapies which he recorded privately. Across town, the Colgems-approved operation had Boyce and Hart producing tracks with ace sessionmen and using Davy for most vocals. Micky managed to straddle the two camps, undertaking lead vocals on tracks that were beyond both Mike and Davy. Peter, who had only ever wanted to be one quarter of a functioning band, was almost completely out of the picture, writing no songs and contributing in only a minor musical way to the activities of the others. When it came to picking tracks for singles, Colgems preferred to pretend that the Nesmith camp did not really exist. He may have won the battle to depose Kirshner but he certainly had not won the war. After a brief diversion, Colgems and RCA were still getting exactly the sort of hit singles they wanted – played and written by reliable professionals. They also got a miserable 500,000 album sales for the dismal 'The Birds, The Bees And The Monkees', released on 22 April.

By early 1968 Screen Gems had finally woken up to the importance of records in the overall Monkees project and officially set aside one or two days each week for recording. The engineer on some of these sessions was Dave Hassinger, who had previously worked with the Rolling Stones and Jefferson Airplane. While the Monkees were in the studio, Colgems issued a sixth American single, without bothering to inform the group. The A-side was *Valleri*, a Boyce and Hart composition and production that had been used in the series. A gutsy, thumping track in its original state, it was reworked for single release with disappointing results. As Tommy Boyce explains, 'Some disc jockeys had taped the song off the television show and were thrashing it on air. Even though it wasn't available on record, it was number one in places like Miami and Florida. So RCA called up Lester Sill and said, 'You've just gotta put out *Valleri* immediately. We'll guarantee you sales of two million if we can get it into the shops right away.' Lester agreed but he thought the sound was a bit flat so he asked us to put some brass on it, which was a mistake.' Nevertheless, RCA sold the two million discs it predicted and scored a number three hit in the process.

Not surprisingly, Mike Nesmith was enraged by the release. 'The Monkees are dead,' he thundered. 'We've been changing our image over the past year. We're still largely obligated to our public and fans who expect us to play our TV roles in real life. Our latest record, *Valleri*, is a reflection of this. It is the worst record I have ever heard in my life.' However, it would not be long before worse tracks would be pulled out of the old tapes barrel, with Mike's approval, to get the group back up the charts. He was not heard to complain publicly about the

placement of his *Tapioca Tundra* on the flip, which perhaps earned him as much publishing profit from the hit as Boyce and Hart.

Tapioca Tundra, with its *Winchester Cathedral*-type megaphone vocals, brisk pace and neat electric 12-string strumming, was easily the best of Mike's four compositions on the album, followed closely by the Byrds-ish *Auntie's Municipal Court*, featuring actual Byrd Clarence White on guitar. *Writing Wrongs* was the longest Monkee recording, and possibly the most tedious. The final track in his quartet of offerings was *Magnolia Simms*, an intriguing excursion into speakeasy music of the twenties. *Magnolia Simms* and *Tapioca Tundra*, were part of a Nesmith frame of mind that had initiated the 'Wichita Train Whistle Sings' project. Apparently the motivation for it all was the purchase in a junk shop of $100 worth of ancient 78 discs.

Davy had tendered two insipid efforts for this album, *Dream World* and *The Poster* which were written with Steve Pitts, a previously unknown musician who suddenly found himself with a royalty cheque for tens of thousands of dollars. 'The songwriting credits have lots of names on them,' explained Davy to *Blitz* magazine in 1978, 'because there'd be people walking through the studio and we'd call out and ask them if they'd like their names on things!' Tommy Boyce expands, 'Davy would show up in the studio with a bunch of street musicians and say, "I just met these guys, they're a great band. I've given them $100 each and I want them to play on the next track".'

The fragmented sessions around 1968 resulted in a surplus of tracks that were used later on the film soundtrack album or, as in the case of *Rosemarie, My Share Of The Sidewalk, Smile* and *Lady's Baby*, left unreleased. Harry Nilsson's *Daddy's Song*, which didn't even approach his *Cuddly Toy* in terms of commercial appeal, was recorded, with Davy on vocals, as a possible follow-up single for *Valleri*, but canned when Nilsson's own version was mooted as a single. It was later released in place of *Porpoise Song* as a single in England, but failed to chart.

The song that was chosen to follow *Valleri* was *D. W. Washburn*, written by Jerry Leiber and Mike Stoller. It was one of the first fruits of their reconciliation with The Coasters, whom they had not produced since 1965. Coasters biographer Bill Millar describes the original version as, 'Just about as perfect as any pop record could possibly be. A beautiful and carefully constructed scenario of city life, it owed much in the way of melodic ideas to the work of the Lovin' Spoonful.' However, the Monkees got the song out on to the market before the Coasters. The circumstances are best described by Mike Stoller in Millar's book *The Coasters*: 'There was one record we made with the Coasters on Date that I thought was really a potential hit. I felt very strongly about it – it was called *D. W. Washburn*. Now CBS said, "We don't think our people can get r and b play on it." I said, "Well it's not an r and b record, y'know, what with the banjo an' all." So because of Columbia's attitude, it stayed in the can for a while. Then I played the tape to our old partner Lester Sill who, at the time, was at Screen Gems. He said, "Man, what a fantastic record," and we said, "Look it doesn't look like they're gonna put the thing out. I mean they just don't seem to know where it's at as far as this kind of production is

Micky with Lester Sill. Colgems was still getting exactly the sort [of] hit single material it wanted.

concerned." Lester said, "If they don't do it I'm gonn[a] grab that song an' I'll do it with the Monkees." W[e] went back to the people at Date and said, "We think w[e] have a big hit here," and they said, "Well, if you wan[t] us to put it out, we'll put it out but y'know, we don'[t] have any faith in it." So I figured it would be better no[t] to have 'em throw it up against the wall and not get an[y] promotion on it. So we let the Monkees have it and, o[f] course, their version became a hit. When they saw wha[t] was happening, CBS released it by the Coasters. It go[t] good reviews, but it was during a CBS convention and [it] never got played.'

The Micky Dolenz vocal was nowhere near a[s] impassioned as Billy Guy's and somewhere along th[e] way the song lost a deal of its magic, despite [a] sympathetic arrangement by the highly-respecte[d] Shorty Rogers. Nonetheless, it deserved better than [a] nineteen charting in America and a seventeen chartin[g] in England. The style of the song was such a radic[al] departure from the cuddly Monkee image that [it] severely affected the popularity of the group. By th[e] time the single was released, the series was just about o[ff] the air and so could not provide convenient promotio[n.] Left to sink or swim on the basis of the group's curre[nt] popularity, the record performed accordingly. It al[so] marked an end to their chart career. No subseque[nt] release entered the American or English top forty.

head

Preparation for the feature film that was first entitled *Changes*, then renamed *Untitled* and finally released as *Head*, commenced in the second half of 1967. Columbia Pictures was then still sufficiently enamoured by the Monkees' ratings and record sales to allocate a modest but adequate budget of $750,000. Columbia paid for and might rightfully have expected a teen exploitation film of the Elvis Presley variety, a ninety-minute version of the television series. This idea was not even entertained by Bob Rafelson, the talented young director who had never made a film; nor by the Monkees, who had buffooned their way through almost fifty increasingly predictable half hour sit-coms.

In an interview in *Sight and Sound*, Rafelson frankly explained, '*Head* was never thought of, by me or Bert, as a picture that would make money. We felt that we were entitled, since we made an enormous amount of money for Columbia, in their record division and in their television sales, to make a picture that would in a sense expose the process. *Head* was supposed to be an exploitation film but it was not that at all. It opened metaphorically with the Monkees committing suicide; it was a complete exposure of my relationship to the group. *Head* is an utterly and totally fragmented film. Among other reasons for making it was that I thought I would never get to make another movie, so I might as well make fifty to start out with and put them all in the

Micky and Peter confer with producers Bob Rafelson (seated) and Jack Nicholson (intruding sideways).

same feature. I was, in a sense, emulating or satirising the styles of various American pictures – there was a kind of history of American movies in there.'

Initially, the Monkees were adamant that they should direct the film themselves. Rafelson, Schneider and Jack Nicholson vetoed this suggestion firmly, but still made allowances for a strong input from the group. The seven creative participants locked themselves in a hotel room in Ojai, California, for a whole weekend, with a tape recorder running endlessly. Peter recalls, 'We discussed what we all wanted from the movie and that's when we all agreed "Let's for God's sake grab a little reality and walk through scenes and talk about ourselves and put a little objectivity behind the whole thing, show the people what it's all been like." Nobody, absolutely nobody, wanted to do it like the television show. Jack and Bob went away and wrote the script from the ideas that we all came up with. That meeting set the tone of the film. We could say anything we wanted to on tape and we knew that any of those thoughts might have been taken up as an idea by those guys. One of the things that came out of it was that Bob decided to do a movie about movies. So then it was obvious to do things like getting Annette Funicello in to play that part she always played. They listened to us and there was a lot of *us* in the film. Even when they had to say no to our ploy to direct it, they compensated by letting us direct episodes of the series.'

Nicholson's association with the Monkees was a result of his growing professional and personal relationship with, particularly, Rafelson and, to a lesser degree, Schneider. Like both of his friends in their pre-Monkees years, Jack was a fringe dweller; an intelligent, thoughtful talent who left industry heavyweights ill at ease in his presence. He had played bit parts and lead roles 'for experience' in Roger Corman films, and had moved into scriptwriting with *The Trip*, which starred Peter Fonda and Dennis Hopper who would figure prominently in his future career.

'Jack had abandoned his career as an actor at this point,' related Rafelson. 'I didn't even know him as an actor. When we were writing *Head* Jack would act out all the parts, as would I, and my eyes were just glued to the expressions on his face and the intensity he brought to the performance in a script conference. I told him the next time I made a picture he had to be in it. Meanwhile I persuaded Bert and Dennis Hopper that he would be right for a role in *Easy Rider*, which led to the role in *Five Easy Pieces*.'

'Nicholson really knew his craft,' Peter remembers. 'Such a good writer, and actor, and director. He'd been paying his dues for so long but had never broken out, so working with Rafelson was like a step up for him. Jack was a really strange personality; that is, the kind of person who is probably genuinely off his rocker yet socially correct at all times. He channelled his mania and craziness into his acting. When you met him on the street he had these crazy eyes, like in *The Shining*, and that was his natural expression. But when you saw him with his eyes hooded and he was smiling, *that* was acting.'

On the first day of shooting, 15 February 1968, only Peter Tork reported for duty. The other three had been advised by their individual managers and attorneys to go on strike as part of a pressure campaign for improved financial arrangements and increased creative control. At the core of the conflict was the lack of any clause in their renewed contracts which covered payment scales or profit sharing for feature films. Screen Gems, secure in their belief that the group would not take the action they were threatening, called their bluff and were so shocked by the result that they sat down at the conference table and renegotiated the contracts within twenty-four hours. On 16 February all four Monkees were at work. The militant three had won their battle but, as later events would attest, they would again lose the war.

This industrial action was met with outright hostility by Rafelson and Schneider, who were willing to support any sort of pedantic bickering over the recording of the music but were not prepared to tolerate any disruption to their baby, the almighty *film*. 'Schneider was very angry,' claims Peter. 'I actually asked him about it. Bert is probably one of the great producers of all time, partly because he can be absolutely blockheaded when he wants to be. He's very hard nosed about his business, nobody can put anything over him. See, he thought of us all as family, like a Cosa Nostra type family – you're in if you're in and you can do no wrong. As long as you come and apologise we'll cover for you and do you right, but step outside the pale and you're out of the picture, that's it, you're no longer part of the family. So when Micky, Davy and Mike struck, Bert no longer thought of them as part of the family and it coloured his whole feeling about the movie.'

In a *Zig Zag* interview in 1974, Mike Nesmith told John Tobler, *Head* was one of the projects that I was involved in that I was the most profoundly proud of. I was just humbly grateful to be involved in the project. A sophisticated film made by sophisticated film-makers, it was the first time I felt a truly creative return during the whole project. It was a true portrayal of what the Monkees were – a creative unit of four with a hub of twelve or so people around them making musical and celluloid artefacts of long lasting value.' Micky Dolenz is quoted as saying, 'I think it was one of the finest things that we ever did as the Monkees. It was a story of the Monkees and the story of Hollywood in a way.' Davy thought it had some 'magical moments.'

Head has been the object of the same sort of dissection and analysis as *Citizen Kane* or *2001*. It has been reviled and revered, deified and dismissed. Scrape away the rhetoric and it stands as a fascinating and ambiguous work, a somewhat flawed masterpiece. On one level, Rafelson is indeed paying a personal tribute to classic film forms – the war movie, the thriller, the spy saga, the slapstick comedy, the desert epic, the potboiler, the western. On a different level he is waging

A break in the trench sequence.

a clever and often devastating attack on the cultural milieu of the late sixties by mercilessly attacking the manipulated and disproportionate success of the Monkees.

The cast list rivalled that of Todd Browning's *Freaks* for sheer improbability. Annette 'Beach Party' Funicello was hired, as was boxer Sonny Liston, Green Bay Packers football hero Ray Nitschke, veteran character actor Timothy Carey, silicone enhanced 'Miss Super Breasts' Carol Doda, similarly endowed ham actor

Davy with Annette Funicello (Minnie).

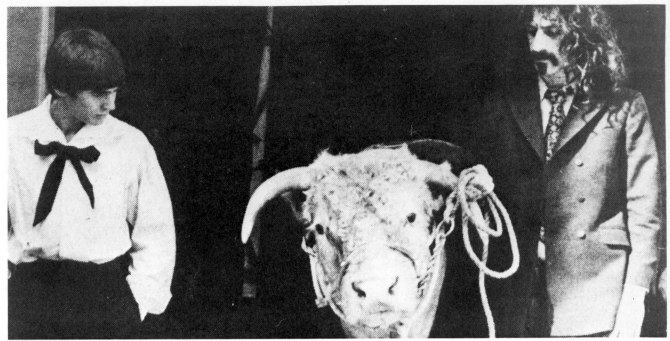

Davy Jones and Frank Zappa in Head.

Victor Mature, Frank Zappa, drag queen T. C. Jones, Abraham Soafer, and Terri Garr. Bert Rafelson cameoed as 'the director' and Jack Nicholson as 'the director's assistant.' Dennis Hopper and June Wilson were seen as extras.

Victor Mature portrays The Big Victor, a forty foot tall Hollywood matinee hero of the 1940s, in whose hair the four Monkees appear as dandruff. Big Victor was in fact a living metaphor for RCA Victor, one of the capitalist interests raking in huge profits from the Monkees. When Mature was given the script, he read it several times and admitted, 'I can't figure it out. All I know is that it makes me laugh.' As shooting commenced, Rafelson told the press, 'What we are doing is not a comedy but it's funny. It sounds campy but it's the enemy of camp. It's a kind of trip. The film is full of solid comedy but it is also laced with contemporary comedy.' Rafelson's 'comedy' opens with the Monkees committing suicide by jumping from a suspension

Peter with veteran actor Victor Mature.

bridge and moves into a live concert sequence, intercut with original film sequences of Vietnam war atrocities. Nesmith's lyrics to *Circle Sky* provide a chilling commentary: 'It's a very extraordinary scene, for those who don't understand,' as villagers run from a bombing blitz, 'but you must believe it if you can' as a Vietcong suspect is shot through the head at short range in a Saigon street. Are the young blonde fans in a state of advance hysteria screaming at the Monkees? Or are they horrified by the war images?

The Monkees strive to convince the world that they are only playing the roles of these over-rated, over-idolised, money-spinning pop idols, and that their real selves oppose the fabricated image. All the technical equipment – cameras, microphones, cables, lights – are made deliberately visible, to destroy any *Summer Holiday* trappings and enhance the anti-movie stance. Micky walks through a fake background pulling fake arrows from everybody in a western scene. Bob Rafelson is seen operating a film camera during a party scene. Davy and Peter are seen in a studio toilet – a location which, in American mass media, just does *not* exist. Later the two are interrogated by a policeman (brutal, of course) against the same lavatory wall. Cultural icons are desecrated with appropriate irreverence. An inoperative Coke machine in the desert is blasted. Television advertisements for Playtex 'Cross Your Heart' bras and Ford gas guzzlers, examples of America's fine cultural identity, are terminated abruptly. Scrupulously and callously, the myth of rock is laid bare; the seemingly natural exuberance and idealism exposed as a calculated business using craft and cunning to produce a basically worthless image for mass consumption.

So much for the self-flagellation. The cinema tributes were handled with a deal more wit and style. Scenes from *Golden Boy*, *Gilda* and *City of Conquest* are seen

Above: Some underwater sequences were filmed in the Bahamas and above right: in a Hollywood pool.
Right: On location at Pasadena Rose Bowl.
Below right: Davy with Carol Doda.

alongside Davy's Fred Astaire dance sequence. White on a black set and black on a white set, as a tribute to director Vincente Minelli, is filmed with choreography by young dancer Toni Basil.

Davy, in knickerbockers, serenades Minnie (Annette Funicello) with a violin on the front steps of a bowery brownstone. A World War Two Italian Army regiment surrenders to a single American soldier (Micky), who appears supremely bored by it all. Davy is beaten senseless in a boxing ring by Sonny Liston, in true Kid Galahad style. Micky and Mike make bets on the fate of a woman poised to jump from a building ledge, exhibiting the brutality of the urban jungle. Every scene was a barb, every cinematic cliché fair game.

There are, as Davy said, some truly magical moments, sublime in fact. Like the underwater sequence (filmed in the Bahamas) backed by the chillingly majestic *Porpoise Song* (written by Goffin and King). Or the four seasonal scenes, backed by Carole King and Toni Stern's elegant *As We Go Along*. The desert sequences were filmed in Palm Springs, on the same location as the chase climax in *It's a Mad Mad Mad Mad World*. The 'War!' sequence was shot in the Pasadena Rose Bowl.

95

Mike, performing Circle Sky *at Salt Lake City*

The live musical performances in the film were filmed at a free concert in Salt Lake City, Utah on 17 May, at the very end of shooting. Public Relations officer Floyd Ackerman, who had worked on the 1967 American tour, had been in town for a week whipping up interest and ensuring an enthusiastic airport welcome. Monkee management had given Radio KCPX four thousand free tickets to distribute to listeners, but the response was so overwhelming that a second 'bonus' concert had to be scheduled and five thousand more passes given away.

The staged concert, for filming, occurred at the Valley Music Theatre at 1pm. Dressed in pristine white, the four rehearsed and repeatedly filmed a sequence which required them to run from their dressing room through a thrusting audience to the stage and then perform a powerful Nesmith original called *Circle Sky*. The prettiest young things that the city had to offer were assembled in the front row and used for tear-stained close-ups. Between the seemingly endless takes, the group knocked out frenetic versions of their hits and did their best to handle a bundle of special requests. That night they played again, at Lagoon Park amusement centre, delivering a crisp forty-five minute set as a 'thank you' to the kids of Salt Lake City.

When the raw sequences were strung together, the disjointed, chaotic film ran about 110 minutes. Bert Schneider took it into the editing room and fashioned a vaguely coherent eighty-six minutes out of it. 'Bert is an amazing artist,' asserts Peter. 'He doesn't think of himself as an artist, he sees himself as a businessman, but I've seen him in a cutting room the size of a kitchen for twelve hours straight, looking at boring sequences a hundred times over, checking out thirteen different camera angles. It's hard work, a lot harder than mixing a record.'

Schneider and Rafelson made no attempt to homogenize the film in the cutting room. The same dichotomy remained – cuddly teen idols make anarchistic, uncommercial film. Scenes seemingly unrelated to the diaphanous plot stand as impressionistic soliloquies on the part of the writer and director, much like the Chorus in ancient Greek tragedy. The credits made plain just whose film it was. There are no opening titles, but brief credits appear at the very end, after the Monkees are carted away in a giant perspex water tank, as props to be filed away in the property department. After the 'Head' title is flashed, the director (Rafelson), writers and producers (Rafelson and Nicholson) and executive producer (Schneider) are credited, *then* the actors take a bow.

While the film was in post-production, the Monkees were given two weeks leave of absence. Two of them, Davy and Micky, headed for England, where they could enjoy a peer relationship in the music world that they were denied back in America. Seemingly oblivious of the media hostility which had begun to manifest itself during Davy and Peter's Christmas visit, Micky gushed, 'From the first time I came to London I've felt at home here. The people are friendly, courteous, real interested in what's going on – and they don't try to put performers down like they do in the States.' He flew in on 22 May to be with Samantha Juste, who had been forced to return to England some weeks previously due to an expired visa. She was, it would soon be revealed, in the early stages of pregnancy.

Unable to arrange for reasonable hotel accommodation in London, as a result of the shattered plate glass window at the plush Mayfair Hotel in January, Screen Gems leased a private flat in Mayfair for visiting Monkees. Micky took up residence and set about proving his own generous words by popping down to the Revolution Club with Georgie Fame, Mickie Most and Chris Barber to see Eric Burdon and the Animals; journeying to Lewisham with Paul McCartney, Jane Asher, David Frost and Bobbie Gentry to catch a concert by the Hollies and Scaffold, and stocking up on new clothes at the Apple Boutique in Baker Street. A visit to a vintage car dealer in Paddington resulted in the purchase of a green Bentley and a 1928 white Rolls Royce, which were shipped back to California. In Regent Street he bought a complete 'landed gentry'

Micky on stage in Salt Lake City.

Davy's secret wife Linda was on display during the filming of Head.

Sunday afternoon motoring ensemble, complete with a deer-stalker hat.

Micky was playing the pop superstar role with fine style. Walking around the West End, tailed by large crowds, he stopped photographing landmarks long enough to sign autographs for police officers and shopkeepers. He accepted the standard invitation to appear on BBC TV's *Top Of The Pops* hosted (as was always the case whenever a Monkee appeared) by Jimmy Savile. More than 500 fans were outside the Lime Grove studios when he emerged after the show. A few days later he hired a Triumph TR4 to take him up to the Scottish Highlands for a spot of fishing.

Davy arrived on 31 May with David Pearl, appeared on *Top Of The Pops*, and went straight on to Manchester to be with his sick father. Worried about the effect of a few hundred screaming fans descending on his father's house, Screen Gems took great pains to tell the media that Jones was staying at a country house in Berkshire. Of course the dedicated few were not taken in by the hoax and dutifully took up their positions on the front lawn in Manchester.

Davy was followed home by a BBC film crew, intent on making a promotional film clip for the new single *D. W. Washburn*, something that would not have been possible when the television series was in production. John Hughes, the *Top Of The Pops* production assistant, wanted to hire professional models for 'decoration' but Davy insisted on using the fans who were patiently waiting outside his house. After borrowing a vintage car from a local resident as a prop, he visited the home of every girl he had chosen to participate, to personally seek the approval of their parents.

Promotional films for singles were rare in 1968. The Beatles usually made a film for each new single to send to Ed Sullivan and other American television outlets because they were really the only chart act which did not undertake public appearances or tours. The *D. W. Washburn* clip was especially unusual as it featured only one Monkee, who was not even the one who sang lead on the track. After the film exercise was completed, Davy visited Basil Foster at his horse training track in the village of Middleham on the edge of the Yorkshire moors. There he worked out on his two thoroughbred horses, Chicomono and Pearl Locker. And, of course, he found the time to talk to the press. Unfortunately, whenever in his native land, Davy felt that he had to issue forth with proclamations on subjects that were not very popular with his bosses, from Monkee inner workings to the fate of the starving millions. This visit was certainly no exception, as *Melody Maker*'s Tony Wilson discovered. 'We're touring from mid-July to about the end of August,' he said. 'We're going to Hawaii, Japan, Australia, New Zealand. Then Holland,

Whenever Davy had some spare time in England he worked out on his horses at Basil Foster's Middleham training track.

Germany, France and Sweden. We would like to finish in Britain, playing in places like Manchester and Edinburgh. When I think about it, the group could probably go on for another ten years. In thirty-five concerts we could make two million dollars between us. But we want to spend the next year proving we're not just a rock 'n' roll band.' So far so good, but Davy never quite knew when to stop. 'I'd like us to get a theatre for about six weeks. We'd be playing guitars, pretty music and some skits – anything we do would be basically comedy. I'm a song and dance man but at the moment I'm playing the role of a rock 'n' roll singer.'

On 3 June Davy met up with Micky in Manchester and the pair flew back to Hollywood the following day. During these rambles, Peter and Mike remained Stateside. Peter formed a film production artist development company in Los Angeles, known as BRINCO (Break Through Influence Company), with experimental film-maker and houseguest Bobby Hammer. With the single exception of some demo recordings with an obscure piano singer called Judy Myhan, BRINCO's activities seem to have escaped entirely without documentation. Peter's days were otherwise filled with one giant houseparty, just like neighbour Elvis Presley. In fact, to facilitate the ever expanding number of guests he purchased a fourteen room cliff-face mansion near Studio City (on the *other* side of the Hollywood Hills), which had once belonged to veteran film comedian Wally Cox. George Harrison and Ringo Star, in town to publicise *Yellow Submarine*, dropped by for a chinwag. The Hollies called in one night when Peter's good buddy Stephen Stills was in residence, facilitating a fortuitous meeting between Stephen and Graham Nash which, one might reasonably assume, led to bigger and better things. Pete Townshend and John Sebastian also met each other there. 'When Townshend showed up,' relates Tork, 'all the Who came along. We had a great time, it was one of the highlights of my life, it was just gorgeous. Like any bunch of guys, they had bits they did together. They pilled up and did these things from *Beyond the Fringe* until we were on the floor. There'd be two of them doing something and suddenly another one would appear at the door, as if on cue, read his line and

Peter's parties were never ending.

beat it to the next room, and it was as if it had all been scripted. Townshend posturing about crazily, it was so funny.'

Mike was unable to wander the world after *Head* because of the duties of fatherhood. Phylliss had given birth to a second Nesmith son, Jonathan Darby, on 4 February. When advised that he would not be required for any film work during the first week of May, Mike took off to Texas for a fishing trip with some of his circle of buddies. While visiting Nashville on the way, he initiated another independent project by which he would be able to assert, in his own eyes at least, his individuality. 'I called up Felton Jarvis, an RCA staff producer who had done some sensational things, not the least of which were Fats Domino and Elvis records. I told him I wanted to come to Nashville and make some records and he said, "Great." I asked him to get a band together for me, and he said, "Do you want a big name, hard line boys?" and I said no, I wanted all new people. He told me there was a bunch of kids up in Muscle Shoals out of work and it would really mean a lot to them if they could work with me. The people he got for me were David Briggs on piano; Kenny Buttrey on drums, Norbert Putnam on bass, Larry Osborne on banjo, Buddy Spicher on fiddle, Charlie McCoy on harmonica, Lloyd Green on steel and Billy Sanford and Wayne Moss on guitar. Of course, they ultimately became Area Code 615 and are now pillars of Nashville session work.

Mike in Nashville in June 1968 with the musicians who played o
Listen To The Band.

Nine powerful, dynamic country rock tracks were recorded during a week of around the clock session; including reworkings of Nesmith chestnuts like *Some o Shelley's Blues* and *Different Drum*. 'Songs that had n place with the Monkees,' says Mike. The best track wa a newer composition called *Listen To The Band* which was the only track to be released. 'I still have the othe tapes . . . if anyone's interested.' Many have bee interested, but the tapes have never been made avail able, not even through Mike's own Pacific Arts com pany. He has seen fit to foist 'The Whichita Trai Whistle Sings' once more upon an unsuspecting world but not his grand Nashville sessions.

Post production on *Head* which was expected to occupy three months, took six. But by the end of 1968 there was still sufficient teen interest in the Monkees for the challenging, iconoclastic film to at least earn enough to cover costs. All it needed was some deft marketing and promotion. There had not been a proper Beatles film in three years and Elvis flicks were playing second bill on double features. The kids were not to know just how oddball the thing really was. All it would have taken was a few cute'n'cuddly stills of Davy splashed about and a bunch of rabid adjectives. The Monkees themselves were waxing lyrically about it for most of the year. 'Our film is going to astound the world,' insisted

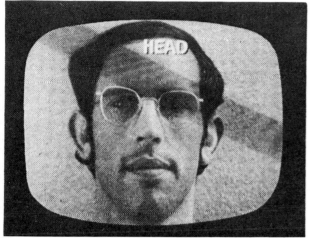

The minute-long television advertisement for Head. *No reference to the Monkees was included.*

Mike. 'Gone is the soft-spoken, puppy dog, pattable Monkee image of yesterday. What you will see is the natural extension of where we were headed in our TV series. . . . Even the Beatles wouldn't be able to duplicate what we're doing in our film.' Micky added, 'It's our rebellion thing. The kids are going to love this movie because they are going to *understand* it. The adults will walk out and say "I wonder what that was all about?" but kids will know *exactly* what it is about. It's fast, surprising and totally kooky. It flashes from one scene to another without any continuity. The truth is that our movie *Head* is the movie of tomorrow!'

It could have worked, but it was never given the chance. Such was the impact of the promotional campaign, that the 'heads' were convinced it was a teenybop film, the teenybops were convinced it was a hippie film and no one in the middle had the slightest idea that it was even a movie! Full page advertisements in the *New York Times* did not include a mention of the Monkees. Peter Tork suggests that 'The *Head* promotion was so strange, so far out that it didn't connect with anybody. They had this sleazy media personality called John Brockman, the sleaziest looking guy you could find. He wrote a great book called *The Late John Brockman*. Anyway, they ran these ads on late night television which was just one minute of this guy's head with complete silence, and at the end he smiled slightly

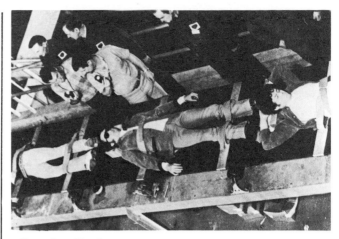

Scene from Head.

and the word 'Head" came up on the screen. That was all, no specific indications that it was a film. Now how the hell was anybody going to connect that with a new movie by the Monkees that they might have heard about?

'If the success of the movie had been terribly important to Schneider he would have left no stone unturned. He might have had psychedelic advertisements but he would have been sure they were slightly middle-of-the-road psychedelia. He would have said, "The Monkees like you've never seen them before." That sort of thing. He would have tried to coax the teenyboppers into the psychedelic image, into seeing the movie. But he didn't, he let things get completely schizoid. I don't think he cared when the movie died.'

Rafelson and Nicholson seem to have been a little more concerned with commercial success. Bob arranged a sneak preview for about a hundred people in Los Angeles to observe reactions, which were polarised. Some did not understand it at all, others thought it was great. He claimed it was just what he expected. Two years later, with an adoring media buzzing around him following the release of *Five Easy Pieces*, he told the *New Yorker* '*Head* made no money, coming out some time after the Monkees decline. Hardly anybody saw it and those who did were mostly mystified by it. One of the pleasing things is that the Beatles and the Stones and other rock groups regarded *Head* as being a minor triumph because it's the story of their lives as well – of the manipulation of rock stars. They all recognise their own story.'

Jack Nicholson was in love with the film and has never lost his enthusiasm. He persuaded Rafelson to go around the streets with him slapping up John Brockman posters, like a couple of kids. In 1970 he told Rex Reed of the *New York Times*, 'Nobody ever saw that, man, but I saw it 158 million times, I loved it! Filmatically it's the best rock'n'roll movie ever made. I mean, it's anti-rock. It has no form and is unique in structure, which is very hard to do in movies.' Nicholson's wild enthusiasm for the film is detailed in his official biography, which recounts an incident, related by Bob Rafelson, that occurred on 6 November, 1968 in New York: 'We knew that we had a strange and unique picture. We also knew that there was not an audience that was going to rush out and see a Monkees movie, so we hired a guy who was then associate professor of communications at Fordham, destined to take McLuhan's seat, to do the campaign. He had never done anything like this before and his idea was that we would just put a head on television with no description, and ultimately, enough people would be curious to find out what this was and when they found out it was connected to a movie, would go out and see the movie.

This campaign Jack and I were a little uncertain of, although we enjoyed the experimentation of it. So, the afternoon of the day the picture was opening, Jack and I were walking around Central Park and down Fifth Avenue and elsewhere. It was opening in a very obscure theatre in New York, Cinema Studio, all through choice, by the way, the idea to kind of sneak this picture out in some way and have everybody curious as to what it was all about. We were talking in overt tones about this brilliant new film that was about to open, thinking that of course we would create a lot of word-of-mouth in the street – this deranged concept we had of public relations – and walking around with these little stickers that just had a picture of the head on it, that said *Head* and slapping them up like pirates all over New York City.

At one point we were on Fifth Avenue and 56th Street and I saw a chestnut salesman in front of Bonwit Teller being busted by a cop for illegally selling chestnuts. I walked over and asked if I could buy the remaining chestnuts. The cop said he couldn't sell them and I said "I want to give him the money for the value of the chestnuts, because you're preventing him from making a living." Meanwhile, Jack was sneaking up behind the cop and taking the *Head* sticker – which was about two by four inches – and trying to paste it onto the back of the cop's helmet. The cop turned around just when Jack was about half an inch away from his helmet and the sticker wound up half on his face and half on his helmet. Two seconds later, both of us were lined up against the wall on Fifth Avenue and being handcuffed for harassing the police.

Jack was carted off to jail. I managed to fanangle my way out of it and rode along with him, thinking that this was just the PR break that we needed. Here we were, the producer/writers of our first film, both of us with an enormous sense of the absurdity of what we were doing. We went down to the jail on 9th Avenue, wherever the precinct was, and then tried to explain that we were opening up this major Hollywood production that very evening. They said, "Where is it?" and we said, "El Studio Cinema," and it was so absurd, because the cop was saying, "What? What is this major movie bullshit?" Finally, we managed to get out and didn't make one line of news.'

The reviews and critiques which followed were notable not so much for their content as for their origin.

Final capitulation in the billing department!

The most respected and admired publications and critics granted the film an honour not extended since *A Hard Day's Night* – they acknowledged its existence. *Cue* magazine described it as, 'Like $8\frac{1}{2}$ made by a flower child." The *New York Times* likened it to other 'Pot Meets Advertising' films, such as *You Are What You Eat*, *Revolution* and *You're A Big Boy Now*. The *New York Daily News* called it, 'A commentary on our times, spoofing politicians, movie making success and intellectuals.' Stanley Kauffman in *New Republic* claimed the Monkees were, 'Virtually devoid of charm, unlike the Liverpool quartet, but they are vigorous and willing. The script was not meant to be described. It's modelled on dreams – a free series of fantasies flow into each other . . . Rafelson directed the film with a well stocked memory and a pretty fair imagination.'

The feared Pauline Kael of the *New Yorker* snarled, 'The doubling up of greed and pretentions-to-depth is enough to make even a pinhead walk out . . . the movie might have worked for bored kids at matinees but the film-makers got ambitious. This is the kind of material, taken from all over, that the Monkees have already worn out on television, only much worse . . . The only novelty is in the selling, in convincing kids that they are sophisticated when they buy old jokes and blackout routines as mind-blowing psychedelia. It borrows as much from Abbott and Costello as Richard Lester – will someone try to sell their old movies, and *Hellzapoppin'* and the *Three Stooges* as marijuana visions too?'

But Kael's review was almost kind in comparison to the drubbing dished out by Renata Adler in the *New York Times*: 'The Monkees, who are one of the least-talented contemporary music groups and know it, are most interesting for their lack of similarity to the Beatles. Going through ersatz Beatle songs, and jokes and motions, their complete lack of distinction of any kind – the fact that fame was stamped upon them, as it might have been on any nice four, utterly undistinguished boys – makes their performance modest and almost brave. They work very hard and they aren't any good. This keeps them less distant from their own special fans than the Beatles or, say, Bob Dylan and the Beach Boys are. They do not have to bridge the distance of talent and style.'

There is little doubt that critiques such as these, in publications and by reviewers that were taken very seriously by film-makers, considerably affected Rafelson and Schneider's attitude toward the Monkees, and their future plans for the group. Their reputation within the film community was obviously of far greater importance than a fun experiment which had plainly run its course.

Head premiéred in Los Angeles on 20 November and in Australia during May 1969, for a short run. Though it was supposed to follow *Candy* at London's Piccadilly Classic Cinema in August, it was not accepted for British release at all and not seen there until March 1977, when the National Film Theatre imported a print to meet massive cult demand. It then ran a successful season at the Electric Cinema on Portobello Road. Reviews for the Australian season were limited and limp, though Griffen Foley in the Sydney *Sunday Telegraph* observed, '*Head* is a film about nothing and yet a film about everything. It is said not to have a story but it is a score of stories rolled into one. Producers/writers Rafelson and Nicholson have created a masterpiece of fast-moving psychedelia which verges on satire.'

Comments from the Monkees in recent times, given the benefit of hindsight, tend to be a little more perceptive than those during production. Micky says, 'It wasn't at all like a typical Monkees show. Consequently the fans didn't have anything to relate to. The arty intellectuals, trying hard to be abstract, heard it was a Monkees movie and weren't interested.' Davy goes so far as to say, 'It had nothing to do with the Monkees. We never even got paid for it.' 'It even took me a long time to get what it was all about,' admits Peter. 'I must have seen it about five dozen times. Every single frame has something of interest to me. But it wasn't instantly accessible. It had to be seen and seen and seen before it began to sink into people's minds. It was a depiction of the four of us against the establishment, but I didn't even get that impression until I had seen it several times. All I knew then was that it was a major nosedive for our careers.'

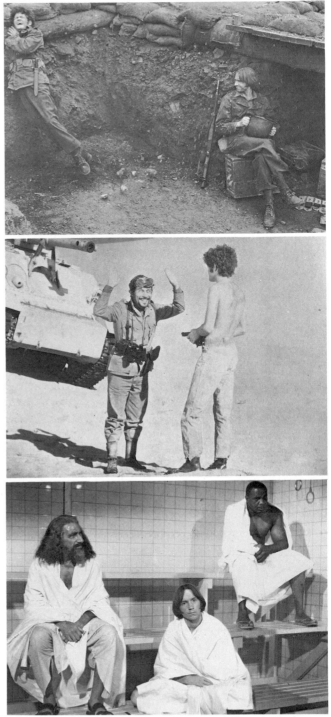

Scenes from Head, *the sauna sequence starred Swami Abraham Soafer.*

After short runs in major American cities, *Head* disappeared from cinemas. It turned up again about three years later as a double drive-in bill with Dennis Hopper's *The Last Movie*. 'Had *Head* been a success,' contends Mike, 'it would have opened up a whole new run for the Monkees. We could have continued on in that vein, making movies. That would have been real interesting, that would have really been us. It came about legitimately, it was not fabricated. But it collapsed and so did the Monkees.'

All the things that had rendered the film impotent were brought to bear on the soundtrack album, which sunk without trace even quicker than the film. The truly superb *Porpoise Song*, was criminally ignored by radio and peaked at a miserable sixty-two. The album fared even worse. Like the film it represented, it was dismally packaged and confusingly assembled. To this day it stands as perhaps the primary source of ill-feeling between Peter and Mike.

On the rear panel of the plain grey jacket, below the 'Album produced by the Monkees' credit, appear the words 'Album Co-ordinator – Jack Nicholson.' Why an out of work actor and occasional scriptwriter should have been given charge of a soundtrack record of rock music is best described by Mike: 'I was putting the album together in the studio and Jack said he wanted to do it – a lot of decisions were made like that – so I said great, you do it, I'm gonna go home.'

Peter however prefers to blame Mike for what he and most fans see as the worst decision made during the assembly of the album – the replacement of the crackling, kinetic live version of *Circle Sky* as heard in the film, with a blurred, insipid studio remake. 'Mike substituted his own studio cut on the record,' Peter snarls. 'That's the kind of guy he was. You could always count on him to do the right thing. He cut it again with his friends, doing all the guitar parts himself. I was really angry about that.' When *Blitz* magazine editor Mike McDowell enthused that the movie version was 'the greatest live performance ever made by a rock band' during a 1978 Nesmith interview, his subject completely ignored the appraisal and launched into a comment about the nature of the lyrics. The live version was eventually issued, to Peter's uncontained delight, in Australia in 1979, along with the original four minute single release of *Porpoise Song*.

'I don't think Mike has any community spirit whatsoever,' observes Peter. 'Not that it's so strange, it's the way he was raised. He wanted to do everything himself. It was he who got the other two guys together to strike. He was gonna be the boss at any price, essentially.' Nowhere is this observation more perfectly manifested than in Nesmith's comment to *Zig Zag* in 1974: 'If I said "Let's do this song" it would get done;' a boast which seems to have no basis in fact.

After being virtually absent from 'The Birds, The Bees and The Monkees', Peter took a high profile on the 'Head' soundtrack album, contributing two songs. *Can You Dig It?* and *Do I Have To Do This All Over Again?* were recorded with Peter on guitars, Lance Wakely on bass and acoustic guitar, and Dewey Martin (from the Buffalo Springfield) on drums. The other songs on the album were reputed to feature such players as John Sebastian, David Crosby, Doug Dillard, Stephen Stills, Bernie Leadon and Chris Darrow. There were only six actual songs in 'Head', and the remainder of the album was padded with incidental music snatches by Ken

Micky and Peter in the studios during the Head/Instant Replay *sessions.*

Thorne and generally nonsensical dialogue bursts. The only worthwhile item was the revealing *War Chant* which neatly summed up the film, the Monkees, and all the great questions of life.

Hey, Hey we are the Monkees, you know we love to please
A manufactured image with no philosophies
We hope you like our story, although there isn't one
That is to say there's many, that way there is more fun
You told us you like action and games of many kinds
You like to dance, we like to sing
So let's all lose our minds
We know it doesn't matter, cause what you came to see
Is what we'd love to give you and give it 1–2–3
But it may come 3–2–1–2 or jump 9 to 5
And when you see the end in sight the beginning may arise
For those who look for meaning in form as they do fact
We might tell you one thing but we'd only take it back
Not back like in a boxback, not back like in a race
Not back so we can keep it but back in time and space
You say we're manufactured, to that we all agree
So make your choice and we'll rejoice in never being free
Hey Hey we are the Monkees, we've said it all before
The money's in, we're made of tin
We're here to give you more.

goin' down

Throughout 1968 speculation had been rife that the Monkees television show was going off the air. The second series had not finished and the Monkees themselves were not saying anything, so the conjecture remained just that. But by the middle of the year the rumours were so widespread that *16*, *Tiger Beat*, *Teen World* and the other teenybop rags were urging readers to send letters and other petitions to NBC-TV, Screen Gems and even the Federal Communications Commission. In June, NBC put the limping dog of a rumour out of its misery by officially axing the show, along with *Batman*, *I Dream Of Jeanie* and *Tarzan*. Raybert went through some token motions of offering a third season to another network and then accepted a Screen Gems compromise offer of three sixty-minute Monkee television specials.

From the Monkees public statements it appeared that the cancellation was entirely to their liking. Davy, of all people, came out with the cocky comment, 'When you start getting Monkee pens and Monkee bubblegum, that's when the fun stops. Micky was still doing his "you dirty rats" thing, I was still falling in love with the same girl. We decided to forget it man.' Could this have been the same Monkee who, years later, lamented, 'My only regret about the Monkees is that I wish we'd gone on for another year. I don't think the quality was dropping. It could have gone on because we had the potential. We could have hosted TV shows, the four of us with guests.' Micky tried to effect the pretence that the group had declined a third series despite corporate pleading. 'There won't be any more Monkee TV shows because we refused to do another series,' he told the British rock press. 'We ended the show because the establishment wanted it to go on exactly the way it was and we didn't.'

The official news fanned derisive flames and set off new rumours that the group were about to disband. Over in England, the knife was inserted and twisted brutally. When *D. W. Washburn* was released on 18 June, it was castigated mercilessly by a panel on Stewart Henry's BBC Radio 1 *Sunday Show*. Carl Wayne of the Move described it as 'A load of rubbish,' while only Bobby Vee claimed to be impressed. Even the studio audience voiced strong disapproval. The venom managed to filter through and its intensity stung the Monkees. 'People who had an axe to grind were willing to take their frustrations out on us,' reasons Peter. 'The public needed a rock'n'roll scapegoat and we were it. . . .

After the first couple of hits I heard from an old Village friend of mine that there was a lot of bad feeling toward us from actors in the New York Little Theatre Group, who were moaning 'What are those four talentless slobs who haven't paid their dues doing with all that success when we've been doing little theatres for five or six years? The criticism was always there and even though we did our best to ignore it, it got to us sometimes.'

Back in March, during the filming of *Head*, the group (without Peter) had attended the Grammy Awards ceremony at the Century Plaza Hotel. Although nominated in every appropriate category, they went home

Micky Dolenz and Samantha Juste were wed on 12 July 1968 in Laurel Canyon.

magazines. Inevitably, Samantha came to wield the same subtle (and no doubt unconscious) divisive force over the Monkees as Yoko and Linda had over the Beatles. 'I'd really like to see Micky move into a serious acting career,' she was soon saying. 'I've felt bad, deep inside, seeing him in some things, some of the television shows, because I felt it really wasn't him. Now I'm convinced he should be an actor. . . . That psychedelic stuff rather aggravates me, a lot of it is rubbish.'

Wedding bells were also being rung over Peter's corner of the Hollywood Hills. His girlfriend, Karen, whom he had been with at Monterey and in England over Christmas, married a fellow called Bob and the couple, with young Justin, moved into the Tork mansion. Peter had by then switched his affections to Reine (pronounced Wren) Stewart, daughter of actor James Stewart.

Davy had started his secret marriage by telling a string of bare-faced lies to conceal it. 'No wedding bells, please get that straight,' he demanded of *Monkee Monthly* a few months after the furtive nuptials. 'I have a girlfriend in New York and she's groovy. There's one or two or three in London and other parts. There are too many beautiful girls in the world and I've only seen some of them. There's plenty of time for marriage but right now it's not my scene.' But by the time Micky tied the knot with nare a concern for loss of following, Davy

Peter with Reine Stewart, daughter of James Stewart.

empty-handed. Davy, called upon to read the nominations for Best Documentary Recording, drew a chilled silence and hostile glances when he read off the near-fascist *Open Letter To My Teenage Son* by Victor Lundberg and blurted out, 'And I hope it doesn't win!' The night was almost a repeat of the Chasen's Restaurant debacle.

On 12 July, in the midst of this doom and desolation, Micky married Samantha Juste in the garden of his Laurel Canyon home. Ric Klein was best man, Coco Dolenz the maid-of-honour. The guest list was strictly limited to immediate family – genetic and professional. Screen Gems were bound to an oath of secrecy and although they sent a photographer, agreed to hold the shots for at least two weeks. This mild piece of deception aside, the whole affair was handled with honesty and few fans were offended. Micky had never hidden his romance but had instead sought to share it with the kids. They were as excited as he was when the wedding finally occurred. Samantha, by this time, was quite a celebrity in her own right and had even recorded a single for England's Go label – *No One Needs My Love*. After the wedding she announced plans to open a boutique in Hollywood called *Two Of A Kind* (Davy's *Zilch* in New York was still doing fair business at this point). In fact she became so independent that she began conducting her own solo interviews with fan had very obviously tired of the masquerade and began dropping blatant hints. First he confided to England's *Melody Maker*, 'I have a girlfriend in California. I used to be a confirmed bachelor but now I've decided I would like to get married one day. I'm mad about children.' A little later he told England's *Fabulous 208* magazine, 'I will tell you about one young lady. Her name is Linda Haines Jones.' Davy and Linda had actually been photographed in cuddlesome company on the set of *Head*. But all the hints went unheeded.

According to a number of media reports, the Monkees were supposed to have spent every Friday, Saturday and Sunday of July and August performing concerts within the United States. These dates did not happen and the group found themselves with some unexpected leisure time – their first break in over two years of frenzied activity and constant pressure. Finally, too, a chance to spend some of the piles of money they were earning. A chance to hob nob with the 'beautiful people' who lived around them. A chance to indulge personal tastes and pet hobbies. A chance to patronise certain needy causes, charitable and otherwise. The first needy cause was the newly-formed group, Three Dog Night, whom the Monkees supported by donating instruments and capital. A Texas blues band called Armadillo was also 'supported' by Monkee Mike.

Mike and Davy both bought Alsatian dogs, which were as cool then as Afghans were in swinging London. Davy collected a few odd sports cars and had Monkeemobile designer Dean Jeffries put together a nifty little roadster. But the real extravagance came from Mike, who embarked upon a staggering spending spree. Inside the Nesmith garage was a Lamborghini 400 2+2 (worth $14,500), Jaguar XKE, Radford Mini, Jeep, Pontiac GTO, Buick Riviera, '57 Chevy, an old pickup truck, assorted motor cycles, a speedboat and dune buggy, both designed by Dean Jeffries. The Nesmith mansion was outfitted with a complete closed circuit video system and, if legend is to be believed, all the doors in the place were wired to open in response to the spoken word 'love'. There was even talk of a Lear Jet being placed on order. And, of course, one must not forget the expensive self-financed recording projects in Los Angeles and Nashville.

In the January 1981 issue of *Playboy*, Mike detailed his descent into compulsive spending. 'The money came quickly and my lifestyle changed so rapidly that I developed an incredible overhead without realising it. I went from paying $300 a month rent to a $2,000 a month mortgage. The numbers didn't seem staggering at the time but what was important was the multiples. I had increased my standard of living by factors of tens. The biggest single problem was that almost no one, outside the oil industry, understood the influx of cash. Because all of a sudden the influx stops and, in my case, I wasn't prepared for it. I had to start telling stories to the tax man as they were putting little red tags on the furniture. Aside from drugs, money has to be the biggest single hazard in the industry.'

Janelle Dolenz-Scott saw that her son kept more of his money than his compatriots.

Lynne Randell recalls her friendship with the Monkees and their wives: 'I got on real well with Samantha and I lived just down the hill from the Nesmiths. They were a strange couple, very intelligent and very different. They were both strong Christian Scientists and never really got involved with much of the wild stuff that the others did. I saw them fight a lot and split up on a couple of occasions. It was always kind of a tense relationship. By this time I was a lot less innocent than I was on the tour and I began to see some things a bit clearer. The Monkees were all pretty careless with their money, particularly Peter, and there was always lots of sharks hanging about them. . . . Davy would invest money in anything that was put in front of him – he made a lot of silly mistakes. Micky didn't get ripped off too badly because his mother ran his accounts for him. But just *everybody* tried to take advantage of the Monkees and then turned their backs when they began to slip: I saw Peter do a real lot of things for Steve Stills but there came a time when Peter wasn't allowed on Stills' property when the Rolling Stones were visiting. Poor Peter, he bought David Crosby a boat and stuff but they all bled him dry with peace signs and bullshit.' Jackson Browne was a resident of Laurel Canyon during the summer of 1968. He recalled a high point of that season during a 1974 *Rolling Stone* interview. 'These beautiful chicks from Peter Tork's house kept coming over with these big bowls of fruit and dope and shit. They'd fuck us in the pool. We'd wake up and see this beautiful sixteen year old flower child, who only knew how to say "fave rave", with a bowl of fruit. She'd get you incredibly high and then take you downstairs to go swimming.'

Doug Trevor, leader of Australian support group the Cherokees, arrived in Los Angeles early in 1969 and took up the Monkees' offer to 'drop by when you're in town.' Now Davy Jones' musical director, with five Japanese tours behind him, he readily recalls his first experiences with the group. 'Peter had just left the group and invited me to stay at his house, which was always full of people. There were stoned hippies laying all over the place, naked girls wandering in and out of the pool and the constant noise of Peter rehearsing his new band Release somewhere downstairs. Barry McGuire and his chick were living in an old VW Combi in the back yard. Peter found a room for me in the attic and the first night I tried to sleep in it I was kept awake by this loud drunk roaring in the kitchen all night. They told me in the morning that it was Jim Morrison.'

'After a couple of weeks of this, Davy came around and asked me to stay over at his house, which was much more sedate. I came in handy then for carrying the baby into restaurants, with Linda by my side and Davy walking a few paces behind. I also started to spend time with Micky, who was the real party giver. . . . A lot of people hung around Micky's place but it wasn't a hippie haven like Peter's. People really liked Micky, they didn't just use him. Kenny Rogers was a regular guest, so was Sal Mineo. Beau and Jeff Bridges were the house table tennis champions.'

While Mike spent mountains of money, Peter gave away just as much and Micky entertained all the right people, Davy was undergoing a period of serious re-evaluation. He was still a sincere kid from the poor British family who viewed his position not so much as an excuse for massive indulgence, but as a transitory phase in his entertainment career. Rather than take out the frustrations of exhaustion on his workmates, Davy began to slip away quietly whenever a break allowed. He would drive down the Pacific Coast for hundreds of miles or take flights to mid-western cities. Once while driving around San Francisco, Davy came upon the Sacramento Delta and its hundreds of houseboats. He struck up a casual conversation with one houseboat family who invited him for dinner. He ended up staying on board for three days, helping with the cooking and cleaning and loving every moment of it. In Phoenix, Arizona he wandered through a shopping centre, chatting with anyone who recognised him. 'The first time I did it I was so nervous,' he later recalled. 'It was like when I left home for the first time. But eventually I realised that the plastic world I lived in was not the real world. There were other things out there and I wanted to get them.'

Micky was the only one who seemed able to take notoriety, wealth and a heady lifestyle in his stride. Hollywood, the film world, famous people and outrageous parties were nothing special to him. He had not come to Hollywood from Texas, Connecticut or Manchester with stars in his eyes – this was his own backyard. Once he had found his feet after the initial surge he wasn't taken in by the fast talkers, gurus and fad sensations to anywhere near the degree of his companions.

The Monkees' rest ended in the second week of September 1968 when they packed their bags for the much-touted Far Eastern tour, which in the end only included Australia and Japan. The Beatles had toured Australia in 1964 and had drawn the largest street crowds ever recorded during the entire span of global Beatlemania. Four and a half years on, the climate was right for an attempt at repeating a similar onslaught. The same promoter lined up the Monkees, the same hotels were booked, the same performance venues secured, the same publicity procedures followed. And if the Monkees roller coaster was on its descent in America and England, the news had not yet reached Australian teenagers. During their lifespan the Monkees had charted seven top forty singles in America and eight in England. In Australia, they had charted fifteen singles and four EP's in the top forty and two Davy Jones solo singles in the top five.

The task force flew out of San Francisco on 14 September and arrived in Sydney just after dawn on the 16th, after a brief stop over in Fiji. An estimated crowd of 500, a good many of whom had taken up their barrier positions almost twenty-four hours before, were on hand at Sydney's Kingsford Smith Airport to extend a frenzied, raucous welcome. The Australian tour party comprised of manager Ward Sylvester, tour manager David Pearl, sound engineer Bill Chadwick, bodyguards/personal attendants Brendon Cahill and Ric Klein, Raybert PR manager Floyd Ackerman, Screen Gems publicist Marilyn Schlossberg, the four Monkees and wives/girlfriends Samantha Dolenz, Reine Stewart and Phyllis Nesmith (who arrived in Adelaide ten days after the tour kicked off). After the touchdown, cooperative airport authorities conducted on-board Health and Immigration checks and then escorted the party into the VIP area of the terminal for a five minute Customs clearance. Casting an eye over the contents of Peter's luggage a Custom's officer spied a copy of William Burrough's *The Naked Lunch* and seized it with the gruff comment, 'I'll have that, it's banned here!' 'But I was just getting interested in it,' the bearded Monkee griped.

Placed in a gold cadillac for transfer to the first Australian press conference, at the Miller's New Brighton hotel at nearby Botany Bay, the Monkees were whisked along the tarmac past the fan barrier. Commonwealth Police Superintendant Davies, who had been the hero of the Beatle 'airport campaigns' in 1964 had given strict instructions to the driver that he was not to stop under any circumstances. However, the vehicle did come to a halt, at Davy and Micky's insistence, and the pair clambered out to meet some fans. Micky retreated when he sighted livid policemen advancing towards him but Davy ran thirty yards along the barrier, operating an 8mm movie camera, pursued by police and fans who had vaulted the barrier.

At the hotel, the four Monkees appeared for an hour before the Australian media festooned with, in one reporter's words: 'Fringes, chains, medallions, embroidered linen sashes and various bits of leather.' Davy got in early with a comment about the airport tarmac incident. 'It was frightening,' he claimed. 'I thought those cops were going to get out of hand'. Asked about their forthcoming feature film, he quipped, 'It's about an itinerant parrot salesman in Florida,' to which Peter

The Melbourne press conference. Right: Melbourne Monkee fans turned out in large numbers to give a noisy airport welcome.

added, 'Yeah, but it's also an allegory depicting the brutalisation of man by the mechanics of society'. Asked about future plans Micky offered, 'The past and future don't exist. We are primitive emerging forms.'

The following day the Monkees gave their second press conference, at the President Hotel in the Melbourne suburb of St Kilda. Another series of quick quips, queer queries and stock statements. While a hundred teenies shrieked out in the street, Davy sermonised 'When those kids stop one day, I'll be back shovelling horse manure. They're my bread and butter. We don't exploit them. We're bubblegum men who give them what they want – a chance to let off steam.'

Australians were unstinting in their expressions of affection toward the Pre-Fab Four. They were accepted as witty, intelligent and entirely credible entertainers. Not even their new physical appearance, which had accelerated their demise back home, seemed to faze their antipodean fans. Bearded Peter was resplendent in his kaftan and beads, Mike was sombre in dark glasses, suit and tie, Micky was sporting an untamed afro and Davy was as neat as Barbie's friend, the Ken doll.

The Monkees performed four concerts at Melbourne's Festival Hall on 18–19 September, to a combined audience of 25,000. They were supported by an all-girl cabaret-pop outfit called Marcie and the Cookies and a versatile pop group called the Cherokees. In a show of strength prior to the commencement of the first concert, thirty-four assorted white-coated attendants and policemen were assembled beneath the stage and the audience were warned that anybody who left their seat would be instantly ejected. Surprisingly the stunt worked and the shows were generally orderly affairs – at least in the stalls. The stage situation was another matter entirely. For a start there were more flowers arranged around the band equipment than at a sacred rite on the banks of the Ganges. Then came thousands of yards of streamers, stuffed native animals, foodstuffs and other offerings from the audience.

The four Monkees added the final brushstroke to this mad mosaic. Like their street clothes, the stage costumes resembled a cross section of the exhibits at Madame Tussaud's Wax Works. Nothing matched, nothing was supposed to. At one point in the show the four appeared in velvet burgundy suits and frilled silk shirts. In other sequences Mike donned a jacket cut from an American flag, Micky flailed away in cheesecloth, Davy dazzled in Paisley, and Peter became the hippie version of the Cigar Store indian. Overall, the stage scene resembled a page from 'Mad Magazine Looks at Flower Power.'

On Friday 20 September the group returned to Sydney for two concerts at the creaking Sydney Stadium the following night. They were accommodated at the Sheraton Hotel, which had been the location of much madness during the Beatles tour. This time the din of encamped fans was exceeded by an anti-war march organised by a body called 'High School Students Against The War In Vietnam'. When the protesters passed the Sheraton *en route* to a Rest and Recreation Centre for American troops, they found unexpected support from the Monkees, who proffered peace signs.

Vietnam was very much on the mind of one Monkee

Davy in Australia.

Micky in Australia.

at the time – Micky announced in Australia that he had received his draft papers and was not at all pleased by the situation. 'I'm scared to death and I'll fight tooth and nail to get out of it,' he admitted. 'I just won't go and at the moment the only way to do that is to avoid staying in America. I have my lawyers investigating the ways that I can avoid being called up.' Upon his return to America Micky did undergo an Army medical but his childhood leg injury saved him.

'We play to eleven or twelve-year-olds because they are the only ones who can save us', Micky insisted during his draft revelation. 'They haven't been taught to hate enough. We've played to young kids in the southern states of America and there was no trouble about integrated audiences. We'd like to say these things at home but nobody has ever asked us. In the beginning they tried to stop us speaking our minds but it wasn't honest and we found that the kids don't like contrived answers.'

The two Saturday night concerts at the eleven thousand capacity Sydney Stadium were fraught with problems. Just about at the end of its long life, the Stadium was simply not able to handle the scope and volume of the Monkees performance. The four tons of sound equipment employed for the event was a hun-

Peter in Australia.

Mike in Australia.

dredfold over that used by the Fab Four and most of the other British acts that had followed them. When the proceedings hit full pitch, furious nearby residents descended upon the box office with hands clasped firmly over ears. There was also the problem of the revolving stage, which ground to a halt under the unaccustomed weight and had to be rotated by hand (many of them) to avoid seat burning in the bleachers.

From Sydney the tour progressed to the northern ultra-conservative city of Brisbane, which managed to live up to its redneck image. The Monkees were just a few minutes into a press conference at Lennons Hotel when Keith Sharpe, a British reporter attached to a television station, asked, 'when do you think you might break up and try something like music?'. Peter began yelling at Sharpe, accusing him of asking provocative questions to create arguments. Davy's response was to pour a glass of water over his head. The reporter retaliated by hurling his glass of water into Jones' face, before being frogmarched from the room by security guards. He later defended his actions, saying that he didn't like 'scruffy individuals who pour water over people,' and that 'you can't do that sort of thing to an Englishman. Especially if you're a little Welsh coalminer!'

After two shows in Adelaide, it was back into Sydney for the third time, in order to play another three concerts, one added by public demand – bringing the combined Sydney audience to over 50,000. The live set, at this point in Monkee history, officially comprised *Daydream Believer, Last Train to Clarksville, Salesman, D. W. Washburn, It's Nice To Be With You, Sunny Girlfriend, I Wanna Be Free, Cuddly Toy, Mary Mary, You Just May Be The One, Stepping Stone* and the solo segments. The final Sydney show on Sunday night seemed no different to the first four. The audience was around eighty per cent female and under fifteen. Everyone there had a fine time, except for thirteen-year-old Jennifer Charlsworth from the suburb of Northbridge, who died. Jennifer's heart stopped three times after she collapsed unconscious at the concert. She was rushed to hospital and died there the following day. The news was deliberately witheld from the Monkees until they reached Japan, where Floyd Ackerman made the details known. Davy, in particular, was shattered by the information.

The tour party flew from Sydney via Hong Kong to Tokyo, where an airport welcoming committee of over five thousand shrill Nippon teenies was on hand. The first two days were devoted to press conferences, publicity duties, shopping in the local Ginza, and guided tours of the Nikon camera and Honda vehicle factories. At night the whole team congregated in a single hotel room to view the Japanese version of the television series, rolling around the floor in hysterics over the dubbing of the voices. For Peter, being in Japan was the ultimate trip. Since the beginning of the year he had become obsessed by the country, was dabbling in Sumi Art and had even taken Japanese language lessons from a private tutor when it seemed likely that some *Head* scenes were going to be shot in Japan and that the Far East tour was going to take place in May. The shows commenced in Tokyo, with a local band called *Floral* filling the same role as the *Candy Store Prophets, Sundowners, Epifocal Phringe* and the *Cherokees*. They performed in Kyoto, Nagya and Osaka, with a total of six concerts, one of which was televised. Tension surrounded some of the shows following bomb assassination threats from a left-wing anti-American political group.

When the final concert in Osaka was over on 8 October, Davy skipped the festivities and jumped on the first available flight to England. Officially he was going to visit his sick father but he was also dashing to

Reine, Micky, Peter and Sammy stopping over in Hong Kong en route to Japan.

Manchester to lay eyes upon his new daughter, Talia Elizabeth Jones, who had been born on 2 October while her father was in Tokyo. Davy spent about ten days in England with his family before reporting for duty at Paramount Film Studios in Hollywood. On 2_ October word came through that his father had died. Absolutely devastated by the news, Davy returned immediately to England with David Pearl to attend the funeral.

On 6 November the four flew to New York for the *Head* première and returned home with the grave verdict, 'We didn't expect most of the film critics to like it but we feel that it will have a rather different reception from young-minded people everywhere when it goes on general release.' On 20 November they dutifully attended a Los Angeles première. Samantha appeared at the premiere in a remarkably rotund state and on _ January gave birth to a 6lb 13oz girl named Ann Bluebell.

The final task before the Monkees for the year of 196_ was production of the first (and last) of three projected television specials – *33⅓ Revolutions Per Monkee*, under the direction of Jack Good and Art Fisher, with War_ Sylvester as executive producer. Good, honoured now as the 'father of rock'n'roll television' was the master of transferring the kinetic energy of rock to the smal_ screen as he had spectacularly displayed with *6._ Special, Oh Boy!, Around The Beatles* and *Shindig*. Th_

The Monkees took a time capsule back to the Paramount Theatre on 7 December 1956. This time with help from Little Richard.

Monkees wrangled a far greater degree of script participation and approval on this special than with any previous project. In fact, when they returned from Japan they complained that the draft was 'too sloppy, too fairy-tale like' and insisted that it be redrafted. *Head* had been Rafelson and Schneider's statement, this was going to be theirs.

If the Monkees' self-mockery went over the heads of their dwindling fans in *Head*, it was brutally shoved down their throats in the television special. With even Davy gleefully participating, they took perverse delight in puncturing, deflating and ridiculing the remaining shreds of their manufactured image. The Buddy Miles Express, Julie Driscoll, Brian Auger and the Trinity, Fats Domino, Little Richard, Jerry Lee Lewis and the Clara Ward Singers were engaged as guest stars, somehow fulfilling each member's personal concept of hipness. Good sent a couple of buses down to Sunset strip to round up about a hundred hippies to comprise a live audience at Paramount Studios.

The story involves Charles Darwin the famous evolutionist (Brian Auger) taking the Monkees through various stages of evolution, until they are ready to brainwash the world through commercial exploitation. Hatched in giant test tubes, they are stripped of all personal identity and names, becoming 'Monkee number one', 'Monkee number two' etc. One wonders how Rafelson and Schneider, who fought so hard to develop and nurture wholly individual and expressive personalities from the very beginning of the series, thought of this interpretation of the process. Almost all of the soundtrack was written specifically for the show. Surprisingly, no soundtrack album was ever issued. Mike sang a memorable country song called *The Only Thing That I Believe Is True* (also known as *As I Play My Guitar*), during an inventive split-screen sequence, which cast Don Kirshner as 'the devil incarnate':

'Now it's quite a while ago that I had a strange intuition
Something was wrong with my old record situation
Well the devil incarnate was planning music to provision. . .
Well tell me Mr. TV Man, just where you make your moral stand
Which way today do you take your pay?
Do you walk straight up or do you face the other way? . . .
And for a while I'll just play my guitar, I'll play you a couple of tunes
I know it may not take me too far
but it's the only thing that I believe is true'

The process was called 'using the system to discredit the system', and if any viewers failed to catch the intent of the lyrics, the tiresome point was pressed home by *Wind-Up Man*, performed by all four in the stiff-legged pose of robots:

'I'm a wind-up man, programmed to be entertaining
. . . Invented by the teenybopper. . .
Turn me on and I will sing a song
about a wind-up world of people watching television
Wind-up man, can you hear me laughing at you?'

The plot, which the four helped to write, allowed
each Monkee to regain his stripped personal identity by
thinking his way out of captivity. Micky Monkee makes
his mark by performing a stunning rhythm and blues,
up-tempo duet version of *I'm A Believer* with Julie
Driscoll. Peter Monkee reclines on a giant cushion in
eastern garb and, to the lilting backing of sitar and
tabla, sings *Prithee*, a gentle song about spiritual values.
By late 1968 Peter had adopted a complete macrobiotic
diet of brown rice, yoghurt, herbal teas and the like,
and had graduated from the *I Ching* to a veritable
library of books on eastern religion and philosophy.

After Mike's country song, Davy cavorts around in
short pants and a frill collar in fairytale land, singing
and dancing to a song called *Goldilocks Sometime*. But
Darwin is alarmed by their fantasies and attempts to
break them down physically by hypnotism. *Only the
Fittest Shall Survive* is a slab of swirling psychedelia
overlaid with conga drums, jungle sounds, cyclonic
winds, explosions and heavy breathing. Regenerated to
Darwin's taste, the Monkees make their debut at the
Paramount Theatre, billed as the 'greatest rock 'n' roll
stars in the world.' Draped, stovepiped and greased,
they hurl themselves into a classic rock medley – *At The
Hop*, *Whole Lotta Shakin'*, *Tutti Frutti* and others. As
backing musicians, Jerry Lee Lewis, Little Richard,
Fats Domino and the Buddy Miles Express take a
backseat to the magnificent Monkees.

The scant *String Of My Kite* is heard as Darwin
decides that he must give the four their freedom – a
liberation that ends in mad shambles. Standing alone on
a giant sound stage, Mike strums *Listen To The Band* on
his beloved Gretsch twelve-string guitar (one of only
three in existence, the others in the possession of Chet
Atkins and George Harrison). As the song progresses,
he is joined by Peter on keyboards, Micky on drums
and Davy on maracas in a final symbolic performance
by The Monkees. As the climax approaches, the set is
invaded by the hundred hippies and by the musicians
from the Trinity and the Buddy Miles Express. The
song ends in a frantic cacophony – similar to the
Beatles' famous performance of *Hey Jude* on the *David
Frost Show*.

Away from the fatherly glare of Rafelson and
Schneider, the Monkees found that making the special
was enjoyable and stimulating. Brian Auger returned to
England full of praise for the musical abilities of the
cardboard kids. He told the press, 'We expected to meet
four actors who happened to make records as well.
Instead we found four switched on musicians; especially
Mike who had a lot of sensible things to say about the

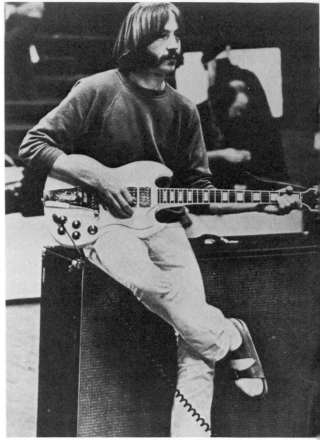

Peter sported a walrus moustache throughout the rehearsals for
33⅓ Revolutions Per Monkee, *his last Monkees project.*

music scene of today.' Drummer Clive Thacker was
fascinated by Micky's technique and set-up, observing
that his kit was arranged for a left handed and footed
player but Dolenz was right handed. Whoever had
conducted Micky's crash course in 1966 had managed
to overlook that matter.

Micky was not the only drummer who impressed.
Peter's girlfriend Reine Stewart filled in when Fats
Domino's drummer failed to arrive. She so impressed
the veteran rocker that he asked her to join his band for
a few dates. It was a deal more credence than Peter
received when he tried to play a piece of Bach's *Toccata*
during a song take. His action was met with the
inevitable outcry which accompanied any attempt by
the Monkees to be musically innovative. 'I really got my
hand slapped for that. I said "I'll play some Bach with
my rock 'n' roll on the piano here" and they screamed
"Horrors!, you can't do that! You're not Jimi Hendrix.
You're not the Nice." They wanted me to say, "Boy,
I'll never innovate again!".'

As soon as production of the special was completed,
Peter announced that he was leaving the group. He had
contemplated departure at the end of the first television
series two years before, but the pleadings of the others
and the binding terms of his contract held him back.
His announcement was greeted with the usual 'Yeah,

And then there were three . . .

Pete, sure, now let's get back to work,' but on 30 December, 1968 he ceased to be a Monkee. It reportedly cost him a staggering $160,000 to break his contract, leaving him virtually penniless. He took with him a cheap watch bearing the engraved inscription 'To Peter from the guys down at work.' The inscribed back is now on its fourth watch.

At a press conference Peter claimed that he was sick of the fighting and lack of definite direction. 'I never cared about the things that were happening; all the acclaim. I hated the work. It was tough and I didn't like it. The pressure was awful. We were working in an incredibly new environment and half the crew on the show was young and had very little experience at that level of work. The concerts were fun but during tours you are removed from your friends, except for the guys. When we did take along a few friends it was only a mild relief. The Far East tour wasn't fun because I felt hideously under-rehearsed. I was constantly pushing for rehearsals and they were constantly saying, later. We could never get together. Also, we didn't play any new music on this recent tour. It was all old tunes, a bore.'

Peter later explained that he wanted to make more collaborative records like 'Headquarters' because the only time he was really happy was when the whole group was working in the studio together. 'I said, "let's go back into the studio" and Micky told me "no, you make your records, I'll make mine, and we'll have four times as much product." As far as I could tell there was no virtue to that attitude. They just didn't understand, the suckers, they still don't. It was obvious that there was going to be a fallow period, but the group that sticks together through that kind of thing and believes in itself can go places. But I couldn't get the other guys to concur. I just wanted to record for all my life.'

Physical deterioration began to catch up with the four of them: 'At first it was a joy,' Peter recalls, 'we were young and full of piss and vinegar and we could really work hard. We could film all day, record all night, carry on heavy romantic lives and be back on the set by 7.30 the next morning, stumbling blindly after about forty-five minutes sleep. But you only have three maybe five years of that life available to you. When you start pulling into your late twenties you've got to start rationing your energies and resources because you've already knocked several years off the end of your life with that sort of lifestyle. Anyway, nobody was paying attention anymore. . . . When we did three behind-the-scenes things in a row – a movie, a far eastern tour and a television special – we dropped out of sight from the public's point of view and that was the end right there. It was over and I was the first to admit it.'

Peter had started covert rehearsals with other musicians some time before, as a preliminary to forming his own group. He began working with guitarist John Anderson, who had been the Assistant Director on the Monkees series. Also involved in these early rehearsals was Hollywood guitarist Lowell George. Lowell had done some uncredited work on the Mothers of Invention 'Reuben and The Jets' album in 1968, and had tried to interest Frank Zappa in his song *Willin'*. Legend has it that Zappa fired the lad and told him to go back to Los Angeles and form a band. He heeded this advice but before the formation of Little Feat in late 1969, Lowell worked with Tork.

'Peter's soul left us about two and a half years ago,' said Davy. 'He was a banjo player from Greenwich Village who was made into an actor and finally decided that he didn't want to be a Marx Brother forever. His heart was back in the Village, that's all.' Davy's suggestion that Peter was always the square peg in the round hole was entirely correct. He had refused to accompany the others on the very first promo trip to London preferring to hide away for the duration. In his absence Micky had said, 'Three of us more or less play ourselves in the series. The odd one out is Peter Tork. Offstage he's a real serious guy who thinks a lot about things like religion and problems in the world. But in the show he throws off all that and becomes a dumb-but-likeable character who is always doing the wrong thing at the wrong time. He kind of moons around with a lovesick expression on his face – not like the real Peter Tork at all.'

Peter now reflects on the Monkees as a union doomed from inception: 'We never had a chance to work out our personality differences in obscurity. We were under the public eye from the beginning so we had to work through our differences behind the scenes, hidden from the public glare. . . . Had we been a group before, we would have been O.K. but we never did get a chance to work out ways of living together. Looking back I have to say that Davy was the one I had the most feeling for, Micky was the one I had the most fun with, and Mike was the one I had the most respect for.'

The others were deterred from following Peter's lead by the cost of buying out their contracts. They kept on with the masquerade, showing a brave face to the world, each realising that the Monkees had ceased to exist when the television series was cancelled. Mike reasons that: 'It was just a show, there wasn't really a group to break up. A character in a television show doesn't have any ongoing life after the show is over.' Micky adds: 'Any TV show, *Bonanza*, *Star Trek*, *The Monkees* or whatever, once it goes off the air, well that's what happens, it goes off the air and the cast don't hang out together anymore; they go and do other shows. Leonard Nimoy and William Shatner didn't run around in their space suits saying 'Beam me up Scottie.' It was just that, with the success we'd had as a rock 'n' roll band, it was very difficult for the public to understand that. It made it almost impossible for us to be accepted as actors, and to be given other shows.'

'Things just weren't the same after *Head* bombed, so we stayed together in an effort to ride the inertia down,' claims Mike, who began to express and manifest a somewhat uncharacteristic loyalty toward the diminished unit. 'It is a fact that Peter's leaving has brought us together. We lean on each other more and now we believe we can develop each of our talents within the context of the Monkees. We are going to try and abandon our collective identity because we are not represented by one idea. By a pattern of record releases and exposure we will be able to make the transition so that each of us will be able to spring out and do what we want within the context of the group.

'In the future we really want to exploit comedy rather than rock'n'roll. Our stock in trade is that we are, simply, comedians. This is what we must concentrate on and probably abandon the music. It's not a question of us shaking off the old Monkees image. We've nothing to escape from. What we've done is valid and honest, I'm not ashamed of it. It's coming alive!'

Trying to relate sections of this statement to the Mike Nesmith who single-handedly took on the entire Screen Gems-Columbia boardroom over a point of musical honour – and won, is incredibly difficult. It was almost as if he was trying to atone for the excesses of his earlier idealism. Ironically, it was Davy who came forward at this point: 'It's not a question of us now being in control of our destinies. It wasn't our destinies we had to worry about in the past, it was our souls. A lot of people have used us in the last three years. There have been many who have bettered their own personalities by taking credit for our success. We've known where we've been since the beginning and the fact that we're now one less only makes us much tighter.'

The first the public saw of the new Monkees trio was a seventh album, 'Instant Replay', which hit the market before *33⅓ Revolutions Per Monkee* was screened. Though few people ever had the opportunity to discover the fact, the album was one of the group's more impressive efforts, considerably more pleasurable over-

all than its two predecessors. Comprised of material from the shelf and some new recordings by the trio, it was a simple, sunny pop collection, with quite bearable country overtones from Mike, who later admitted that: 'What I was doing with the Monkees at the time of the last two albums I appeared on was to try and move us in the direction of country rock. I had no intention of leaving the group at that time, I had long term goals for us in that respect.' However Micky counters with 'Mike kept saying "Country and western is going to be huge!" and the executives would say "No no no no!" or "Country what?".'

The older material, generally of Brill Building origin, gave 'Instant Replay' an overall sound of a cross between the first album and 'Pisces Aquarius Capricorn and Jones Limited'. From the Goffin and King catalogue came *A Man Without A Dream* and *I Won't Be The Same Without Her*. *The Girl I Left Behind Me* was a Carole Bayer and Neil Sedaka ditty in the same mould as *When Love Comes Knockin'* from the second album – both probably recorded at the same session.

The band had come such a full circle by 1969 that it was not easy to isolate the old from the new. However there was no difficulty when it came to the choice of a single to follow the disastrous *Porpoise Song*. In an attempt to pull off another *Valleri* trick, Colgems dug up Boyce and Hart's *Teardrop City*, a dreary and previously rejected clone of *Clarkesville*. It did manage to chart to fifty-six in America and forty-four in England, but sealed their image as top forty has beens. Mike referred to it as, 'a concession on our part to certain people. You could call it a corporate swansong.'

Critically, the tracks which gave 'Instant Replay' sufficient appeal to climb into the top thirty were the likes of *Shorty Blackwell* (recorded during the *Head* sessions), a five minute, eerie ode to the Dolenz family cat. Or Mike's country ballad *Don't Wait For Me*

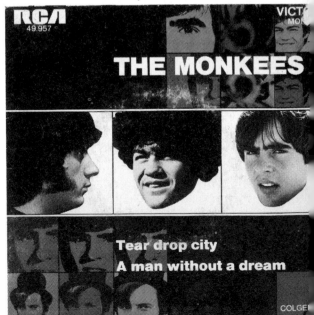

which sounded almost identical to what he would produce with the First National Band in the following year. Of note was *Me Without You*, a Davy-sung Boyce and Hart song that borrowed rather heavily from the Beatles' *Your Mother Should Know*. Davy's surprisingly tough *You and I*, written with Bill Chadwick, was yet another piece of guilt therapy, with the lines, 'In a year or maybe two we'll be gone and someone new will take our place. There'll be another song, another voice, another pretty face.'

As it happened, Davy's words were remarkably prophetic. The new crop of kids grew quickly bored with yesterday's heroes and switched their allegiance to Michael Cole of the *Mod Squad* and new hearthrob Bobby Sherman, a *Shindig* regular who had once appeared on *The Monkees*. The original Monkee fans had become self-consciously 'heavy' and were contemplating the wonder of their navels to the accompaniment of Iron Butterfly and Vanilla Fudge. Special Monkee issues of teen magazines could no longer be counted on for huge sales.

Just as 'Instant Replay' was released, Screen Gems gave the trio official artistic control over their recordings and quite neatly wiped their hands of what had become a liability. The corporation still held the power of veto over 'inappropriate' activities but adopted a benign attitude toward most projects put to them for approval. A tally of overall record sales up to mid-1969 showed that the Monkees had sold sixteen million albums and eleven and a half million singles in just two and a half years. No doubt some executives were of the opinion that the golden goose had gone off the lay and the quicker it was boiled down for broth the better.

The most notable area of new flexibility was television appearances. Although they had made an appearance on *The Ed Sullivan Show* in 1967, more to join the honoured ranks of Elvis Presley, The Beatles and The Rolling Stones than to promote themselves, the Monkees were not made available to variety shows. Now they found that they needed these outlets to maintain anything near a high profile. First, Davy performed a cameo on *Rowan and Martin's Laugh In* during 1968 and then the whole group (including Peter) turned up on *The Glen Campbell Show* for a loony appearance that included the unreleased song *Everybody Loves A Nut*. During Davy's Christmas sojourn in England, he taped a spot on *The Tom Jones Show*, singing the Cockney staple *Consider Yourself*. Then in the first half of 1969 the trio were seen on *The Johnny Carson Tonight Show* and *The Andy Williams Show*, promoting their new singles. Mike appeared solo on *The Johnny Cash Show* and Davy on *The Tennessee Ernie Ford Show*.

Rafelson and Schneider had disappeared from sight after the *Head* fiasco and were busy with other projects. Schneider was investing his Monkee profits in Fonda and Hopper's *Easy Rider*, on which he was executive producer and editor. Rafelson was directing Jack Nicholson in *Five Easy Pieces* during 1969. Steve Blauner, the pair's new partner in BBS Productions

Davy encountered Goldie Hawn on his first solo appearance on Laugh In.

(Bert, Bob and Steve) produced the soundtrack album for *Five Easy Pieces* and then went on to produce such films as *The King Of Marvin Gardens* (directed by Rafelson) and *Drive He Said* (directed by Nicholson).

The Monkees' new masters Cahill and Pearl's approach to 'riding the inertia down' was to match the still saleable trio with the seven-piece black rhythmn and blues outfit Sam and the Goodtimers, fresh from the Ike and Tina Turner Revue. An ambitious two and a half hour 'revue' show was staged, with a backdrop of loony silent film footage shot by Micky and Mike. Simple but compelling comedy sequences were introduced to the show while retaining the solo performance spots that had always been so well received. Mike stubbornly clung to his guitar, while the other two surrendered their musical roles to the Goodtimers and hit the front of the stage as Vegas-style entertainers.

The first audience of their first tour as a trio gave them enormous confidence. Opening at the Pacific Coliseum in Vancouver on 28 March (the location of Elvis Presley's most famous 1957 concert appearance), they performed to 5,200 enthralled fans who howled their heads off. Reviews were strong and the vibes were high. On the following nights when they hit Seattle and Alberta, the audiences were just as fervent but half in number. The shows in Chicago, Augusta, Birmingham and Honolulu reinforced the low attendance pattern – just one short year after they had turned down a lucrative Shea Stadium date because they did not want their fans to 'Pay good money to see tiny dots on a far away stage.' To save face, Screen Gems eventually cancelled all the remaining dates.

This was an unfortunate knee-jerk reaction which denied the Monkees the chance to fight their way back on the strength of their talent and ability to adapt to changing situations. Janine Gressell, writing in the *Seattle Times*, gave their new show this appraisal: 'The change in format has allowed each of the members to develop himself in his own direction. Since there aren't the restrictions of conforming to a group image, each is given the opportunity to explore his own capabilities, interests and abilities. This has been a challenge to the trio because there is no chance to mask a lack of creativity behind a group facade. . . . On the whole their show is immensely interesting. It is exciting to see three performers who could have rested on their laurels have the nerve and artistic integrity to change a successful style. The new Monkees have risen to the challenge and are succeeding beautifully.'

Billboard also commented on the tour, selecting a Charleston, West Virginia show (which just happened to have a full house of 6,000) on 12 April. 'In the first Peter Tork-less tour, the Monkees are popping their bubble-gum image and evolving rapidly into a young-adult act. . . . The Monkees are carefully bridging two images. They performed enough of their hits to avoid alienating the vast teenybopper market, while adding enough new material to stake out a claim on a more mature market.' Around the same time, the trade magazine announced that, 'The Monkees are redubbing the music from their old NBC-TV series to a more contemporary vein for the show's re-runs on CBS, which will debut on Saturday mornings in September. The reruns will be redubbed to give the Monkees an opportunity to sing compositions written by the Beatles, Donovan and Jimmy Webb among others.' This extensive musical overhaul never occurred but, according to Peter, the shows *were* tampered with. 'There was a minute or two cut out in the reruns to allow more time for commercials. They cut out a lot of the side gags, so the show became a little duller. I don't think anybody has the original shows. All the private video copies are the cut versions.'

Billboard also announced that Mike had 'signed an exclusive five year production contract with Dot Records to produce a minimum of eighteen masters each year under the American Wichita Company logo. He also formed National Mod Records and Runner Music (BMI). Artists to be produced by Nesmith are singer Bill Chadwick, country-rock group the Corvettes and a female vocalist not yet signed.' The female vocalist never was signed and the required ninety masters failed to materialise. The only products to hit the market were two singles: *Back Home Girl/The Lion In Your Heart* by the Corvettes, and *Talking To The Wall/If You Had The Time* by Bill Chadwick. What became of National Mod Records and Runner Music is a secret no doubt held close to the chest of the Nesmith legal and accounting department.

33⅓ Revolutions Per Monkee was broadcast in April NBC, in all their wisdom, put it up against the Academy Awards telecast and it rated disastrously. Mike ironically remembers that, 'I'd already seen it so watched the Oscars like everybody else.' However, the time difference allowed it to screen without such competition on the Eastern seaboard and reviews there were pleasing. *Variety* said, 'It was anything but a conventional norm rock 'n' roll and in some respect made *Laugh In*, which it was pre-empting, seem almost conventional television by comparison.' Nonetheless network executives let it be known that the two remaining planned television specials would almost certainly never see the light of day.

To compound the woes, a new single drew ecstatic review upon release and then took a nosedive into oblivion. *Listen To The Band*, one of the nine songs that Mike recorded with the nascent Area Code 615 in Nashville, had been relegated, in usual style, to the flipside of single number ten, after being displaced as single number nine by *Teardrop City*. Colgems pushed Paul Williams' *Someday Man* (for the first time, a non-Screen Gems copyright), but critics and radio programmers began raving about the great flipside and turned it over. Mike's victory was a small one. His song limped to sixty-three, while William's formal effort

peaked at eighty-one (forty-seven in the UK). In Australia the powerful, countryfied *Listen To The Band* hit a responsive chord and made it to number fifteen.

Single number eleven made it one place higher than *Someday Man*. *Good Clean Fun*, the first ever official Monkee-composed American A-side, was country and western style, without the rock leaning of *Listen To The Band*. Banjo runs, pedal steel glistening, fiddle flourishes – all the Nashville accompaniments. On the other side was Micky Dolenz's best song since *Randy Scouse Git*, the compelling, atmospheric *Mommy and Daddy*, recorded in the brassy style of *Goin' Down* and *Steam Engine 99*. Once more, loyal Australia came to the aid of the Monkees, giving them a double-sided top thirty hit.

The Monkees as 'Wind Up Men' in 33⅓ Revolutions Per Monkee – Peter's final performance with the group.

The Monkees' status in England was in tatters by this point. *Someday Man* had made it to position forty-seven for a single week, but that was it. No other Monkees record appeared on the British charts until a reissue EP made it to number thirty-three in 1980. *Daddy's Song* was snatched from the archives and rushed to revive some of the flagging interest in July 1969, against the group's wishes. It missed the chart completely and drew venomous reviews. In a *Melody Maker* 'Blind Date' listening session Robin Gibb pronounced it 'quite repulsive really,' and the rest of the country appeared to share the verdict. In May, RCA had taken out a full page advertisement in *New Musical Express* broadly hinting at a May tour by the trio, which never came about.

The final nail was hammered into the coffin on 7 June, when relentless Monkees antagonist Don Short, a reporter with London's *Daily Mirror*, who had once described them as 'plastic people,' did the arithmetic that everybody else in the world seemed incapable of and announced in giant headlines that Davy Jones was

German picture sleeve

married to twenty-four-year-old Linda Haines, the daughter of an American airline company executive, had been so for eighteen months, and was the father of an eight-month-old daughter.

Davy was stunned and not a little hurt by the unexpected backlash from the revelation. Sobbing fans wrote to magazines accusing him of deception and thoughtlessness and even *Monkees Monthly* ran an editorial titled 'Davy: You Should Have Told Us!' Davy took time out to explain his actions to his fans, readily conceding that the whole incident had been badly handled. He had only lied to protect their feelings in the first place, not to shield the downsliding group from adverse fan reaction. 'I kept my marriage a secret because I believe stars should be allowed a private life,' he explained to *Tiger Beat* magazine, 'I feel I have a lot to offer in a professional sense and I've offered it *all* for my fans and for everyone else to see. But I've always tried to remove my personal life from sight, as it really isn't anyone's concern but mine and those close to me.' In the same issue, a Miss Vicki Yasser of Clinton, North Carolina, echoed the predominant fan sentiment at the time: 'Why did Davy keep his marriage a secret? I'll tell you. It was because he was afraid of losing his fans. Well, Davy doesn't have to worry anymore, because he's lost half of them already.'

The motives were almost certainly as pure as he claimed, for Davy Jones was a rare creature from rock's black lagoon. Genial, inoffensive, punctual, unpretentious and consistently sincere, he was a prime target for the barbs of critics who refused to acknowledge that anybody who attracted pre-pubescent females could possibly possess any real talent or artistic merit. With a wide-eyed innocence that was never quite naïveté, Davy suffered the criticism silently, fighting back with a degree of zealous professionalism his detractors could not hope to match. A faultless dedication tinged with pathos.

In many ways, Davy Jones *was* the Prince Charming his fans saw him to be. Far from being embarrassed by his level of appeal, he cared passionately for the welfare and feelings of his followers. Instances of outstanding kindness and generosity were regular. When twelve-year-old Rhonda Cook of Phoenix, Arizona, was struck by a car while carrying a Monkees album and pleaded for Davy to be with her before a leg amputation operation, he jumped on the first plane and then returned a week later. When he saw an elderly woman fall on a sidewalk, he rushed her to hospital and then visited her every day for a week, without her ever becoming aware of who he was. Whenever Davy spotted small girls being trampled in autograph crushes he instructed David Pearl to extract them from the crowd and bring them to him for private meetings where he handed over concert tickets, autographed records and even taxi fares. Star-struck teenybops would never have a better friend.

A real-life Prince Charming.

Like most objects of overpowering adoration, Davy found himself very much alone within a vacuum, as he tried to explain to Jackie Richmond at *Monkees Monthly*. 'When my mum died when I was young I felt like it was the end of the world. Then when my dad died not so long ago I realised that I was in a strange position. Right in the middle of a whole lot of people when it came to my work, but right in the middle of nothing when it came to my own life. I needed a family, I wanted roots. With my sisters being married and having their own lives to lead I felt like some kind of orphan. I don't think anyone realises just how much family life means to me.'

His impressive honesty was to no avail. The Davy

Jones comet plummeted to earth dragging the remnants of Monkee popularity with it. If there was any demand remaining for cuddly teen idols by mid 1969, then Bobby Sherman and David Cassidy were ready to meet it. The cute jockey from England was very much yesterday's papers. So much so that it went virtually without notice that he had been making selected solo concert appearances for some months. In Birmingham, Alabama, he headed the bill at a radio station-promoted show starring Boyce and Hart, Andy Kim, Billy Joe Royal, Gary Puckett and the Union Gap and Four Jacks and A Jill.

Davy and Linda Jones with daughter Talua, the best kept secret in showbiz.

Once the furore had died down, Davy visited England with his family and tried to repair a little of the damage. He publicly forgave Robin Gibb and planned to record some of his songs, with Gibb as producer. It was also revealed that George Schlatter, producer of *Rowan and Martin's Laugh In*, was hoping to incorporate the three Monkees into the show. 'It's the sort of improvised material we could handle well,' enthused Davy. 'He's also thinking of a show for me that would cover news events. I guess we could even find something funny to say about the riots in Ireland.' These words were printed in an August issue of *Melody Maker* which also carried, on the same page, arrival details for Bob Dylan, The Band, Ritchie Havens and Tom Paxton, who were flying in for the Isle of Wight Festival later in the month. With British Rail preparing for a 'second Dunkirk' as half a million hippies packed their love beads and hash stash, the affairs of Mr Jones and his Monkee cohorts were of massive insignificance.

The Monkee 'boom industries' were painfully aware of this level of insignificance. In September *Monkees Monthly* discontinued publication after its thirty-second issue. Davy's face on a fan magazine cover could no longer be relied upon for even moderate sales. In any case, the Monkees were now far more interested in the company of recording engineers than celebrity photographers.

In 1968 Davy had spoken in an interview of a proposed four album set titled 'The Monkees Present', which would feature a solo album by each member. The basic idea of this preposterous strategy was retained and implemented in the creation of their eighth album, which borrowed the same title. Having scooped the cream off the handy reservoir of unissued early material, the second album as a threesome needed new material. This material came from Mike Nesmith, Micky Dolenz and Davy Jones. It did not come from the Monkees. The three performers who hid under the banner had *nothing* musically to do with each other. After the title 'The Monkees Present' came the sub-title 'Micky, David, Michael'. The album was in every respect a compilation, of three different acts. Which is not to say that it was worthless; the three had amassed enough experience for each to produce interesting and appealing music. In fact, 'The Monkees Present' is a fine late sixties American pop album, with tinges of country, rock, pop and jazz.

The second album as a trio.

Tommy Boyce and Bobby Hart contributed two more of their polished pop efforts. *Looking For The Good Times*, written for Paul Revere and the Raiders, was potentially a high quality hit single that was never given the chance to become one. *Ladies Aid Society* was a quirky little thing that featured a Salvation Army marching band snatched off the street. Both were sung by 'their boy' Davy, who took his other two vocals on Bill Chadwick's compositions *If I Knew* and *French Song*, which he co-produced. In this very democratic arrangement, Micky was also heard on four lead vocals: *Mommy and Daddy*, *Little Girl* and *Bye Bye Baby Bye Bye*, which he wrote and produced, and *Pillow Time* which he produced. Helped in the arrangement by Shorty Rogers, Micky turned out the best third of the album with his restrained, well sung commercial pop

songs. Mike twanged away with his down home boys on four of his own productions. *Listen To The Band* and *Good Clean Fun* had been heard on singles. *Never Tell a Woman Yes* was an overlong and very ordinary country plodder from his own pen. *Oklahoma Backroom Dancer* came from Michael Murphy, and though graced with nice honky tonk piano came over as a lacklustre workout.

During the second half of 1969 the trio undertook a number of irregular performances, mainly in two thousand seater clubs. Details of this period are sketchy, but apparently they did a few shows around Toronto and one in Mexico City. By this point Mike had accepted an offer by John Ware who was then drumming for Linda Ronstadt, to form a country rock band with John London and Orville 'Red' Rhodes. He gave his notice and was working out his time with the least possible good humour. What would appear to be the final Monkees concert took place in San Francisco, a scene of former glory, early in November. It was reviewed by the most unlikely of journals – *Rolling Stone* (forever referred to by Micky as Rolling Stain) – who prefaced the piece with the condescending qualification that reviewer Ed Ward 'surprisingly admits to having dug their *Last Train to Clarksville*.' Ward's review says about all there is to say about the dying moments of the Monkees: 'Oakland Coliseum is a big place; it holds 24,000 or 30,000 people plus ushers and program hawkers. Unlike a week earlier when the Stones had played, there were only 1,500 (my guess) or 2,000 (the guard's guess) people lost in the dim recesses of this huge plastic hall. Most of them seemed to be between ten and sixteen, although there were a goodly percentage of over twenties with slicked-back hair and Woolworth's bell-bottoms, and, as might be guessed, the parents.

They sat through some of the worst bands I've ever heard, some of whom played only two numbers, and they applauded them. These two Bossjox from KYA appeared on stage in between and tried to get the audience to applaud more, but they knew what they wanted and from time to time various sections erupted with cries of "Monkees". One of the Bossjox said, "The Monkees asked me if I thought San Francisco would still go for them, and I just said ho-ho-ho just wait and see."

'Finally it happened. Some cardboard music stands, just like the sax section had used in the high school dance band I'd played in, were set up. The word "Monkees" was apparent on the front of them. And out walked these six black guys, five of them in black tuxes, one in a purple tux – Tony and the Goodtimers, formerly backup band for Ike and Tina Turner.

'They played a tight, slick, professional, derivative rhythm and blues set. Tony did some lovable imitations of Otis Redding, some lovable soul routines – "Lemme hear you say "Yeah!" ", and some lovable introducing of the band, and then they left the stage, the lights went up, the tension mounted, the audience pleaded, the

Bossjox wasted time, the audience keened, the Bossjox wasted time, the audience shrieked, and suddenly, there they were. Micky, Davy and Mike.'

It was strange. Micky and Davy up there trying to do exactly what the band had just gotten through doing with infinitely more finesse (well professionalism anyway), and getting ten times the response. And Mike, up against the amp, trying to hide behind the band, back to the audience, tuning his guitar, which was inaudible during the entire concert.

In between were sandwiched little bits of comedy – imitation Smothers Brothers routines, Micky getting sent backstage for messing up a song and coming back wringing out a handkerchief and putting on a crybaby act. The audience was eating it up!

Mike Nesmith introduced *Listen To The Band* by saying 'I'm gonna sing this song, "cause that's what I'm getting paid to do"'. Davy Jones sang *For Once In My Life* and Micky Dolenz sang *Summertime* with considerable histrionic effort. By the time Nesmith did *Johnny B. Goode* I was thoroughly confused. They really did think they were doing an R 'n' B Show. And girls were *screeeaming* and rushing up to take pictures and being held back by security men and throwing beads and candy and notes and *screeeaming*. Somebody threw up a brightly coloured sign, which Dolenz picked up and showed to the audience. It said "We Still Love You".

Backstage Micky freely admitted, 'There'll be Monkee records in the future but they'll be done by Davy and me,' at the same time informing Ward of Nesmith's future plans. Davy repeated his aspiration to tackle Broadway shows; Micky said he was keen to move into film-making. After the interview the pair mingled freely with fans at the hotel, handing out scarves, cigarettes and personal oddments. Mike was nowhere to be found. After filming a Kool-Aid television commercial, his last contracted commitment, Mike was a free man, his decree nisi becoming official on 1 March, 1970, by which time he had almost completed the debut album by the First National Band and had apparently done a short stint with the Byrds as a pedal steel player.

Like Peter, Mike eventually reflected on his years as a Monkee with a mixture of pride and regret. 'Do me the gracious favour,' he asked *Zig Zag*'s John Tobler, 'of not pointing me out as the most talented Monkee. You see, you can't turn a sow's ear into a silk purse. David, Micky and Peter were very heavy cats. They were no dummies, there wasn't a dummy among them. I didn't get along with them, none of us got along, because we were all very different, but they weren't fools. Peter is a remarkably spiritual and good guy, a very heavy cat. David and Micky in their own ways are consummate professionals. They're dedicated artists, dedicated to their craft. They express themselves lucidly and with great poise and they are indeed very different. If you're in the company of somebody who's got heavy chops, just because he plays piano and you play saxophone, it

doesn't mean that somewhere along the line it can't work. In the case of the Monkees we weren't playing the same tune, in fact we weren't playing the same scale!'

There was no immediate announcement of Mike's departure. When Davy flew into London for Christmas 1969, he spoke at length about his own future and touched but briefly upon the Monkees. 'I've been sitting around the States doing nothing for two months,' he complained. 'I want to act again. We just did our last concert of the year as the Monkees and now we're free to do our own things. Micky and I are currently working on a screenplay for another television series, which would star just the two of us. Mike's not interested in the film end though, he wants to concentrate solely on recording. The three of us are under contract to Screen Gems for another two years yet. And this means we must do at least thirty-six concerts, four singles and four albums a year. Personally, I want to get my solo career worked out at the moment. While in Britain I'm looking out for people for a spectacular I'm getting together – a variety hour sort of thing with an audience. I've already got a coloured singer/pianist called Charlie Smalls and a group called Poco, who play great country and western type rock.'

With the two musicians in the group gone, the two actors were easy prey for the master manipulators – this time Jeff Barry who, with co-writers Andy Kim and Bobby Bloom, dished up an insipid serving of tired bubblegum and trite lovesongs. Ten of the twelve songs were recorded by producer Barry and engineer Mike Moran, the team responsible for the Archies and their assembly line recordings. Though the playing is competent, the songs of the ninth and final Monkees album 'Changes', sound empty, emotionless and banal, like the 'filler' songs on Archies albums. Though Don Kirschner's name is nowhere to be seen, the product bears his unmistakeable stamp. *Do You Feel It Too?* was

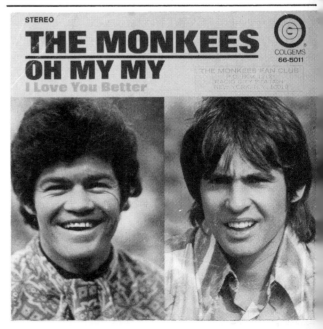

Mike debuted his First National Band at the Troubadour: 22 March 1970. Left to right: Red Rhodes, John London, John Ware and Mike.

simply a copy of a failed Andy Kim single. There were some better moments though. The single *Oh My My* was a chunky thumper with quality vocals. Dolenz composed and produced *Midnight Train* which was as good as his other cuts on the previous two albums. Boyce and Hart's *I Never Thought It Peculiar* is remembered by Tommy Boyce as one of his favoured works, though for a decade he was unaware of the Monkees version of it ever being released. It is the only track on the album for which musician credits are

available: Louie Shelton, Wayne Irwin and Boyce on guitars, Joe Osborne on Bass, Billy Lewis on drums, and Bobby Hart on keyboards. *Lady Jane* and *Do It In The Name Of Love*, album leftovers, were issued as a Bell label single in 1972 under the name of Dolenz and Jones.

With its almost pathetic cover of just two battered members, 'Changes' was, as *New Musical Express's* Alan Smith describes, 'A cheapskate epitaph, a cardboard tombstone.' Certainly, it was a tatty end for a group which, maligned and misunderstood far more than it deserved, brought a freshness and vitality to pop music just as it was being dragged under by dark forces which would come close to destroying all the charm it ever possessed. Delivered to Colgems to fulfil a contractual obligation, the LP gave birth to the industry joke that one of the dwindling group would eventually milk the well dry with an album titled 'The Monkee'.

There were occasional signs of life during 1970. On 22 March Micky, Davy and most of the old television crew got together at the Troubador to cheer on the debut performance by the First National Band. Mike whipped through a brisk set of hip country songs like *Smoke That Cigarette* and a bunch of new originals, giving the distinct impression of being absolutely in his element. A month later, Micky and sister Coco got up on the same stage with Peter for a twenty minute Hoot Night set, 'for old time's sake.' There was no formal announcement of disbandment. The two remaining Monkees just watched *Oh My My* and 'Changes' fall off the end of the pier, shook hands politely, and quietly walked out of each other's lives.

do i have to do this all over again?

Monkeemania left a permanent scar, of varying degrees, upon its protagonists. All four suffered broken marriages, and it took at least two years for each to recover physically from the enormous pressures that had beset them for more than three intense years. In 1973 Davy recalled that, 'After the show went off the air nobody wanted anything to do with us. One day we were so hot and the next day all the doors were shut and we were standing in the cold all alone.' Micky confirms that, 'The negative criticism affected us all. It wasn't until years later, when the television series was still being shown and the records were still selling that I was

brave enough to venture out of my house and say "Is anybody going to throw anything at me?" As an artist you try not to believe critics, but you do.'

Mike was the only one of the four to achieve any significant commercial and critical success in the immediate post-Monkee perod. The First National Band lasted no more than a year, but that year was highlighted by two sizeable international hits — *Joanne* and *Silver Moon*. There were also two albums issued during 1970, 'Magnetic South' and 'Loose Salute'; which were poor sellers despite good reviews received from the 'serious' rock press. No less an authority than *Rolling*

The original First National Band, (left to right) John London, Red Rhodes, Mike Nesmith and John Ware.

Mike during sessions for his third solo album, 'Nevada Fighter'.

Stone decreed, 'Mike Nesmith? Well, hang onto your wool hats cats and kitties, because this album is *good...* Mike's straightforward, no bull-shit vocals are a welcome change from the usual Byrds-y constipated singing style generally preferred by country hippie bands. I have never considered myself a real Monkees fan but I think "Loose Salute" is one of the hippest country-rock albums in some time, certainly the most listenable. Mike Nesmith? Well, why the hell not?'

In September 1970 the First National Band toured England and Europe, where a sizeable, critic-led cult following had emerged. The group broke up during the recording of the 'Nevada Fighter' album in 1971 and extra players were called in to finish it. The project was notable for a modification of Nesmith's obsessive country music interest and the infiltration of eccentric and often aggressive songs which would characterise some of his later work. After writing virtually all of the first two albums, he drew material for this album primarily from Monkee-era writers such as Harry Nilsson, Murphy and Castleman, Lewis and Clarke, along with Eric Clapton and Red Rhodes.

The Second National Band lasted for just one album in 1972, the erratic and indulgent 'Tantamount To Treason Volume 1'. The unit comprised of bassist Johnny Meeks (ex Gene Vincent's Blue Caps), keyboards and synthesizer player Michael Cohen, drummer Jack Ranelli and pedal steel guitarist Red Rhodes. After the commercial and critical failure of the album, Mike recorded 'And The Hits Just Keep On Coming' with just himself and Rhodes. A curiously compelling and melodic exercise, it presented interesting new versions of two songs from Mike's Troubadour-era, *Different Drum* and *Two Different Roads*. During the early seventies, Mike is reputed to have cut some tracks with the Nitty Gritty Dirt Band, under producer Mac

Gayden, assuming the collective identity of the Aspen Falls Musical Preservation Society. Apparently United Artists chose not to release the material.

1973 saw the formation of Nesmith's own Countryside label which was financed by Elektra Records. The initial concept was to establish a studio with a house band and run it as a country version of the Stax/Volt style of operation. However, only two albums were ever issued on Countryside — 'Pure Country' by bar picker Garland Frady and 'Velvet Hammer In A Country Band' by Red Rhodes. Ian Matthews' 'Valley Hi' was issued by Elektra, though Matthews disclaims it to this day as being more Mike Nesmith's album than his own. It featured the short-lived Countryside house band of Billy Graham (bass and fiddle), Danny Lane (drums), Jay Lacy, Bobby Warford and Mike Nesmith (guitars), Red Rhodes (pedal steel and dobro) and David Barry (piano). They also played on the final RCA Nesmith LP, 'Pretty Much Your Standard Ranch Stash', which featured an entire second side of traditional country music. Countryside Records ceased to exist in 1974 when wonderboy David Geffen took over at Elektra. Mike returned to live performancing with Red Rhodes, when he accepted an offer to headline at *Zig Zag's* Anniversary Concert at the London Roundhouse. Asked about the Monkees during the visit, he stated sharply, 'I've seen no-one from the Monkees, I have nothing to do with anyone from the Monkees, I never talk to anyone from the Monkees.' While in London he produced demos for the pub band Chilli Willi and the Red Hot Peppers, which were apparently so bizarre that they almost broke up the group. During this trip, Mike also produced Bert Jansch's dark, brooding 'L.A. Turnaround' album, and received a BMI songwriting award for *I Never Loved Anyone More*, which he had written with Linda Hargrove.

Following the demise of Countryside, Mike established his own Pacific Arts Corporation label and introduced it with a boxed set entitled 'The Prison' which contained a single disc and a lavish sixty-five page book, with text in both English and French. Billed as a 'Book with a sound-track' the release had merit as a piece of contemporary art, but the point was somehow lost in distributing it as a rock record. The engaging, intense and ponderously serious music was highly regarded by loyal critics, but it nevertheless sold poorly.

From his years as a Monkee, Mike had developed an incredible passion for film and visual arts. With the freedom of having his own company he was able to pursue that interest by experimenting with the then new medium of creative video. During 1976 he spent $22,000 on the production of a promotional clip for his new single, *Rio*. A long and truly off-the-wall opus, the song became a huge hit in Australia and a moderate hit in England, almost solely on the basis of the stunning promotional clip. *Rio* was the opening track of 'From A Radio Engine To The Photon Wing', Nesmith's eighth album and the first not to feature Red Rhodes. It was recorded in Nashville with the likes of Weldon Myrick,

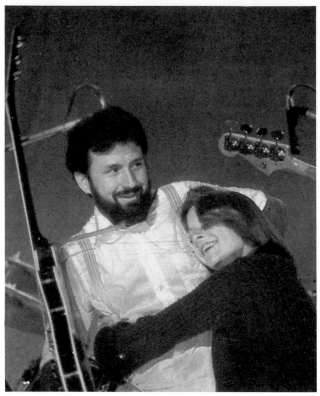

Some Australian fans tried to repeat the hysteria of peak period Monkeemania.

David Briggs and Lonnie Mack. However, it became clear that Mike's acceptance in Nashville was strained to say the least when the band flatly refused to record *Navajo Trail*, without offering a reason. 'I'm not a popular man,' he admits. 'I was once criticised for writing a song with the word "impelled" in it, c'mon man! What he didn't know was that I have written songs with words like "bereft", "preclude" and "prism".'

On the basis of his top ten Australian hit with *Rio*, Mike toured Australia in November 1977 with a tight band that included John Ware from the First National Band, Al Perkins from Manassas, David McKay and James Trumbo. The Melbourne concert was captured for a live album the following year, 'Live At The Palais', highlighted by a storming encore of Chuck Berry's *Nadine* and a powerful version of his alienation anthem *The Grand Ennui*.

'Infinite Rider On the Big Dogma', his 1979 album, presented Michael Nesmith as a hard rocker. It was well reviewed internationally and it sold over 40,000 units in America, considerably more than all of its predecessors. It also marked, for the time being at least, Mike's departure from music and the beginning of his exclusive involvement in video production. His 1980 *Popclips* television show introduced the regular screening of rock films and videos to American network television and led to him producing clips for Kim Carnes and providing rock clips for ABC-TV's *Fridays show*. His first long-

form production, *Elephant Parts*, won the first Grammy ever awarded for video, in 1982. It also earned him some glowing reviews, including one by David Crook in the Los Angeles Times which stated, 'It is glitzy, flashy, a gaudy display of the flesh and sequins and irreverence shining in the rock'n'roll borealis. Nesmith has emerged as one of the principal philosophers and entrepreneurs of the new wave of video.' Brendon Tartikoff, NBC Television's programming chief, was also greatly impressed and invited Nesmith to produce a series of half-hour comedy shows under the title of *Michael Nesmith In Television Parts*. Typical of the style is one sequence in which comic Martin Mull lectures on domestic safety procedures, such as what to do if your house is struck by an iceberg.

In 1979, Bette Nesmith sold her patent for Liquid Paper to the Gilette Corporation for $47 million. She died in the following year, leaving Michael as her sole heir. 'You don't go from five zeros to seven zeros without some changes' he admitted. 'Now there's more to do and manage, and also a certain amount of freedom that comes with it.'

The inheritance would appear to have financed the massive expansion of the Pacific Arts operations. *Elephant Parts* and *Timerider* (which he wrote and scored) were followed by the highly-acclaimed, ultra-contemporary film *Repo Man*, and in 1986 Nesmith announced the formation of a new company, Pacific Arts Pictures, to produce five feature films a year. First into production was *Square Dance* with Rob Lowe and Jason Robards, followed by *Tapeheads*, the story of two high school kids who stumble into directing rock videos. Like everything he has ever done, Mike takes video *very* seriously. He once told *Billboard*, 'To me it's the single most important event in the history of the rock'n'roll music industry — bigger than the Sun recordings of Elvis. There is only one segment of the entertainment business that will understand what a video record is — the record business. The record business understands retail sales and that's where all this is going.'

Mike divorced Phylliss in the mid-seventies and is now married to the very able Kathryn Nesmith, who also undertakes his management and zealously protects him from enthusiastic (female) fans. Always intelligent, he seems to have become impressively articulate over the past few years. He now appears to be a little more comfortable with his Monkee past, recently telling an interviewer, 'It was a tremendous training ground, a positive experience, and people who don't see it as such are missing the point.' However, Mike's recollections of the Monkees tend to be tailored to suit and are, accordingly, the least reliable of all.

☆ ☆ ☆ ☆ ☆ ☆ ☆ ☆ ☆ ☆ ☆ ☆ ☆ ☆ ☆ ☆

For an artist as versatile and confident as Davy Jones, the relative failure of his post-Monkees activities is puzzling. Immediately after the split he set up a New York street market called 'The Street', which cost him

$40,000. He also collaborated with his new musical director, Doug Trevor, on a one hour television special *Pop Goes Davy*, featuring new sensations the Jackson Five and the Osmonds.

Bell Records, then successful with *The Partridge Family*, signed Davy to a very inflexible solo recording deal in 1971. They picked the songs and hired Bobby Sherman's producer, Jackie Mills. Davy's second solo album, resulting from this deal, was without any real direction or style; just a bunch of simple ditties thrown together to cash in on whatever vestiges of appeal remained. Bell was probably far more interested in the recording career of David Cassidy at the time. However, the first Bell single, *Rainy Jane*, charted quite respectably at fifty-two, although the follow-up, *I Really Love You*, expired at 107. Single three, *Girl*, did not chart at all, and the fourth and final Bell single, *Road To Love*, was another flop.

For all his cocky predictions to the press about his future plans, Davy fell into a directionless heap when left to his own devices. Doug Trevor, who stayed with him for about three years recalls that 'We put together a band with B.J. Smith on bass, Dennis Larden on lead guitar, myself on rhythm and Lindy Getz on drums. We played a few Army base concerts in England and then went over to California for a charity show at the L.A. Forum and an appearance on the *Merv Griffin Show*. Davy and I also did a disastrous tour of Ireland, backed by a band called Harmony Grass. There wasn't much money around and Davy didn't have a lot left from the Monkees. He'd never been properly advised on how to invest his earnings. There were two small Japanese tours in 1972, in July and December. Although there were a lot of screaming kids at the airport, we never

The second of three Davy Jones solo albums, 1971.

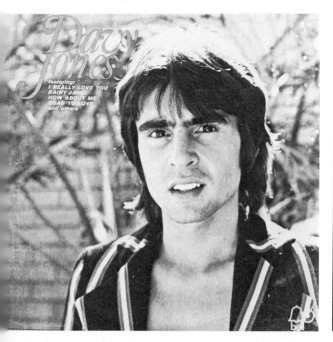

really played to them. We just did some Army bases and small clubs, and made a few supermarket appearances. Davy went back to Japan a few times after I left him, but only for celebrity tennis matches and stuff like that.'

Davy switched from Bell to MGM in 1973 and recorded two singles. His version of Peter Skellern's *You're A Lady* (in both English and Japanese) was beaten to the charts by the writer's own. Alan O'Day's *Rubberene* was another dose of the turgid British Music Hall style gunk which Davy has such a passion for. MGM let Davy go after both singles flopped and he resorted to occasional theatre engagements to pay the rent. He also appeared on an episode of Disneyland called *The Bluegrass Special*, as well as undertaking guest spots on *The Brady Bunch* and *Love American Style*.

In 1975 all four Monkees met at Davy's house to discuss the possibility of a reunion for concerts and a McDonald's television commercial. Mike would only participate if the deal included a feature film and Peter as a vegetarian was not prepared to do the advertisement. Only Micky and Davy were interested in working together again and so accepted an offer from entrepreneur Tony Ricco to tour American ballparks and fairgrounds. Tommy Boyce and Bobby Hart, bored out of their wits opening for Zsa Zsa Gabor in Las Vegas, were offered the roles of the other two hesitant Monkees to make the package into a nice saleable quartet. Young Texan guitarist Keith Allison, a former member of Paul Revere and the Raiders, was engaged as leader of the band which, in the studio, included Chip Douglas, Neil Norman, Jerry Yester and Louis Shelton.

The Golden Great Hits of The Monkees Show — The Guys Who Wrote 'Em And The Guys Who Sang 'Em did exceptional business across America during 1975 and 1976, drawing up to 22,000 kids at amusement parks such as Disneyland and Magic Mountain. Signed to Capitol by Al Coury (just a week before he moved over to RSO), the outfit cut one reasonable album that was mercilessly outsold by an Arista reissue of a scant 'Greatest Hits' package which charted at number fifty-eight. Two singles, *I Remember The Feeling* and *I Love You (And I'm Glad That I Said It)*, both written by Boyce and Hart, failed to reproduce the act's live popularity in the charts. Micky devised, scripted and directed a fairly dire thirty minute video production called *The Golden Great Hits Of The Monkees Show*, which pops up occasionally in video catalogues. Capitol in Japan taped a Japanese tour by the act and issued a posthumous live album in 1981.

Boyce and Hart eventually tired of, in their own words, 'The road and jailbait' and the outfit dissolved. However, the collaborations continued. Peter had joined them on stage at Disneyland during Bi-Centennial Week in 1976. He was handed a bass and a microphone to join in on *Last Train To Clarksville* and *Theme From The Monkees*. Strangely, he claimed then that he had never been asked to join the half-reformed

The 'posthumous' live DJB&H album, never released outside Japan.

group and probably would have if the opportunity had arisen.

Davy, Micky and Peter were herded into the studio at the end of 1976 by producer Chip Douglas to record a Christmas single, his own *Christmas Is My Time Of Year*. Davy had begun to record a rough version of the song with Douglas in Micky's home studio and, inevitably, Dolenz joined in on harmonies. As Davy recalls, 'Chip hears us and says, "Ah, another five million records!" thinking of *Daydream Believer*. He hadn't been in the studio for five years, he'd been living off his royalties too. Chip suggested we call it a Monkees record so we called up Peter and told him he could throw in a couple of Auntie Grizelda's in the middle. Then we got the original Monkees record drummer Eddie Hoe to help out. It was getting to be a real family thing so we rang Mike and asked him if he wanted his name on it. He didn't, so it just went out to the kids in the fan club.'

Davy continued to work with Micky. Their new *Micky Dolenz and Davy Jones Show* debuted at Hollywood's Starwood Club in March 1977. Not surprisingly, Peter Tork joined in on banjo for a few songs. During 1977 the pair appeared as Tom Sawyer (Davy) and Huck Finn (Micky) for a season in a Sacramento theatre. In June they made a Telethon appearance in the Australian city of Perth, where the fan response was so frenzied that the studio walls were almost pushed down in the crush.

A chance meeting with Harry Nilsson, while Davy was adding back-up vocals to a commercial for Simple Life suits that Ringo Starr was making for Japanese television, led to Jones being offered the role of Oblio in the British stage production of Nilsson's *The Point*. At Davy's insistence a role was also found for Micky (as the

Count's Kid and the Leafman) and the two set off for London in 1978. *The Point* had a highly successful run and spawned a soundtrack album, featuring Dolenz and Jones.

After *The Point* Davy obtained a divorce from Linda Haines, with whom he had two children, Talia Elizabeth and Sarah Lee. Early in 1982 he married playboy bunny Anita Pollinger and his third daughter, Jessica, was born. His work after that was rather patchy. He played in a pantomime of *Jack And The Beanstalk*, starred in a British television mini-series, *Horse In The House*, hosted the *American Hot City Disco* television show and undertook a guest role on *The Love Boat*.

Since late 1979 Davy has worked sporadically with a band called Toast with Peter Doyle and Arlan Green of the New Seekers. He wrote a book with Arlan Green called *They Made A Monkee Out of Me*, which has yet to see publication.

The saving factor of Davy Jones' very shaky career has been his always-loyal market in Japan. The fortuitous use of *Daydream Believer* in a Japanese television commercial for Kodak in 1980 sparked off an unbeliev-

In 1982 Davy married his second wife, former Playboy Bunny Anita Pollinger.

able revival of Monkeemania. The first seven albums were reissued there, along with various repackagings which all sold in the hundreds of thousands. In one eighteen month period, from mid 1981 to late 1982, Davy toured Japan on five occasions. 'I got a call out of the blue,' relates Doug Trevor, 'asking me to be musical director for a Japanese tour. We went there in March '81 and played 3,000 seater auditoriums with a Japanese band and the response was unbelievable — just like the Monkees at their peak. It was so successful that we went back in June, September, December and the following March. Every visit was amazing; thousands of screamers at the airport, fans waiting outside the hotel, the whole thing.'

Davy was signed by Japan Records and managed to crack the charts with a number of singles, including *It's Now*, *Dance Gypsy* and *Sixteen*. The label issued a live

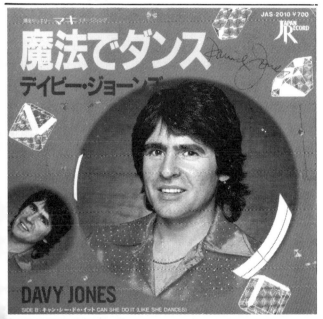

album, comprised almost entirely of reworked Monkees' hits, titled 'Davy Hello'. It was his first solo album since 1971. In February 1982 Davy joined Tommy Boyce on stage at P.J's in New York and was so buoyed up by the response that he repeated the guest spot over the next three nights. He then returned to England, where he now resides, for a *Coronation Street* 'Old boys night'. A racehorse owner and trainer in his non-performing hours, Jones attempted the occasional return to riding. He once came fifth on his mount El Cito at Brighton and later rode before the Royal Family at Epsom.

For almost five years, Davy subsisted on a varied schedule of minor appearances and projects. A regular guest on British television and radio chat shows, he also hosted episodes of the TV shows *Puzzle Trail* and *Pop Quiz*; starred in stage pantomimes *Cinderella* and *Puss 'n Boots*; portrayed Jesus in a season of *Godspell*; appeared at benefit shows for the Society for the Prevention of Cruelty to Children; ran in the London

Marathon and played seasons at swank English country clubs; such as Lakeside in Surrey.

In 1984 Davy undertook the first of three passages to New York on the cruise liner Queen Elizabeth II, as an on-board entertainer. Upon arrival in the Big Apple, he appeared on *Hello America*, *Good Morning America* and, Peter Tork's favourite outlet, *Uncle Floyd's Show*.

✩ ✩ ✩ ✩ ✩ ✩ ✩ ✩ ✩ ✩ ✩ ✩ ✩ ✩ ✩ ✩

As Micky had predicted, there were few television openings for characters as powerful as the Monkees. George Reeves, television's *Superman*, had committed suicide in the same state of despair that the Monkee now found himself. Almost out of necessity, he turned his full attentions to music and signed a recording contract with MGM. His first single, *Easy On You/Oh Someone*, was recorded in his own home studio. The B-side was written by David Price and co-arranged by Peter Tork. This was followed by a fine version of Randy Newman's *A Lover's Prayer*, which the radio stations had absolutely no right to refuse to play. Sadly, although MGM had signed Micky with great enthusiasm and high hopes, the company tucked him away in a corner and seemed to forget about him.

1973 saw two Micky Dolenz singles on the independent Romar label. *Daybreak* was written and produced by Harry Nilsson, who also appeared in the promotional film. Nilsson and Dolenz, who had remained friends since *Cuddly Toy*, hung out together a great deal during the early seventies and Micky sometimes went along on Harry and John Lennon's legendary crazed bar crawls. After a second Romar single, the unsuccessful *Buddy Holly Tribute*, Micky worked with teen idol studio svengali Michael Lloyd, in a group called Starship. Although they are believed to have recorded a considerable amount, only one single was released, *Johnny B. Goode/It's Amazing To Me*. A second single, reputed to have been *Where Did All The Good Times Go?*, was apparently cancelled just prior to release.

After one despairing failure after another with records, Micky diverted his energies back into television and film. He auditioned for the role of the Fonz in *Happy Days* and then picked up voice roles in the

Jones, Dolenz, Boyce and Hart, circa 1975.

cartoon series *Scooby Doo, Where Are You?* and *Funky Phantom*. A variety of 'bit' parts included *Adam 12* and *My Three Sons* on television and the films *Linda Lovelace For President* and *The Night Strangler*. In Chicago he played a straight dramatic stage role in *Remains To Be Seen*. In between these diverse assignments he established a small production company for television commercials.

Micky didn't need much convincing to join in on the Dolenz, Jones, Boyce and Hart venture. 'I'm no fool,' he said, 'you can make a lot of money on the road.' But he was also far from disappointed when it came to a natural end; 'We were playing Las Vegas and I found myself looking at an audience of losers. I realised they're the only people who watch the shows in Las Vegas.'

Seven years after their storybook marriage, Micky and Samantha were divorced. This coincided with Micky's emergence in Hollywood as a 'face about the place.' He was photographed with John Lennon, seen at Swan Song Records' opening celebrations with Groucho Marx, at Keith Moon's birthday party and at the opening of Alice Cooper's Beverly Hills restaurant in 1976. Micky and Davy even accepted offers to compete in celebrity tennis tournaments, where Micky would entertain the crowds with his tightrope walking stunts. During a visit to Chicago he met another English beauty, Tina Drew, who became the second Mrs Dolenz, with whom he had three more daughters, Charlotte, Emily and Georgia.

Micky had participated eagerly in the Dolenz, Jones, Boyce and Hart exercise, the Christmas single and *The Point* but was adamant that his future lay in a serious career as a television and film producer/director. In 1977 he was handed an assignment to direct a BBC show called *Premiere*. 'It was an incredible opportunity and I've never looked back.' In 1979 he settled permanently in London and, just to keep his hand in, signed a recording contract with Chrysalis Records, the sole product of which was a solitary single of Bob McDill's *Lovelight*, backed with his own *Alicia*.

Since 1979, Micky has earned a great deal of respect for his visual production work. He has directed plays for the BBC, including *Story Without A Hero*, an ITV show called *Pop Gospel*, a documentary on the advertising industry called *The Persuaders*, rock videos for Virgin Records, a television advertisement for Lulu, a short film called *Gateway To The South* and a one week theatre run of Stephen Sondheim's *Company* for charity. By far his most well-received effort has been directing a Monty Python television film called *Buchanan's Finest Hour* later entitled *The Box*, written by Michael Palin and Terry Gilliam.

His most recent projects include a television series called *Metal Micky*, a million dollar West End stage production of Bugsy Malone, a children's television series called *Junior Classics* which were adaptations of *Treasure Island* etc, and a six-episode science fiction series called *Luna*, based on his own original story.

Micky refused an offer from Davy and Peter to join them for a 'reunion' tour, claiming that his new career was so successful that he no longer had to rely on his Monkee legacy to survive. To date he has been responsible for more than sixty British television productions and obviously has a rewarding career, for as long as he wishes to pursue it, in the most demanding and distinctive television industry in the world.

✩ ✩ ✩ ✩ ✩ ✩ ✩ ✩ ✩ ✩ ✩ ✩ ✩ ✩ ✩ ✩ ✩

Release: (left to right) Judy Myhan, Reine Stewart, Peter Tork and Riley Wyldeflower.

Peter's post-Monkees saga was pathetically predictable. All the grandiose aims expressed at the time of his departure from the group withered and died in a stoned stupor. His group, *Release* — featuring Reine Stewart on drums, Riley Wyldflower on bass, Judy Myham on keyboards and vocals, and Peter on guitar — had a fan club, lots of smiling faces in the fan magazines, but no idea of what they were doing. When record company executives came to the Tork mansion to talk business, they would be confronted by scores of naked hippies disrupting discussions with absurd noises and offensive acts. The group endured for about a year, with just a few unannounced bar gigs and a bunch of 'basement tapes'. They did tender a song for the *Easy Rider* soundtrack, but its fate was similar to everything else Peter was associated with at the time. Peter recalls that, 'We played it to Bert Schneider, Dennis Hopper and Peter Fonda and they loved it! But they went with Roger McGuinn and Bob Dylan. Ours was a much better song; ... we could have gone somewhere if we'd stuck to it. Everyone knew it wasn't just *any* garage band. It was a high priced garage band, I still perform one of Riley's songs, *Good Looker*, in my solo set to this day. But Judy just wasn't into success.'

During his first year away from the Monkees, Peter opened a New York soup kitchen and threw open his house to every freeloader in Hollywood. These 'guests' made home movies of their poolside orgies, fed and intoxicated themselves, and removed a good many objects of value from the premises. When Peter's money was siphoned off completely, he sold his house to Stephen Stills and moved into a $25 a month basement room in David Crosby's house, with a pregnant Reine Stewart. A daughter, Hallie Elizabeth, was born on 25 January, 1970. Peter and Reine ended their relationship soon after.

By 1972 Peter was at rock bottom. Drifting across America, he was caught with three dollars worth of hash in El Paso, Texas, and sentenced to four months in the El Reno Federal Penitentiary in Oklahoma. This was not long after some local courts in the south were handing out thirty year jail terms to long-hairs found in possession of a single joint. 'Fortunately I was nabbed by the Feds,' he reveals 'and I was sent to a youth prison where twenty five was the maximum age and fifteen years the maximum term. I was not actually sentenced. I was committed for examination under a federal statute. The final outcome was that I have no criminal record and may legally represent that I have never been arrested or sentenced.' Doug Trevor remembers seeing a photo of the prison band with Peter in work clothes, picking guitar with 'A twelve foot black guy and a few weasels.' Peter is far from bitter about the experience. 'They lined the walls the first morning I went to breakfast but that didn't last. It was not the worst thing that ever happened to me.'

After his release, Peter pulled his life back together and moved back to Southern California, where he took out an unsuccessful law suit against Columbia Pictures for $13 million, claiming that he was owned $8 million

Peter Tork and girlfriend Reine Stewart in an advanced state of hippiedom.

in unpaid royalties. While that was stewing he became one of the thirty-five voices in the Fairfax Street Choir and played guitar for a non-recording group called Osciola. He then took up teaching posts (Social Studies and English) at Pacific Hills School in Santa Monica, California, and a private school in Venice, California. 'I consider myself a professional has-been,' he candidly told *National Enquirer*. 'When I was with the Monkees we used to reach millions of people every day. Now I just reach a handful each week and the satisfaction is much greater.' With his new stability came a new girlfriend, teacher Barbara Iannoli, who became his wife and bore him a son, Ivan. 'There I was,' he recalls, 'a married father of two with a nice square teaching career, coaching volley ball and basketball.'

Inevitably the academic world could not hold him for long. After guesting on stage a couple of times with Davy and Micky, Peter began to take a little more

advantage of his past status. In July 1977 he played a few solo performances at New York's punk palace CBGB's. Accompanying himself on guitar and piano he worked his way through *Pleasant Valley Sunday, I'll Spend My Life With You*, some Jimmy Cliff numbers and a snatch of Bach's Prelude from *The Well Tempered Clavier*. The response was enormous and *Variety* magazine reviewed him in the 'New Acts' column. In one of a spate of fanzine interviews at the time he explained his situation in the early seventies: 'To the outside observer I'm sure it looked as though I had succumbed to the extremities of a given culture. To me, I simply exhibited moderate good sense. Basically, I lived at poverty level, scratching for odd jobs. I wore a beard, my hair was past my shoulders and I was working in a restaurant singing folk songs and waiting tables… I tried to make some demos but it didn't go anywhere. The mass media has a tendency to distort. Its way of thinking is a picture of Peter Tork as a burned-out hippie, a hopeless case who can't lift his hand to his face to use a razor and who has no interests except stealing to support his drug habit. It's what sells, so they print it. The truth of the matter is, my primary concern was and is self-realisation in a social setting.'

By late 1978 Peter's musical comeback had only got him as far as a singing waiter job at the American Food and Beverage Company on La Cieniga Boulevarde in Hollywood. From 1979 to 1981 Peter worked sporadically with a number of bands including Cotton Mouth, and The Back Street Boys; his vocals were as flat and limited as ever. He also began appearing on the popular *Uncle Floyd TV Show*, once announcing that the Monkees would reunite for the Emmy Awards ceremony in September, 1980. In the same year Peter did some demos for Sire Records, which included the tracks *Good Looker* and *Lady's Baby*. During 1981 Peter

assembled the New Monks (Vince Barranco on drums, Phil Simon on guitar, Nelson Bogart on guitar and trumpet and Phil Ill on bass), and in November toured Japan with some reports suggesting a bigger airport welcome than even Davy has been afforded. They released one single, an update of *Stepping Stone*, with the B-side Jackie Wilson's *Higher and Higher*. This was Peter's first official record product since 1968.

Like Davy, Peter has spoken of writing a book to 'expose' the whole Monkee story. However, the shelves remain bare.

The grey cloud that hovered over the Monkees began to dissolve toward the end of the seventies. Suddenly they were 'hip' and 'cool' all over again. Their original albums began to fetch up to $70 in auctions, a new generation of fans gathered together at 'Monkee Meets' to sell T-shirts and swap memorabilia, and some quality repackagings of their recordings began to appear. From Australia came the forty-track 'Monkeemania' album, stuffed full of hits, misses, rare mixes, foreign language recordings and unreleased songs, concert tracks and other delights. Its export sales were truly enormous. In 1982, America's Rhino Records issued a fascinating picture-disc album of tracks deemed 'rare' Stateside. The label then set about re-issuing all nine original albums each in its original jacket except for the 'Head' soundtrack. 'Monkeeshines', a superbly packaged bootleg of impressive audio quality also hit the market and was eagerly snapped up by fans who had been burned by a number of appalling-quality multiple-disc bootlegs emanating from Hawaii. The twenty-seven tracks (some less than a minute in duration) drew together most of the available rarities, including the 1976 Christmas single *Mustang*, Mike's *All the King's Horses* and Peter's *Tear The Top Right Off My Head* and *Lady's Baby*, and Davy's *Her Name Is Love*. Monkee fan clubs, fanzines and newsletters have been circulating around the world

since about 1975. They dutifully inform the devoted of the latest developments in each Monkee's life, no matter how trivial.

Of the great many major figures involved with the Monkees project, there is no doubt that it is the non-music participants who have used it best as a springboard. Bob Rafelson and Bert Schneider blossomed into remarkable film-makers, their collective and individual credits including *Easy Rider*, *Five Easy Pieces*, *The King of Marvin Gardens*, *Drive, He Said*, *The Postman Always Rings Twice* and *A Safe Place*. Jack Nicholson remained closely aligned with the pair, while pursuing his hugely successful independent career as an actor winning an Oscar for his performance in *One Flew Over The Cuckoo's Nest*, in 1975. Paul Mazursky achieved even more impressive successes than the Raybert team. With Larry Tucker he scripted *I Love You Alice B. Toklas*, *Bob And Carol And Ted And Alice*, and *Alex In Wonderland*, directing the last two. Mazursky really hit his stride as a writer and director with *Blume In Love* in 1973, followed by *Harry And Tonto*, *Next Stop Greenwich Village*, *An Unmarried Woman*, *Willie and Phil*, *Tempest* and *Moscow On The Hudson*.

Don Kirshner's power in the music industry was not diminished at all by his forced departure from the Monkees project and Colgems Records. In 1969 he devised a foolproof method of stopping musicians from rebelling against his iron rule by creating the Archies, and laughed all the way to the bank as *Sugar Sugar* became one of the biggest selling singles in history. This project followed a disastrous attempt in 1968 to duplicate the Monkees formula with a group called Toomorrow which included a pretty young Australian singer called Olivia Newton-John. Although they made a feature film and a number of singles for Decca, the project came to naught. However, there were successes, and quite substantial ones. In 1978 he discovered the group Kansas, signed them to his own Kirshner label and sold millions of albums, six months ahead of the equally bland hard-rock band Boston. *Don Kirshner's Rock Concert* rated highly on American network television for many years.

Tony Basil, the *Head* choreographer and dancer, carved diverse swathes through the next fifteen years, appearing in films, choreographing David Bowie's *Diamond Dogs* tour, some of Bette Midler's sleazy extravaganzas, and notching up an international Number One hit in 1982/3 with *Micky*. Songwriters Harry Nilsson, Paul Williams, David Gates, Michael Murphy, Carole Bayer-Sager and Neil Diamond all surfaced strongly in the seventies, establishing independent performance careers which ranged from the achievement of superstardom to solid respect.

Lester Sill is now the senior executive of Screen Gems/Columbia Music. Samantha Juste is a partner in a leading Los Angeles public relations firm. Harvey Kubernick was the American West Coast Correspondent for England's *Melody Maker*. Doug Trevor, with Paul O'Gorman, won the 1977 Tokyo song festival.

The fortunes of Tommy Boyce and Bobby Hart seem inextricably entwined with those of the Monkees, or at least two of them. After the demise of the most lucrative outlet for their songs, the pair settled into a comfortable songwriting niche, often working with other partners. Bobby Hart paid his bills with *Keep On Singing*, recorded by Helen Reddy and Austin Roberts. Tommy Boyce recorded an album in 1973 under the alias of Christopher Cloud, wrote a book called *How To Write A Hit Record And Sell It*, and created the concept album 'The Willie Burgundy Five' with writer Melvin Powers. Following the demise of Dolenz, Jones, Boyce and Hart, Boyce became primarily involved in record production in London, generating hits for Showaddywaddy, the Darts, the Pleasers and Matchbox. He formed the short-lived Tommy Band and recorded one single for RCA, a remake of *I Wonder What She's Doing Tonight*. During a month-long stay in Australia in 1981 he licensed a four-track twelve-inch EP to an obscure television marketing record company. Unfortunately the company went bankrupt a few months later and 'Tommy Boyce and His Rockin' 60's Band' never made it onto the general marketplace. After Australia he went to New York to produce three tracks on Iggy Pop's 'Party' album. Hart, in the meantime, had recorded 'The First Bobby Hart Solo Album' the release of which seems to have been restricted to a handful of European territories.

A four track Monkees EP, issued on Arista in England early in 1980, swept into the singles chart in acknowledgement of the new wave of popularity for the defunct group that had been evident since Dolenz, Jones, Boyce and Hart brought it back to general attention. Soon after, the Japanese Monkees explosion occurred and reissues began appearing all over the world — much to the disgust of a number of 'auction list pirates.'

International interest in the group was continually revived by reruns of the television series, which generated armies of new young fans every year. As a social document of its era, The Monkees is a precious artefact, but like the perpetual popularity of the Marx Brothers, Abbot and Costello, Charlie Chaplin and Monty Python, there is an aspect of Monkees humour that has proved timeless.

Monkee music, given the benefit of a twenty year perspective, comes over in the eighties with a vibrant buoyancy, far from the mindless pop its detractors claimed it to be. In the vast spectrum of thirty years of rock'n'roll, the Monkees hold an elevated position.

postscript...

During 1985 the first signs of a substantial international Monkee revival began to appear. The twentieth anniversary of the group's first entry into the American charts was approaching and, as demonstrated by the exuberant festivities for the refurbished Statue Of Liberty in July 1986, Americans love nothing more than a convenient anniversary to justify a round of celebrations.

In May 1986, Davy Jones and Peter Tork undertook a low-key tour of Australian pubs and clubs, delivering a set comprised primarily of Monkee hits. Every date was jammed not only with teary-eyed original and faithful female fans who almost dissolved when Davy sang *Daydream Believer* and crooned through *I Wanna Be Free*, but wildly enthusiastic teenagers who appeared to sing along with the lyrics of every number. Each show was laced with the slapstick lunacy that the audience would have recognised from the television series, which had been rerun in Australia over the previous two years.

'It's like the sixties again' Tork observed with honest surprise after the first week of shows. 'Last night a girl came walking onto the stage like there was nobody else in the room and wrapped her arms around Davy. Then the kids invaded the stage; they screamed, they pleaded, they flung themselves at us.'

Tork was in uncommonly good form throughout the tour. He seemed to have come to grips with the Monkees' place in history and gave his all to a series of remarkably entertaining performances. Faced with a

fairly limited repertoire of original Monkee tracks on which he had sung lead, he mugged his way through *Auntie Grizelda* and *Gonna Buy Me A Dog*, plucked his sixties concert stalwart *Cripple Creek* on banjo and blended his voice with Davy's to provide passable renditions of many Dolenz-sung hits. Offstage, he was more than prepared to discuss the Monkees at length and to drop a few tasty titbits, such as the revelation that Plas Johnson played the honking saxophone on *Goin' Down*; that Davy was the Monkee who fed hash to the kangaroos during a headline-grabbing visit to an Australian nature park in 1968; that he had introduced John Lennon to the pot-LSD psychedelic STP at London's Speakeasy Club; and that Nesmith wrote the horn and cello parts and Tork the Bach-like opening on *Shades Of Grey*.

'I don't think anyone should take the Monkees too seriously,' he offered in Sydney, 'We would have suffered less criticism if we'd pretended to be a fake from the start and made a big joke of it; like recording *We're Only In It For The Money* on the second album or something. When we got the first lot of clippings back from the interviews we gave when we arrived in Australia, it looked to us amazingly like it didn't matter what we said, they were going to see us the way they always have. The bulk of it was the same old stuff — the Monkees aren't any more talented now than they were twenty years ago. All that matters less to me now. Bad press doesn't keep people away in droves. People come to see us because of how they feel, not what they've read.'

Tork's change of heart as regards the Monkees was gracefully explained. 'I look up and see that this is my life. My only serious acquired skill is that of an entertainer. I did disassociate myself for many years because of a misplaced idealism. I was buying all that stuff about the Monkees not being musicians or real human beings. Back then I was entirely too malleable. I now do not have the remotest idea why I did many of the things I did. In recent times I have had to grunt, groan and strain to become a genuine businessman and take control of my career. The ultimate responsibility lies with me and I have recently agreed with God to do it, however poorly. That is the change in me.

'Davy and I have had to re-establish a relationship that we haven't worked on for eighteen years. We've discovered places where we work together and places where we have no communication. We still have to figure out if there is enough common ground for us to create a situation we can live with. Likewise, if Micky joins us later on in America. We all know that we don't have to live with each other and have enduring psycho-sexual relationships. We can just work together for a few months and then go our separate ways, which is fine.

'You see, none of us knew anything about what you do after your first flush of success, how you wait out the inevitable fallow period before you can claim a kind of fame and fortune. I look now at all the great careers and realise that every single one of them had that fallow period. It is whether that breaks you up or whether you can regroup and gather the enduring values that got you to the top, discard the temporary ones that were the fashions of the moment and carry on that decides your future. Look at Frank Sinatra, Judy Garland, Elvis Presley, Elton John, the Beach Boys, the Bee Gees.

During the Australian tour, news came through to the surprised musicians that America's MTV cable rock television network had screened every episode of *The Monkees* series continuously, calling the day 'Pleasant Valley Sunday.' At this stage, American oldies promoter David Fishof, whose 'Happy Together' tours of

hit acts from the Sixties, had been big money spinners for two years, was well underway in his negotiations to stage a 120 date/100 city, North American 'Monkees Twentieth Anniversary Tour'. When Fishof first approached the new, business-minded Peter Tork, he was advised that 'A million people have approached me' and that the others probably wouldn't be as interested as he was. Nesmith was, as expected, frigid about the idea, but Dolenz was sufficiently attracted by the economic package presented, with the promise of a reunion album and a television special, to leave his stately Nottinghamshire home.

After rehearsing with an eight-piece band, the singing (and occasionally playing) Monkees hit the road at the head of a package which included Herman's Hermits (without Peter Noone), the Grass Roots and Gary Puckett and the Union Gap. As in Australia, the fan response was extraordinary. 'Suddenly,' as David

Frickie from *Rolling Stone* pointed out, 'a whole new generation weaned on pseudo-art clips by Duran Duran has been seduced by the world's first true video-rock group.' Like Tork, Dolenz was now keen to talk about the Pre-Fab Four and its new wave of popularity, 'If you listen to the music that is successful today, it is very similar to the stuff that was happening in the sixties. The Bangles' *Manic Monday*, Huey Lewis' *Power Of Love*, stuff by Wham!, Culture Club and the Thompson Twins, all those songs are things the Monkees could have done. It's all highly melodic with strong hooks and very group-sounding.'

Although the 'golden-oldie' trappings of the tour did not sit too comfortably with Micky, the warmth of the fans was more than a middle-aged Monkee could have asked for. 'The kids are so enthusiastic, it's like a time warp. It's as if we went out for a burger in 1967 and we just got back to do another show.'

Asked repeatedly when the Beatles were going to re-form, Paul McCartney once snapped, 'You can't reheat a souffle.' But, insists Peter Tork, 'Spaghetti warms over very well.' So well in fact, that a double Arista greatest hits album, 'Then And Now, The Best Of The Monkees', sold half a million copies in two weeks. *That Was Then, This Is Now*, one of three new recordings included on the set, debuted on Billboard at number 57.

By July 1986, America was besotted by The Monkees. Fred Bernard, proprietor of the Dallas Rock

Specialities store claimed he'd never seen anything like the scramble for Monkee collectibles in twenty years in the record business. RCA/Columbia capitalised on the MTV exposure by issuing two video tapes, containing two episodes each of the television series.

NBC-TV was not slow in appreciating the significance of these events and has sent out a casting call for four unknowns – male or female – to star in *The New Monkees*, an updated weekly musical situation comedy series. Amongst the hopeful auditionees; Bobby Darin's son, Dodd; Donovan Leech's son, Donovan; Frankie Avalon's son, Frank Burt – and Jason Nesmith, son of Michael Nesmith.

discography

Singles

		US Releases	UK Releases
8/66	Last Train to Clarksville/Take A Giant Step	Colgems 1001	RCA 1547
11/66	I'm A Believer/(I'm Not Your) Stepping Stone	Colgems 1002	RCA 1560
3/67	A Little Bit Me, A Little Bit You/Forget That Girl	Colgems 1003	
3/67	A Little Bit Me, A Little Bit You/Girl I Knew Somewhere	Colgems 1004	RCA 1580
7/67	Pleasant Valley Sunday/Words	Colgems 1007	RCA 1620
10/67	Daydream Believer/Goin' Down	Colgems 1012	RCA 1645
3/68	Valleri/Tapioca Tundra	Colgems 1019	RCA 1673
7/68	D.W. Washburn/It's Nice To Be With You	Colgems 1023	RCA 1706
10/68	Porpoise Song/As We Go Along	Colgems 1031	
3/69	Teardrop City/A Man Without A Dream	Colgems 5000	RCA 1802
7/69	Listen To The Band/Someday Man	Colgems 5004	RCA 1824
10/69	Good Clean Fun/Mommy And Daddy	Colgems 5005	RCA 1887
6/70	Oh My My/Love You Better	Colgems 5011	RCA 1958
1972	Last Train To Clarksville/Monkees Theme	Flashback 70	
1972	Pleasant Valley Sunday/I'm A Believer	Flashback 71	
1972	Daydream Believer/Stepping Stone	Flashback 72	
1976	Daydream Believer/Theme From The Monkees	Arista AS0201	
8/86	That Was Then, This Is Now/Theme From The Monkees	Arista AS1-9505	

Note: Eight Monkee singles were pressed on the back of cereal packets – Last Train To Clarksville, I Wanna Be Free, Forget That Girl, Papa Gene's Blues, The Day We Fall In Love, Theme From The Monkees, Valleri and Teardrop City. The last two tracks were made available on these cardboard discs well in advance of official release.

Notable Foreign Singles

United Kingdom

Alternate Title (Randy Scouse Git)/Forget That Girl	RCA 1604
Daddy's Song/Porpoise Song	RCA 1862
I'm A Believer/Theme From The Monkees	Bell 1354

Australia

I Wanna Be Free/You Just May Be The One	RCA 101789
Alternate Title (Randy Scouse Git)/Forget That Girl	RCA 101793
Mary Mary/What Am I Doing Hangin''Round?	RCA 101831

Canada

A Little Bit Me, A Little Bit You/She Hangs Out	RCA 66-1003

Germany
Theme From The Monkees/Mary Mary   RCA 6615005

Italy
Tema Dei Monkees/Valleri   RCA 1546

Japan (Davy Jones)
Dance Gypsy/Can She Do It (Like She Dances)   JAS 2010

Mexico
Do You Feel It Too?/Acapulco Sun   RCA

Yugoslavia
Theme From The Monkees/I Wanna Be Free   RCA 41.932

Ep's

United States
No commercially released EP's but
three 6-track Jukebox discs issued
(CGLP – 101, 102, 103)

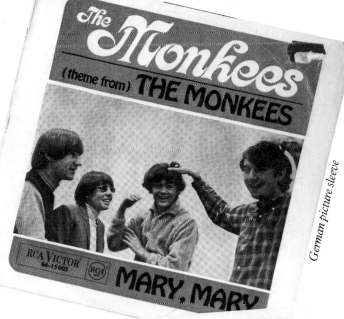

German picture sleeve

United Kingdom
The Monkees Vol. 1.   Arista 326
I'm A Believer/Last Train To Clarksville/Daydream Believer/
A Little Bit Me, A Little Bit You
The Monkees Vol. 2.   Arista 402
Alternate Title (Randy Scouse Git)/ What Am I Doing Hangin'
'Round?/Stepping Stone / Pleasant Valley Sunday

Australia
The Monkees Vol. 1.   RCA 20414
Theme From The Monkees/ Saturday's Child/Tomorrow's
Gonna Be Another Day/Take A Giant Step
The Monkees Vol. 2.   RCA 20415
I'm A Believer/Let's Dance On/Papa Gene's Blues/This Just
Doesn't Seem To Be My Day
She   RCA 20468
She/Sunny Girl Friend/Look Out/ Gonna Buy Me A Dog
Cuddly Toy   RCA 20473
Cuddly Toy/Laugh/You Told Me/No Time
Davy Jones 1   RCA 20541
Hold On Girl/The Poster/We Were Made For Each Other/
She Hangs Out
Davy Jones 2   RCA 20542
I Wanna Be Free/Cuddly Toy/Valleri/ Daydream Believer
The Monkees   Arista K7882
I'm A Believer/Last Train To Clarksville/Daydream Believer/
A Little Bit Me, A Little Bit You

France
Last Train To Clarksville   RCA 86.95OM
Last Train To Clarksville/Take A Giant Step/Monkees Theme
Tomorrow's Gonna Be Another Day
Stepping Stone   RCA 86.952M
Stepping Stone/Sweet Young Thing/ I'm A Believer/
Saturday's Child

Portugal
The Monkees   RCA TP 345
Words/When Love Comes Knocking/ She/Hold On Girl
**Pisces, Aquarius, Capricorn And
Jones Ltd 1**   RCA TP 396
Love Is Only Sleeping/She Hangs Out/Salesman/The Door
Into Summer

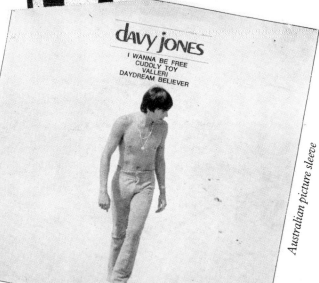

Australian picture sleeve

Australian picture sleeve

**Pisces, Aquarius, Capricorn And
Jones Ltd 2**   RCA TP 397
Cuddly Toy/What Am I Doing Hangin' 'Round?/Star
Collector/Hard To Believe
Pleasant Valley Sunday   RCA TP 344
Pleasant Valley Sunday/Your Auntie Grizelda/Mary, Mary/
Papa Gene's Blues
Teardrop City   RCA TP 465
Teardrop City/A Man Without A Dream/D. W. Washburn/
Valleri

Albums

10/66 **The Monkees**   Colgems 101
Monkees Theme/Saturday's Child/I Wanna Be Free/
Tomorrow's Gonna Be Another Day/Papa Gene's
Blues/Take A Giant Step/Last Train To Clarksville/
This Just Doesn't Seem To Be My Day/Let's Dance
On/I'll Be True To You/ Sweet Young Thing/ Gonna
Buy Me A Dog

1/67 **More Of The Monkees**   Colgems 102
She/When Loves Comes Knocking/ Mary Mary/Hold
On Girl/Your Auntie Grizelda/Stepping Stone/Look
Out (Here Comes Tomorrow)/The Kind of Girl I
Could Love/The Day We Fall In Love/Sometime In
The Morning/Laugh/I'm A Believer

6/67 **The Monkees Headquarters**   Colgems 103
You Told Me/I'll Spend My Life With You/Forget
That Girl/Band 6/You Just May Be The One/Shades
Of Grey/ I Can't Get Her Off My Mind/For Pete's
Sake/Mr Webster/Sunny Girlfriend/Zilch/No Time/
Early Morning Blues And Greens/Randy Scouse Git
(Alternate Title)

11/67 **Pisces, Aquarius, Capricorn And
Jones Ltd**   Colgems 104
Salesman/She Hangs Out/The Door Into Summer/
Love Is Only Sleeping/Cuddly Toy/Words/Hard To
Believe/ What Am I Doing Hangin' 'Round?/ Peter
Percival Patterson's Pet Pig/ Daily Nightly/Don't Call
On Me/Star Collector

4/68 **The Birds, The Bees And The
Monkees**   Colgems 109
Dream World/Auntie's Municipal Court/We Were
Made For Each Other/Tapioca Tundra/Daydream
Believer/Writing Wrongs/I'll Be Back Up On My Feet/
The Poster/PO Box 9847/Magnolia Simms/Valleri/Zor
And Zam

12/68 **Head (Soundtrack)**   Colgems 5008
Opening Ceremony/Porpoise Song/ Dilly Diego/Circle
Sky/Supplicio/Can You Dig It?/Gravy/Superstitious/
As We Go Along/Dandruff?/Daddy's Song/Do I Have
To Do This All Over Again?/Swami Plus Strings Etc

2/69 **Instant Replay**   Colgems 113
Through The Looking Glass/Don't Listen To Linda/I
Won't Be The Same Without You/Don't Wait For Me/
You And I/While I Cry/Teardrop City/The Girl I Left
Behind Me/A Man Without A Dream/Shorty Blackwell

9/69 **The Monkees Greatest Hits**   Colgems 115

TP - 344

10/69 **The Monkees Present Micky, David**   Colgems 117
And Michael
Little Girl/Good Clean Fun/If I Knew/Bye Bye Baby Bye
Bye/Never Tell A Woman Yes/Looking For The Good
Times/Ladies And Society/Listen To The Band/French
Song/Mommy And Daddy/Oklahoma Ballroom Dancer/
Pillow Time

5/70 **Changes**   Colgems 119
Oh My My/Ticket On A Ferry Ride/ You're So Good To
Me/It's Got To Be Love/Acapulco Sun/99 Pounds/Tell
Me Love/Do You Feel It Too?/I Love You Better/All
Alone In The Dark/ Midnight Train/I Never Thought It
Peculiar

1979 **Monkeemania**   Arista L70157
(40 track collection featuring rare tracks: Love To Love/
Steam Engine 99/Circle Sky (live)/Tema Die Monkees.)

8/86 **Then And Now . . . The Best Of The**   Arista
Monkees

Bootlegs

Monkeemania (Hawaiian triple with diabolical sound)
Monkee Rarities (another Hawaiian triple, in box, just as
   diabolical)
Monkee Rarities II (Hawaiian double featuring solo material,
   still diabolical)
Monkeeshines (magnificent rarities collection with notes, pics
   and great sound) (US)
She Hangs Out (Canadian boot of 'Pisces, Aquarius, Capricorn
   And Jones Ltd, Koala label)

Compilations

Literally dozens exist, including:The Best (Japan), Golden
Story (Japan), The Monkees (UK), Best of Davy Jones (Japan),
Best of Micky Dolenz (Japan), The Monkees Golden Hits
(RCA Collectors Club, US), Barrel Full Of Monkees (US),
Refocus (US), The Monkees (Laurie House, US), Monkee
Business (Picture Disc On Rhino, US)

SOLO RECORDINGS (PRE AND POST MONKEES

MIKE NESMITH
Singles

1965	Just a Little Love/Curson Terrace	Edan 1001
1965	A Journey With Michael Blessing/A New Recruit★	Colpix CP 787
1965	Until It's Time For You To Go/What Seems To Be The Trouble★	Colpix CP 792
1970	Little Red Rider/Rose City Chimes	RCA 47–9853
1970	Joanne/One Rose	RCA 74–0368
1970	Joanne/Crippled Lion	RCA 2001(UK)
1970	Silver Moon/Lady Of The Valley	RCA 74–0399
1971	Nevada Fighter/Here I Am	RCA 74–0453
1971	Texas Morning/Tumbling Tumbleweeds	RCA 74–0491
1971	Propinquity/Only Bound	RCA 74–0540
1972	Mama Rocker/Lazy Lady	RCA 74–0629
1973	Roll With The Flow/Keep On	RCA 74–0804
	★As Michael Blessing	

Israeli picture sleeve

Japanese picture sleeve

1975	Joanne/Silver Moon (reissue)	RCA	447–0868
1976	Rio/Life, The Unsuspecting Captive	P.Art	WIP6373
1976	Navajo Trail/Love's First Kiss	P.Art	SIP6398
1978	Roll With The Flow/I've Just Begun To Care (both live)	P.Art	PAC-101
1979	Rio/Casablanca Moonlight	P.Art	PAC-104
1979	Magic/Dance	P.Art	PAC-106
1979	Cruisin'/Horserace	P.Art	PAC-108

Albums

1970	Magnetic South	RCA	LSP-4371
1970	Loose Salute	RCA	LSP-4415
1971	Nevada Fighter	RCA	LSP-4497
1972	Sounds Like The Navy (Interview LP with Sam Riddle)	USNavy	72–37
1972	Tantamount to Treason Vol I	RCA	LSP-4563
1972	And The Hits Just Keep On Comin'	RCA	LSP-4695
1973	Pretty Much Your Standard Ranch Stash	RCA	APLI-0164
1975	The Prison (with book, in box)	P.Art	11–101A
1975	Blue Angels – Soundtrack (sings 'The World is Golden Too')	Tam(Japan)	YX5002
1976	The Best Of The Monkees (Australia and UK only)	RCA	RS-1064
1977	Compilation	P.Art	PAC7106
1977	From A Radio Engine To The Photon Wing	P.Art	PAC7107
1978	Live At The Palais (Melbourne, Australia)	P.Art	PAC7118
1979	Infinite Rider On The Big Dogma	P.Art	PAC7130
1979	The Michael Nesmith Radio Special	P.Art	PAC71300

EP's

| 1976 | Nesmith (Joanne/Silver Moon/ I Fall To Pieces/Some Of Shelley's Blues) | P.Art | IEP4(UK) |

Note: The quad 8-track cartridge of the 'Loose Salute' album has a version of 'Silver Moon' which is a minute longer.

DAVY JONES

Singles

1965	Dream Girl/Take Me To Paradise	Colpix	CP 764
1965	What Are We Going To Do/This Bouquet	Colpix	CP 784
1965	Theme From A New Love/Girl From Chelsea	Colpix	CP 789
1967	It Ain't Me Babe/Baby It's Me	Pye	7N17302
1971	Rainy Jane/Welcome To My Love	Bell	45.111
1971	I Really Love You/Sittin' In The Apple Tree	Bell	45.136
1971	Girl/Take My Love	Bell	45.159
1972	Road To Love/I Believe In You	Bell	45.178
1973	You're A Lady/Who Was It?	MGM	K14458
1973	Rubberene/Rubberene	MGM	K14524
1978	Happy Birthday Mickey Mouse/You Don't Have To Be A Country Boy	WB	K17161
1982	It's Now/How Do You Know?	Japan	JAF2007
1982	Dance Gypsy/It's Now	Pioneer	K . ?
1982	Sixteen/Sixteen	Pioneer	K1517

Albums

1965	David Jones	Colpix	493
1971	Davy Jones	Bell	6067
1982	You're A Lady (one side only)★	MGM	20MM0040
1982	Hello Davy! Davy Jones Live★	Pioneer	K10025

★Japanese releases

EP

| 1967 | Davy Jones (Australia only) | Astor | AEP4013 |

PETER TORK (AND THE NEW MONKS)

| 1982 | Stepping Stone/ Higher And Higher | Claude's Music Works | MW1001 |

MICKY DOLENZ

1966	Don't Do It/Plastic Symphony III (instrumental)	Chall.	59353
1967	Huff Puff (another artist)		59372
1971	Easy On You/Oh Someone	MGM	K14309
1972	A Lover's Prayer/ Unattended In The Dungeon		K14395
1973	Daybreak/Love War	Romar	R0710
1973	Daybreak/Love War (reissued with clearer mix)		R0710
1974	Buddy Holly Tribute/Oh She's So Young		R0715
1979	Alicia/Lovelight	Chrysalis	2297
1982	To Be Or Not to Be/?		

DOLENZ AND JONES

Singles

1971	Lady Jane/Do It In The Name Of Love (Japan)	7RS	19
1972	Lady Jane/Do It In the Name Of Love	Bell	986
1978	Lifeline/It's A Jungle Out There/Gotta Get Up (maxi)	MCA	

Albums

| 1977 | The Point – Soundtrack | MCA | 2826 |

DOLENZ, JONES AND TORK

Single

| 1976 | Christmas Is My Time Of Year/White Christmas (fan club release) | CDS 700 | |

DOLENZ, JONES, BOYCE AND HART

Singles

| 1975 | I Remember The Feeling/You And I | Capitol | 418(|
| 1976 | I Love You/Saving My Love For You | | 427 |

Albums

1976	Dolenz, Jones, Boyce And Hart	Capitol	11513
1977	Live In Disneyland (Bootleg)		
1981	Concert In Japan 1976. Japan		91018

WICHITA TRAIN WHISTLE
Singles

| 1968 | Tapioca Tundra/Don't Cry Now | | Dot 17152 |

Albums

| 1968 | Wichita Train Whistle Sings | | Dot DLP25861 |
| | (Reissued on Pacific Arts label, PACB 7–113, in 1977) | | |

STARSHIP (Dolenz and Michael Lloyd)
Singles

| 1972 | Johnny B.Goode/It's Amazing To Me | | Lion 132 |
| 1972 | Where Did All The Good Times Go?/Monkees Medley | | Lion (unr'lsd) |

MIKE, JOHN AND BILL
Single

| 1963 | How Can You Kiss Me?/Just A Little Love | | Omnibus 239 |

THE MISSING LINKS
Single

| 1966 | I Told You I Love You/ When I See My Baby (*may* feature Micky) | | Jowar 105 |

DENNZY EZBA AND THE GOLDENS
Album

| 1980 | Sings His Greatest Hits | | Texas R. 1001 |
| | (Mike appears on 'Go Somewhere And Cry') | | |

JAN AND DEAN
Single

| 1968 | In The Still Of The Night | Warner | WB7240 |
| | (features Davy on spoken interlude) | | |

MISCELLANEOUS

a) Peter plays bass on the track 'Help Me Sing The Sun Down' on the Wendy Erdman album 'Erdman' (Audio Fidelity AFSD 6243), 1970.
b) Micky and Peter are heard on the Albert Brooks comedy album 'A Star Is Bought'(Asylum 7E-1035), 1975.
c) A bootleg version of Jan and Dean's *Laurel And Hardy* features Davy on lead vocals (Sitchen BREP001), 1982.
d) Davy Jones backing vocals on acetates and test pressings of JAKKO's 'Judy Get Down' (MDM 11), 1986.

Unreleased Tracks Known to Exist
All The Kings Horses   Nine Times Blue   Wind Up Man   Riu Chiu   Rosemarie   Prithee   Apples Peaches   Bananas And Pears   Smile   String Of My Kite   My Share of the Sidewalk   If You Have The Time   50's Rock Medley   St Valentine's Angel   Merry Go Round   Goldilocks Sometime   Tear The Top Right Off My Head   Lady's Baby   The Only Thing That I Believe Is True

Everybody Loves A Nut   Only The Fittest Shall Survive   Mustang   Shake A Tail Feather (with Jools)

Unreleased Tracks Believed to Exist
Rock And Roll Music   Michigan Black Hawk   I Go Ape   She'll Be There   I'm A Man   The Crippled Lion   So Goes Love   Eve Of My Sorrow   Sugar Man   Where Has It All Gone?   Hollywood   Naked Persimmon   Don't Say Nothin' Bad About My Baby

Unreleased Solo Tracks Believed To Exist
Micky Dolenz: Family Of Man/Love Is All I Have/A Long Time/Since I Fell For You/Mockingbird/Long Way Since St Louis/Splish Splash/Purple People Eater/Wing Walker/I Hate Rock And Roll/It's Amazing

Davy Jones: Tears On My Pillow/Manchester Boy/I'm Coming Home/Hit Record

Peter Tork: Shades Of Grey/Since You Went Away/Good Lookcr/Hi Hi Babe/Pleasant Valley Sunday (plus numerous live concert tapes of the Peter Tork Band, Cottonmouth and the New Monks, which circulate freely among fans).

French picture sleeve

THE TELEVISION SERIES

SERIES ONE

1. *ROYAL FLUSH:* The Monkees rescue the Princess of the Duchy of Harmonica from her evil uncle Archduke Otto.

2. *MONKEE SEE, MONKEE DIE:* The Monkees spend the night in a haunted house in order to collect an inheritance.

3. *MONKEE V's MACHINE:* The Monkees go job hunting in a computerised toy factory.

4. *YOUR FRIENDLY NEIGHBORHOOD KIDNAPPERS:* A shady publicity man kidnaps the Monkees to stop them winning a talent contest.

5. *THE SPY WHO CAME IN FROM THE COOL:* The Monkees get mixed up with a spy ring. As foreign agents, they try to recover microfilm concealed in Davy's Maracas.

6. *SUCCESS STORY:* Davy's grandfather visits, and the Monkees try to convince him that his grandson is wealthy and successful.

7. *MONKEES IN A GHOST TOWN:* Stranded in a ghost town, the Monkees meet up with a musically appreciative female gangster.

8. *DON'T LOOK A GIFT HORSE IN THE MOUTH:* Davy is given a horse, which the Monkees have to hide from the landlord. It is returned to a heart-broken child and father after Davy rides it to victory.

9. *THE CHAPERONE:* Davy's feelings for a retired general's daughter leads Micky to pose as a female chaperone.

10. *HERE COME THE MONKEES:* The pilot episode. The Monkees play at a sweet sixteen party and help the birthday girl with her studies.

11. *A LA CARTE:* The Monkees save a restaurant owner from a gang of crooks.

12. *I'VE GOT A LITTLE SONG HERE:* Mike is fleeced by a phoney song publisher.

13. *ONE MAN SHY:* Peter tries to win the heart of a debutante.

14. *DANCE MONKEE DANCE:* The Monkees sign up for lessons at a local dancing school and then find that their contracts are for life.

15. *TOO MANY GIRLS:* A stage mother pushes her daughter into a showbiz career via a double act with Davy.

16. *SON OF GYPSY:* A band of gypsies force the Monkees to steal a valuable sculpture called the 'Maltese Vulture'.

17. *CASE OF THE MISSING MONKEE:* Peter becomes involved with the disappearance of a scientist and then disappears himself.

18. *I WAS A TEENAGE MONSTER:* The Monkees are hired by a crackpot scientist to teach an android to play music and find themselves involved in an evil experiment.

19. *ALIAS MICKY DOLENZ:* Micky impersonates his lookalike, the famous gangster 'Baby Face'.

20. *IN THE RING:* Davy competes in a championship boxing match.

21. *THE PRINCE AND THE PAUPER:* Davy is the image of a shy young prince and his charm wins the prince a bride.

22. *AT THE CIRCUS:* The Monkees join an unsuccessful circus troupe and leap to stardom.

23. *CAPTAIN CROCODILE:* The Monkees' appearance on a children's TV show is sabotaged by the host, who fears that his guest's popularity is diminishing his own (a parody of Captain Kangaroo).

24. *MONKEES A LA MODE:* A teenage magazine runs a bogus article on the Monkees which moulds them into a false image of clean cut Americans.

25. *FIND THE MONKEES:* When a TV producer hears a tape of the Monkees, he frantically stages auditions in the hope of finding them.

26. *MONKEE CHOW MEIN:* Peter finds a secret message in a fortune cookie and is pursued by Chinese gangsters. Monkeemen come to the rescue.

27. *MONKEE MOTHER:* Millie, a middle aged widow, moves in as a new tenant so the Monkees set about finding her a husband.

28. *MONKEES ON THE LINE:* The Monkees operate a telephone answering service.

29. *GET OUT MORE DIRT:* The four Monkees fall in love with April, a girl who works at the local laundromat.

30. *MONKEES IN MANHATTAN:* The Monkees go to New York with their manager to find some work.

31. *MONKEES IN THE MOVIES:* When the starring role in a 'beach party' movie goes to Davy, the others have to bring him down to earth.

32. *MONKEES ON TOUR:* Concert sequences and on-the-road interviews from a real Monkee concert in Phoenix, Arizona.

SERIES TWO – 1967

1. *IT'S A NICE PLACE TO VISIT....:* The Monkees go to Mexico where they are forced to join a bandit gang.

2. *THE PICTURE FRAME:* Believing they are only making a film, the Monkees rob a bank and get into heavy trouble with the police.

3. *EVERYWHERE A SHEIKH, SHEIKH:* Davy is kidnapped and almost forced to marry an Arabian princess.

4. *MONKEE FOR MAYOR:* Mike runs for mayor on a ticket of cleaning up city hall and stopping property developers from tearing down old buildings to put up car parks.

5. *ART, FOR MONKEES SAKE:* Peter's talents are used by the wrong people – to pull off an art robbery.

6. *I WAS A 99 POUND WEAKLING:* Micky undertakes a body building course to impress a beach beauty interested only in physical perfection.

7. *DOUBLE BARREL SHOTGUN WEDDING:* The Monkees become involved in an Ozark family fued. For his intervention, Davy is expected to marry young Eli-May.

8. *MONKEES MAROONED:* While tracking down lost treasure with the aid of a map, the Monkees become marooned on a desert island, where they encounter an Australian Robinson Crusoe.

9. *THE CARD CARRYING RED SHOES:* A visiting Russian ballerina falls in love with Peter and defects from the troupe until the Monkees persuade her to return.

10. *THE WILD MONKEES:* The Monkees imitate Marlon Brando and gang by becoming motorcycle freaks to impress some girls. Disaster strikes when the girls' boyfriends, real bikees show up.

11. *A COFFIN TOO FREQUENT:* The Monkees are forced to witness a man's return from the dead.

12. *HITTING THE HIGH SEAS:* As shiphands, the four find themselves under the orders of an embittered old sea captain (Chips Rafferty).

13. *MONKEES IN TEXAS:* During a visit to Mike's Aunt the Monkees become involved in a family feud.

14. *MONKEES ON THE WHEEL:* The Monkees become involved in a gambling fraud in Las Vegas.

15. *THE CHRISTMAS SHOW:* The Monkees try to teach a cold-hearted youngster the true spirit and meaning of Christmas.

16. *FAIRY TALE:* Each Monkee acts out his favourite fairytale in pantomime, with Mike portraying a bad tempered Princess.

17. *MONKEES WATCH THEIR FEET:* Alien beings from Outer Space invade Earth and Micky is lured into their spaceship.

18. *MONSTEROUS MONKEE MASH:* When Davy becomes romantically involved with the daughter of a mad scientist, the others visit a haunted house to rescue him.

19. *THE MONKEY'S PAW:* A bad luck Monkey paw charm causes Micky to lose his voice.

20. *THE DEVIL AND PETER TORK:* Peter sells his soul to the devil for a harp.

21. *MONKEES RACE AGAIN:* The Monkees assist a veteran racing driver against his villainous arch enemy.

22. *MONKEES IN PARIS:* The Monkees engage in madcap adventures (without dialogue) around Paris, while their masters try to find them.

23. *MONKEES MIND THEIR MANOR:* The Monkees visit an English country estate. (Directed by Peter Tork).

24. *SOME LIKE IT LUKEWARM:* When the Monkees compete in a talent quest they find that all the groups must be of mixed sex, so Davy dresses as a girl.

25. *THE MONKEES BLOW THEIR MINDS:* Oraculo, the great Mentalist, feeds Peter and Mike with a magic potion that induces hypnosis. (Frank Zappa guests).

26. *THE FRODIS CAPER:* An evil wizard hypnotises the city, using a television test patter and the powers of Frodis, an alien visitor he has captured. Only the Monkees can save Frodis and the world. Tim Buckley appears. (Directed By Micky Dolenz).

Acknowledgements

The author is grateful for the kind assistance rendered by Peter Tork, Micky Dolenz, Michael Nesmith, Davy Jones, Tommy Boyce, Lynne Randell, Doug Trevor, Louis Shelton, Rodney Bingenheimer, Kim Fowley and Harvey Kubernick, who granted interviews; and to John Tobler, Pete Townshend, Ken Barnes, Greg Shaw, Jayne Moore, Steve Hessling, Mike McDowell, Pauline Muncey, Mary Griffith, Bobbi Boyce, Nancy McGlamery, Roger Dilernia, Stuart Coupe, Bob King, John Clayton, Peter Carrette, Larry McGrath, Stephen McParland, Colin Beard, Bruce Anton, Gary Carlson, Mike McDowell, David Fricke, Derek Taylor, Gavin Kelly, James Manning, Norm Lurie, Dave Botterell, Ruth Bailey, Helen Sudell, Lisa Hardy and Lorelle Baker for other invaluable services. Thanks to Bob King for photographic work, Rhonda Barton and Karen Peat for typing the manuscript.

Some of the quotes used herein have been taken from features carried by a wide range of publications, including: *Bomp, Blitz, Goldmine, New Musical Express, Record Mirror, Zig Zag, Let It Rock, Go-Set, 16 Magazine, Tiger Beat, Teenset, Billboard, Rolling Stone, Variety* and *The Daily Insider*.

Thanks to everyone at Plexus and a special thank you to Phil Smee for designing the book.

Finally, thanks to everyone who contributed to the making of 'The Monkees' and in turn to the making of this book, especially Raybert Productions Inc, Arista, RCA, Colgems, Screen Gems, Columbia, Colpix, and Challenge.

It has not been possible in all cases to trace the copyright sources and the authors would be glad to hear from any unacknowledged copyright holder.